The Russo-German War
June 1941 - June 1943

edited by

W. Victor Madej

Game Publishing Company
Allentown, Pennsylvania 18103

Library of Congress Catalog Card: 83-081814
Germany, 1 Heer-Evaluation.
2. Soviet Union, Army-Evaluation.
3. Germany, Heer-History-World War, 1939-1945.
4. Soviet Union, Army-History-World War, 1939-1945

ISBN: 0-941052-13-3

Books by Game Publishing:

JAPANESE ARMED FORCES ORDER OF BATTLE (2 volumes)
ITALIAN ARMY ORDER OF BATTLE AND HANDBOOK
GERMAN ARMY ORDER OF BATTLE (4 volumes)
SOUTHEASTERN EUROPE AXIS ORDER OF BATTLE AND HANDBOO
U.S. ARMY ORDER OF BATTLE, 1941-1945
THE RUSSO-GERMAN WAR, June 1941-June 1943
GERMAN MILITARY DICTIONARY OF TERMS AND SYMBOLS
GERMAN OPERATIONS IN THE BALKANS
GERMAN OPERATIONS AGAINST RUSSIAN BREAKTHROUGHS

Most of the book is an edited version of two Department of the Army pamphlets. The first part of the book largely reproduces *The German Campaign in Russia - Planning and Operations (1940-1942)*, published in March 1955, as DA-Pam-20-261a. Maps for the period between September 1942 and June 1943, were taken from E.F. Ziemke's *Stalingrad to Berlin: The German Defeat in the East*, published by the Office of the Chief of Military History (USA) in 1968 **The last part of the book reproduces a portion** from *Small Unit Actions During the German Campaign in Russia*, published in July 1953, as DA-Pam-20-269. The editor acknowledges his indebtedness to the original authors of this material.

TABLE OF CONTENTS

PART FOUR - TURNING POINT

PART FIVE - SMALL UNIT ACTIONS

MAPS

CHARTS AND TABLES

plus photos

INTRODUCTION

This book largely reproduces material from two Department of the Army Pamphlets, Numbers 20-261a and 20-269; titled the *German Campaign in Russia - Planning and Operations (1940 - 1942)* and *Small Unit Actions During the German Campaign in Russia.* It also includes some of the maps and many facts presented in E.F. Ziemke's *Stalingrad to Berlin: The German Defeat in the East.* All three books provide excellent information on the campaign in Russia and I found it useful to present the information again in a combined form to provide a less disconnected perspective.

The purpose of the *German Campaign in Russia* volume was to describe German planning and operations in the first part of the campaign against Russia. The narrative starts with Hitler's initial plans for an invasion of Russia but, unfortunately, ended with the time of Germany's maximum territorial gains prior to the Russian siege of Stalingrad. This historical study was published in March 1955. The second volume completed in 1966, and published in 1968, described the course of events from the Russian November 1942 counteroffensive at *Stalingrad to Berlin* in April 1945. The rest of the latter title is *The German Defeat in the East.* The unfortunate gap between the two volumes is not clear to me, but I suspect it was for political reasons and a reluctance to give the Russian devil his due in defeating Germany.

By culminating this volume in June 1943, I think a new perspective will clearly emerge. It should become obvious that Germany was decisively defeated prior to mid 1943. The remainder of the campaign in the East consisted of the destruction of the German Army and not really its "defeat". The fact is that in the course of World War 2, about five out of six German combat deaths resulted from Russian action (See our *German Army Order of Battle,* vol. 1) The battle of Stalingrad destroyed a German Army (of Army Group size) with twenty-two divisions, but also included the destruction of most of four Axis Allied armies. The destruction of two more armies in Africa confirmed German defeat. There would be no more German offensive victories. Stalingrad marked the beginning of German military destruction. Hence, Mr. Ziemke's title is inaccurate. The recent work by Erickson, on the same subject, repeats this error.

The material for the *German Campaign in Russia* was obtained from German military records in the custody of the U.S. Department of the Army. German sources used in preparing this study included those Fuehrer directives, fragmentary diaries, and records of the Armed Forces High Command that pertained to planning and operations in Russia; the official records of the Organization, Intelligence, Operations, and Logistical Divisions of the Army High Command: selected war diaries of the army group and army headquarters that participated in the Russian campaign; and the Halder War Diaries.

In describing the preparation and execution of the German summer offensive of 1942, extensive use was made of the *Kaukasus* (Caucasus) files of the Planning Branch, Operations Division, Army High Command. The records of the *Technische Brigade Mineraloel Russland* (Technical Brigade, Mineral Oil, Russia), directed by the Armed Forces Economics Office, were also consulted.

Another source of information was the "Strategic Survey of the German Campaign in the East," a postwar study prepared by a group of German general officers under the supervision of General Halder, former chief of staff of the German Army. The memoirs and postwar writings of such outstanding German military leaders and historians as Greiner, Guderian, Heinrici, Heusinger, Kesselring, Rundstedt, Tippelskirch, and Warlimont were also used. In addition, the original author conducted a series of interviews with former German Army and Luftwaffe officers in order to fill a number of gaps in the sources.

The study was originally written by Mr. George Blau of the Special Studies Division, Office of the Chief of Military History. His presentation gives an objective account of Germany's efforts to conquer Soviet Russia in World War II. It provides a clear lesson to those who are overawed by modern Soviet power. Mr. Ziemke's volume also provides many excellent facts and outstanding maps. Unfortunately it is marred by efforts to fog the extent of Soviet perponderance in causing German defeat. The statements are to this effect in General Pattison's foreword, and the conclusion claims that "on the balance the Allied and Soviet strategic accomplishments were about equal" (503). The volume fails to destroy important myths about the war. For example nothing is said about the Soviet myth of a great "patriotic" war, despite clear evidence that in a population only about 55% Russian, nearly 90% of the war effort after 1941 to 1944 was borne by the Russian ethnic group. Little is said of Soviet minority forces that fought on the German side, and the inept American handling of these staunch anti-communists. The relative weakness of the western allies compared to Russian forces is deliberately ignored despite its obvious postwar political implications, and impact on the western bargaining position during the war. Perhaps these flaws will be corrected in future editions or in the subsequent official volumes.

Besides editing the material in the aforementioned volumes, I have added some material at the end of Chapter I plus most of Chapter XV, and some divisional order of battle information on the Germans. Chapters XIII and XV also include original research from other sources.

The sections on *Small Unit Actions* are included to provide added detail on the German method of war. Chapters XVI-XVIII are based solely on German source material, primarily in the form of narratives of personal experience. These also were written under the supervision of General Halder. These were screened and rewritten into English under the direction of Lt. Col. M.C. Helfers, Chief of the Foreign Studies Branch, Special Studies Division, OCMH. The work was done by Mr. George E. Blau, Chief, and 1st Lt. Roger Reed, 1st Lt. Gerd Haber, Mr. Charles J. Smith and Mr. George W. Garand of the Writing and Translation section. Despite considerable revision, the group made every effort to retain the point of view, the expression, and even the prejudices of the original.

June 1983   W. Victor Madej

PART ONE - PLANNING

1

STRATEGIC PLANNING

Initial Discussions (July 1940)

After the conclusion of the French campaign in June 1940 Hitler devoted his attention to initiating plans for the seaborne invasion of England—Operation SEELOEWE. On 16 July he issued the directive for the operation. Three days later, in a speech before the Reichstag, Hitler made peace overtures to Great Britain. When they did not produce the expected reaction in Britain, he could only conclude that his last remaining enemy was continuing the war hoping for a change in the U.S. attitude and for future assistance from the Soviet Union.

On 21 July, after discussing the invasion of England with his military advisers, Hitler asked Field Marshal Walter von Brauchitsch, the Commander in Chief of the Army, to study the Russian problem and submit plans for a campaign against the Soviet Union. In regard to the latter the following was mentioned:

1. The concentration of attack forces would take 4 to 6 weeks.
2. The military objective would be to defeat the Russian Army or at least to seize so much Russian territory that the armaments plants in eastern Germany, particularly those in Berlin and Upper Silesia, and the Romanian oil fields would be beyond the range of Russian air attacks. At the same time the German ground forces would have to advance far enough to bring important production centers of European Russia within striking distance of the Luftwaffe.
3. The political aims would include the creation of an independent Ukraine and a confederation of Baltic States under German domination.

The following day, Brauchitsch informed Generaloberst (Gen.) Franz Halder, Chief, Army General Staff, of the discussions that had taken place at the previous day's conference and asked him to study the various problems involved in an operation against Russia. Halder thereupon requested Lt. Col. Eberhardt Kinzel, Chief, Eastern Intelligence Division, to brief him on Russian troop dispositions and asked Col. Hans von Greiffenberg, Chief, Operations Division, to assign a special assistant to the preparation of a tentative plan for a campaign against the Soviet Union.

On the basis of data provided by Kinzel on 26 July, Halder concluded that an attack launched from assembly areas in East Prussia and northern Poland toward Moscow would offer the best chances for success. After the seizure of Moscow the Russian forces defending the Ukraine and the Black Sea coast would be compelled to fight a series of battles with reversed front. [See *map 1.*]

The first draft of the Operations Division plan placed the main effort south of the Pripyat Marshes. The plan also called for 100 divisions. Halder, however, preferred to place the main effort north of the Pripyat.

Two days later, 29 July, Generalmajor (Brig. Gen.) Erich Marcks was temporarily assigned to Army High Command headquarters to draw up a campaign plan against the Soviet Union. General Marcks was chief of staff of the Eighteenth Army, which had recently been assigned to the Russian border and was preparing plans for defense against a possible Russian attack.

4. The Army would need approximately 80-100 combat divisions; the Soviet Union had some 50-75 good Russian divisions in Europe. If the campaign against Russia was launched that autumn, some of the German air power committed against Britain would have to be transferred to the East.

3

The same day General der Artillerie (Lt. Gen.) Alfred Jodl, Chief, Armed Forces Operations Staff, informed Col. Walter Warlimont, Chief, National Defense Division, and a group of officers working on his staff that Hitler had made up his mind to start a preventive war against Russia. The Army and Luftwaffe were to employ all available forces to eliminate forever the Bolshevist danger in the East. Since an eventual conflict between the National Socialist and Communist ideologies was inevitable, the Fuehrer preferred to extend the war into eastern Europe right then to being forced to resume hostilities after a few years of intermittent peace. Originally, Hitler had intended to invade Russia in the autumn of 1940, but Field Marshal Wilhelm Keitel had pointed out the difficulties of a winter campaign in Russia and had presented convincing evidence that the existing road and rail net in the newly acquired Polish territories would not be capable of supporting the assembly of strong German forces. Hitler had thereupon postponed the campaign, setting the tentative invasion date for mid-May 1941.

The first task confronting the officers present at the conference was to draft a directive—later issued under the code designation AUFBAU OST (BUILD-UP EAST)—stipulating the requirements for a prompt concentration of forces in western Poland. Strict secrecy concerning the plan was to be observed by everybody. The conferees queried Jodl whether it was assumed that Great Britain would be completely subjugated by spring 1941 or whether Germany was to become involved in a two-front war by its own volition. Jodl replied that the campaign against Russia would be conducted independently of developments in the West. He added: "In the autumn of 1941, after the consummation of the Russian defeat, our Luftwaffe will appear in the skies of western Europe in greater strength than over before."

On 29 July, also, data provided by the Navy made it obvious that the seaborne invasion of England could not be undertaken before the middle of September 1940 because of the Navy's inability to carry out and secure landings on a sufficiently wide front. The invasion was to be indefinitely postponed on 17 September.

Chart 1. GERMAN CHAIN OF COMMAND (December 1940)

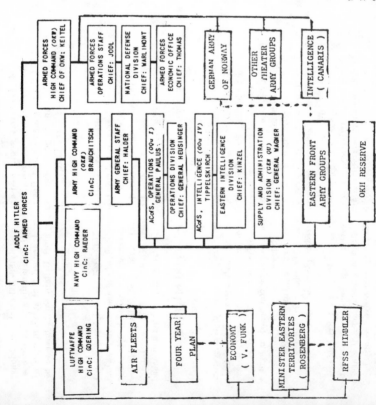

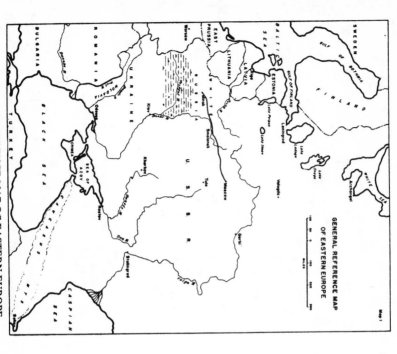

GENERAL REFERENCE MAP
OF EASTERN EUROPE

Map 1

1. GENERAL REFERENCE MAP OF EASTERN EUROPE

On 31 July, toward the end of a conference at Berchtesgaden that was mainly concerned with Operation SEELOEWE, Hitler declared that a showdown with Russia would have to take place the following spring. The quicker the USSR was defeated, the better. The entire campaign made sense only if the Soviet Union was smashed in one fell swoop: territorial gains alone would prove unsatisfactory, and stopping the offensive during the winter months might be dangerous. Therefore, it was best to wait until May 1941 and then bring the campaign to a successful conclusion within five months. It would have been preferable to conduct the operation during the current year, but that solution did not seem practicable. Two converging thrusts were envisaged—a southern drive toward Kiev and into the Dnepr bend, with the Luftwaffe neutralizing the Odessa area; and a northern one across the Baltic States in the direction of Moscow. A secondary operation, by which the Baku oil fields were to be seized, was to take place later. To realize this plan Hitler directed that the strength of the Army, instead of being cut as recently ordered, was to be increased by the activation of 40 divisions.

It remained to be seen to what extent Finland and Turkey might be interested in such an operation. After the successful conclusion of the campaign the Ukraine, White Russia, and the Baltic States would come under German domination, whereas Finland could expand its territory toward the White Sea.

On 1 August Marcks and Halder discussed the campaign: the objective, rail and road communications, and the possible course of operations as well as the missions of the Navy and Luftwaffe. Two large forces were to be formed, one for the drive on Kiev, the other for that on Moscow. Halder pointed out that the Kiev force would operate from insecure bases if it jumped off from Romania. Also, the seizure of the Baltic States would have to be a secondary operation that would not interfere with the drive on Moscow. Halder then asked Marcks to put his plan in writing, including details pertaining to organization, logistical support etc.

5

The Marcks Plan (5 August 1940)

On 5 August Marcks submitted his plan which read essentially as follows:

a. Objective. The objective of the campaign was to defeat the Russian armed forces so that the Soviet Union could not threaten Germany in the future. German troops would have to seize all territory west of the line Rostov–Gorki–Archangel to eliminate the danger of Russian bombing attacks on Germany.

From the military-economic viewpoint Russia's most valuable regions were the food and raw-material producing areas of the Ukraine and the Donets Basin as well as the armament-production centers around Moscow and Leningrad. The industrial areas of Asiatic Russia were not greatly developed. The principal objective was Moscow, the nerve center of Soviet military, political, and economic power; its capture would lead to the disintegration of Soviet resistance.

b. Terrain. To the north and west Moscow was screened by huge forests and swamps which extended from the White Sea past Leningrad through Vitebsk to a line Kobrin–Slutsk–Kiev. [See *map* 2.] The Pripyat Marshes, forming the southern part of this forest and swamp area, divided the western border region of Russia into two separate theaters of operation. The most extensive forests were between Leningrad and Moscow and in the Pripyat Marshes. The intermediate area was crossed by the main highways extending from Warsaw and East Prussia via Slutsk, Minsk, and Vitebsk to Moscow. South of the Pripyat Marshes were the lightly wooded regions of eastern Poland and the Ukraine. The terrain was favorable, but mobility was limited by the scarcity of good roads—only one main west-east highway via Kiev—and by the Dnepr River which constituted a major obstacle.

Because of its better road net the area north of the Pripyat permitted greater mobility, whereas the Ukraine offered better terrain conditions. In the north the fighting would, of necessity, be largely restricted to roads.

c. Russian Tactics. The Red Army would adopt defensive tactics, except along the Romanian border, where it might attack in an attempt to seize the Romanian oil-production centers. In any event heavy air attacks on the oil fields would have to be expected.

On the other hand, the Russians could not repeat the maneuver of 1812, by which they had avoided giving battle. A modern force of 100 divisions could not simply abandon its sources of supply. It was therefore to be assumed that the Red Army would take up defensive positions which would protect most of European Russia, including the eastern Ukraine. The general line Dvina River–Polotsk–Berezina

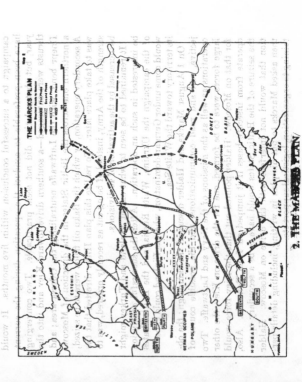

2. THE MARCKS PLAN

River—eastern edge of the Pripyat Marshes—Prut or Dnestr Rivers would serve this purpose, especially since it was partly fortified from earlier days. A withdrawal to the Dnepr also seemed feasible. West of their prepared positions the Russians would probably fight a delaying action.

d. Strength Estimates.

2. RUSSIAN MILITARY STRENGTH, ESTIMATES (August 1940),

Distribution of forces	Infantry divisions	Cavalry divisions	Mechanized brigades
Total	151	32	38
Border defense	55	9	10
Forces total:			
Facing Japan	34	8	8
Facing Turkey	6	1	
Facing Finland	15	---	2
Available for use against Germany	96	23	28

By spring 1941 the German Army would have 24 panzer, 1 cavalry, 12 motorized infantry, and 110 infantry divisions, or a total of 147 divisions, available for a campaign against Russia. This figure did not include the occupation forces to be left in western and northern Europe.

e. Disposition of Russian Forces. As of August 1940 the main concentrations were in the Baltic States in the north and in the Ukraine in the south. In general, the Russian troops in the west were about equally divided between the areas north and south of the Pripyat Marshes with a reserve force around Moscow. It could be assumed that the same disposition would hold in any war with Germany. Whether a point of main effort would be formed in the north or south would depend upon political developments. In all probability the troop strength in the north would exceed that in the south. Once the Russian lines had been pierced, the Red Army, being spread over a wide front, would no longer be able to coordinate its maneuvers and would be destroyed piecemeal.

The Russian Air Force was a redoubtable opponent whose attacks against the few major highways might be very effective.

f. Conduct of Operations. In view of the dimensions of the theater and its division into two parts by the Pripyat Marshes, it seemed unlikely that a decisive victory over the Russian Army could be scored in one single operation. During the initial phase two separate offensives would have to be launched against the main concentrations of Russian forces; later, beyond the extensive forests, the operation could be unified.

The German Army would have to concentrate its forces in the northern part of the theater, crush all opposition, and capture Moscow. To this end it would build up its main effort between Brest Litovsk and Gumbinnen and advance first toward the line Rogachev–Vitebsk. Weaker German forces assembled between Jasi and Jaroslav, south of the Pripyat, were to attack in the direction of Kiev and the Dnepr southeast of that city. They would thus forestall a Russian offensive on Romania and form the southern arm of a pincers that would be closed east of the upper Dnepr. To the north of the main effort, a secondary attack force would thrust toward Leningrad and seize the Russian naval bases.

1. *The Offensive in the South.* An attack against the Russian forces in the Ukraine would have to be launched to protect the Romanian oil fields. If the main effort could have been made from Romania and secondary thrusts from northeastern Hungary and southeastern Poland, this operation might have become the principal attack across the Dnepr toward Moscow. But neither the political

situation in the Balkans nor the road and rail nets in Hungary and Romania would permit the assembly of the necessary forces prior to the tentative date set for the launching of the campaign. A thrust from southeastern Poland in the direction of Kiev and the middle Dnepr, though quite feasible, could not possibly be made the principal operation because the maneuvering space was too narrow and the distance to Moscow too great.

This southern thrust, however, would have to be executed with sufficiently strong forces to destroy the Russians in the western Ukraine and gain the east bank of the Dnepr. Any further advance would have to be coordinated with the principal operation in the northern part of the theater and could be conducted either due eastward toward Kharkov or northeastward. In any event, the main effort of the offensive in the south would have to be on the left, with Kiev the principal objective. A secondary attack force, jumping off from Romanian territory, could link up with the main-effort grouping along the middle Dnepr. Three major roads would be available for the advance toward the river line between Dnepropetrovsk and Cherkassy. The Romanian Army could participate in the occupation of Bessarabia, Odessa, and the Crimea.

2. *The Main Effort.* The main effort was to lead to the destruction of the Russian forces west of Moscow by a direct thrust on the capital. Once in possession of Moscow and northern Russia, elements of the main-attack force would turn south and seize the Ukraine in conjunction with the southern groups.

The principal attack would have to be directed from East Prussia and the northern part of Poland toward Moscow because no decisive operation could be launched from Romania and an initial sweep toward Leningrad would only lengthen the distance to be covered and lead into the dense forests northwest of Moscow.

During the advance on Moscow the left flank would be protected by a special force that was to be committed across the Dvina River toward Pskov and Leningrad. After capturing the latter important industrial city this force might operate in conjunction with the main-attack force.

The road and rail nets west of the Russian border were capable of supporting the advance on Moscow. The terrain that had to be crossed by the forces jumping off from East Prussia was difficult. They would have to traverse a forest and lake belt between the Dvina and Dnepr. There, the battle for the traffic arteries would be decisive. Airborne troops would have to take possession of the eastern exits from large forest areas and thus keep the roads open.

3. *Movements.* Since surprise and speed were of the essence, armored and motorized infantry forces supported by tactical air power were to break through the enemy lines, with ordinary infantry divisions following closely to encircle and destroy the isolated enemy forces. The strength of the first attack wave was limited by the relatively small number of through roads. At most, two division-size units could advance abreast on any one road. The bulk of the infantry with its horse-drawn vehicles would have to march on such side roads as were available. As a result, all units would have to be deployed in great depth. The enormous width of the funnel-shaped theater necessitated keeping strong motorized forces in reserve and so distributing them that they could easily be shifted within the theater.

9. *Primary Missions of the Ground Forces.* The primary mission of Army Group South was to destroy the Russians in the western Ukraine and to establish bridgeheads across the Dnepr from which the army group forces could continue eastward or northeastward.

Army Group North was to seize Moscow. To accomplish this, motorized units would have to drive through the forest areas between Rogachev and Vitebsk with airborne troops assisting them at the forest edges. If the Russians chose to make a stand between the jump-off line and the forests or the Dvina, they would have to be pushed northward, away from the direct route to Moscow. While the reduction of these enemy forces was under way, the armored and motorized units were to move on until they reached the Russian capital.

h. GERMAN FORCE DISTRIBUTION

Distribution	Divisions				
	Total	Panzer	Mtz. Inf.	Inf.	Cav.
Totals	147	24	12	110	1
Army Group South Total	35	5	6	24	
Twelfth Army	12	2	4	6	
Sixteenth Army	17	3	---	14	
Army Group Reserves	6	---	2	4	
Army Group North Total	68	15	2	50	1
Fourth Army	19	6	---	12	1
Sixth Army	20	6	---	14	
Eighteenth Army	15	3	---	12	
Army Group Reserves	14	---	2	12	
Army High Command Reserves	44	4	4	36	

i. The Mission of the Air Force. The Luftwaffe was to neutralize the Soviet Air Force, disrupt rail and road communications, prevent the concentration of Russian ground forces in the forests areas, support the German spearhead units with dive-bomber attacks, prepare airborne operations, and secure the air above traffic bottlenecks.

j. The Mission of the Navy. The Navy was to neutralize the Russian fleet in the Baltic, safeguard the iron ore shipments from Sweden, and transport supplies across the Baltic as soon as the Army had seized the ports.

k. Logistics. A special staff was to be formed to coordinate supply problems and establish bases behind the two army groups. It was anticipated that the Russians would attempt to carry out large-scale demolitions and destroy supply dumps, rail lines, and bridges. This could be partially prevented by keeping them off balance and by preparing appropriate countermeasures. In the Ukraine, Lithuania, and Latvia agents might be able to seize bridges and railroad installations and thus prevent their destruction. All railroad tracks beyond the former Polish border would have to be converted from the Russian wide to normal gauge.

A military administration would have to be set up for the occupied areas. In the Baltic States, White Russia, and the Ukraine the military government agencies would have to work toward turning their authority over to autonomous, non-Communist local governments.

l. Time Phasing. The most favorable season for the campaign was from mid May to mid-October. After a mild winter, it might be possible to start as early as the beginning of May.

It was anticipated that all units needed for the initial operations would be assembled before the outbreak of hostilities. In the event of an unexpected outbreak of fighting, the forces scheduled to be assembled in the Army Group North area would need approximately 10 days to arrive in their designated areas and those in the south 9 days.

During the initial phase of the German offensive the Russians would probably fight delaying actions over distances of up to 250 miles, until they reached their prepared positions. The German infantry divisions would take three weeks to cover this distance. The panzer divisions would have to advance so rapidly and penetrate so deeply that the Russians would be unable to man a continuous defense line. The issue of the entire campaign would depend on the success of the armored thrusts.

The struggle for the forest areas and river courses would dominate the second phase. Since the depth of this zone was 60–120 miles, it would take 2–4 weeks to cross it. At this stage the German forces would either achieve a decisive breakthrough or destroy the previously shattered Russian forces individually.

During the third phase Moscow and Leningrad would have to be seized and the drive into the eastern Ukraine initiated. The distances to be covered were 250 and 200 miles respectively. Whether this phase could be executed immediately after the second would depend upon the condition of the railroads, the serviceability of the track-laying and wheeled vehicles, and the degree of success hitherto achieved. If the Russians were beaten, a few armored or motorized divisions would suffice to keep them off balance, and to seize Moscow and Leningrad and thrust deep into the eastern Ukraine. This would require one or two weeks if sufficient tanks and motor vehicles were available. If, however, the bulk of the Red Army was still capable of offering organized resistance, the start of the third phase would have to be delayed until sufficient supplies were brought up to support the continuation of the offensive. In this case it might be 3-6 weeks, depending on the time needed for the supply buildup.

The fourth and last phase of the offensive would see the Germans pursuing the Russians to the Don, the Volga, and the Severnaya Dvina. The distances to be covered were 250 miles in the south and up to 500 in the center and north. After the Germans had captured Kharkov, Moscow, and Leningrad, the Soviet command would have lost control over its forces but complete occupation of the territory acquired during this phase would be neither possible nor necessary. Motorized forces and rail-transported infantry would be responsible for this operation. The time needed for this phase was estimated at 2-4 weeks.

The total time required to attain the designated objective would therefore vary between a minimum of 9 and a maximum of 17 weeks.

In the event that the Soviet government did not collapse or make peace, the offensive might have to be continued to the Ural Mountains. After the destruction of their armed forces and the loss of their most valuable European territories, the Soviets would probably no longer be capable of conducting military operations but could still set up a government in Asia and maintain a state of war for an indefinite period.

To this plan General Marcks added recommendations for the preparation of the campaign, including details regarding signal communications; the construction and improvement of roads, bridges, railroad facilities, and billeting areas; the organization, equipment, and training of troops; and the procurement of cartographic material.

General Marcks discussed his plan with General der Kavallerie (Lt. Gen.) Ernst Koestring, the German military attaché in Moscow, during the latter's presence at Army High Command headquarters. Koestring did not agree that the seizure of Moscow would be the key to victory. In his opinion the capture of Moscow would not be decisive because the Soviet Union had vast industrial resources beyond the Urals. Moreover, with their ability to improvise, the Russians would be able to reorganize their transportation net without Moscow.

Staff Work (August–September 1940)

At the beginning of August the National Defense Division of the Armed Forces High Command completed the directive for AUFBAU OST. It stated that greater military use was to be made of those German-occupied territories of Poland which had not been incorporated into the Reich. The increasing threat of air attacks on western Germany made it imperative to utilize the comparatively safe eastern territories for the activation and training of new units. The necessary accommodations and facilities had to be built; supply depots had to be transferred from west to east; and road, rail, and signal communications had to be improved. The directive was signed by Keitel and issued to all interested military and civilian agencies.

The Army General Staff and technical service divisions were particularly interested in implementing the directive, and a number of organizational measures were initiated by General Halder and his assistants. In September, personnel of the Operations Division under the direction of the new Assistant Chief of Staff, Operations, General-leutnant (Maj. Gen.) Friedrich Paulus, began to work on a strategic survey based on the Marcks plan.

General Jodl had meanwhile asked his subordinates in the National Defense Division to prepare a campaign plan for his own information. This study was to be drawn up without recourse to the plans that were being prepared by the Army, because Jodl wanted to check the Army plans before they were submitted to Hitler. The National Defense Division plan, submitted to Jodl on 19 September, stressed the need for concentrating the attack forces north of the Pripyat Marshes so that they could take the shortest route to Moscow via Smolensk. Three army groups were to be employed; after Army Group Center had seized the Smolensk area, the continuation of the offensive was to depend upon the progress made by Army Group North. If the latter proved to be sufficiently strong to sustain the drive on Leningrad, Army Group Center would employ all its forces on the continuation of its thrust on Moscow. In the event, however, that Army Group North should be unable to make satisfactory progress, Army Group Center would have to halt its advance and divert forces to lend assistance.

In the Finnish Theater of Operations the National Defense planners wanted to concentrate all available German and Finnish forces in the south; no attack in the direction of Murmansk was contemplated. The thrust from southern Finland was to be coordinated with the advance of Army Group North and was to be directed across the Karelian Isthmus toward Leningrad or from east of Lake Lodoga toward Tikhvin.

The strategic survey then being prepared by the Operations Division of the Army probably influenced the National Defense Division plan because of the close relationship between the Armed Forces and Army High Command personnel on the operating level.

Admiral Raeder's Suggestions (26 September 1940)

On 26 September the Commander in Chief of the Navy, Adm. Erich Reader, suggested to Hitler that Germany should support the Italian attempt to seize the Suez Canal, whose possession would be vital for a farther advance across Palestine and Syria. Once this had been achieved, Turkey would be at Germany's mercy. The Russian problem would then have an entirely different aspect, since the Soviet Union was basically afraid of Germany. Under such circumstances it would be doubtful whether an invasion of Russia from the north would still be necessary.

In expressing his approval of Raeder's ideas, Hitler stated that Russia would have to be tempted to turn toward Persia and India, where she could gain access to the open sea. That would be far more important to Russia than her position in the Baltic. Hitler, also, was of the opinion that the Soviet Union was apprehensive of Germany's power.

Strategic Survey (October 1940)

During October 1940 the Operations Division completed the preparation of a strategic survey which was submitted to General Halder on 29 October. In this study the Army General Staff formulated its own ideas regarding the most appropriate strategy for a campaign against the Soviet Union. The authors of the study realized that the Red Army's numerical strength, the vast terrain to be covered, the adverse conditions of the Russian theater, and the necessity of defeating the Soviet Union with a minimum of delay raised a series of problems for which in many instances no fully satisfactory solutions could be found. On the other hand, ever since the Red Army had performed so badly during the campaign against Finland in the winter of 1939-40, the average German General Staff officer had a low opinion of the military potential of the Soviet Union. Moreover, it was generally assumed that the people in areas recently occupied by the Soviet Union were anti-Russian and anti-Communist, and that disaffection in the Ukraine, the Crimea, and the Caucasus was equally widespread. The purges of 1937 were considered as evidence of the vulnerability of the Soviet Union.

The major factors considered in the study were as follows:

a. Manpower. The ratio of strength between German and Russian forces was not at all favorable. Against the approximately 170 Soviet divisions plus ample reinforcements estimated to be stationed in western Russia the Germans could at best put only 145—including 19 armored divisions—into the field. Small contingents of Romanian and Finnish forces could be added to this total, but their equipment, capabilities, and combat efficiency were below the German. In other words, the German offensive forces would not have the advantage of numerical superiority. The only method of compensating for this deficiency was to mass forces at crucial points and take risks at others. The relative combat efficiency was not as clear cut. To be sure, the German forces had had more combat experience; their leaders were experienced in maneuvering large motorized forces, and the individual soldier was self-confident. The Russian soldier, however, was not to be underestimated, and it remained doubtful whether the Red Army would show immediate signs of internal disintegration. On the other hand, Russian leadership was certainly below the German average, particularly in making quick decisions in a war of movement.

The element of surprise in launching the attack would probably compensate for some of the German numerical inferiority. Extensive deceptive measures were to be taken to achieve surprise, but Hitler's pretext that preparations along the Russian border were merely a deliberate deception to divert British attention from an imminent invasion of England could not be maintained indefinitely. In the final analysis, surprise was limited to the timing and direction of the German attack; to hope for more seemed unrealistic.

b. Space. The tremendous width and depth of European Russia was another problem that deserves serious consideration, especially in view of the disproportion of strength. Everything would depend on the German Army's ability to prevent the Russians from exploiting this space advantage. Whether they would give battle near the border or attempt an organized withdrawal could not be foreseen. In any event, it was essential to engage the enemy as soon as possible, if his quick destruction was to be achieved. The distribution of the German forces and the application of deceptive measures had to conform with this intention. The Russians had to be denied any opportunity to withdraw into the depths of European Russia where they could fight a series of delaying actions. This objective could be attained only by strict application of the principles of mass, economy of force, and movement. Substantial Russian forces were to be cut off from their rear communications and forced to fight on reversed fronts. This was

the only method by which the German Army could cope with the factor of space during the offensive operations. Lacking the necessary forces, the German Army could not mount an offensive along the entire front at the same time, but had to attempt to open gaps in the front at crucial points, envelop and isolate Russian forces, and annihilate them before they had a chance to fall back.

c. Time. The problem of selecting the most propitious time assumed far more importance than on any previous occasion. For operations in Russia the May-to-October period only seemed to offer a reasonable guarantee of favorable weather. The muddy season began in late October, followed by the dreaded Russian winter. The campaign had to be successfully concluded while the weather was favorable, and distances varying from five to six hundred miles had to be covered during this period. From the outset the German campaign plan would be under strong pressure of time.

d. Intelligence Information. The intelligence picture revealed two major Russian concentrations—one in the Ukraine of about 70 divisions and the other in White Russia near and west of Minsk of some 60 divisions. There appeared to be only 30 divisions in the Baltic States.

The disposition of the Red Army forces did offer the Soviets the possibility of launching an offensive in the direction of Warsaw. But, if attacked by Germany, it was uncertain whether the Russians would make a stand in the border area or fight a delaying action. It could be assumed, though, that they would not voluntarily withdraw beyond the Dnepr and Dvina Rivers, since their industrial centers would remain unprotected.

e. Analysis of Objective Area. The almost impassable forests and swamps of the Pripyat Marshes divided the Russian territory, west of the Dnepr and Dvina Rivers into two separate theaters of operation. In the southern part the road net was poor. The main traffic arteries followed the river courses and therefore ran mostly in a north-south direction. The communication system north of the Pripyat Marshes was more-favorable. The best road and rail nets were to be found in the area between Warsaw and Moscow, where the communications ran east and west and thus in the direction of the German advance. The traffic arteries leading to Leningrad were also quite favorable. A rapid advance in the south would be hampered by major river barriers—the Dnestr, the Bug, and the Dnepr—whereas in the north only a single river, the Dvina, would have to be crossed. By thrusting straight across the territory north of the Pripyat one could strike at Moscow. The Red Army would not simply abandon the Russian capital and in the struggle for its possession the Germans could hope to deliver a telling blow.

By contrast, the area south of the Pripyat region was of minor military importance; there the Soviets could more readily trade space for time and withdraw to a new line, possibly behind the Dnepr River. On the other hand, the south offered tempting economic targets, such as the wheat of the Ukraine, the coal fields of the Donets Basin, and the faraway oil of the Caucasus. The Army's immediate interest, however, was to attain military victory, not economic advantages. The quicker the campaign was over the more decisive the victory, the more certain would be the eventual accrual of economic advantages.

For these reasons the Operations Division arrived at the conclusion that the main effort should be concentrated north of the Pripyat Marshes and that the principal thrust should be directed via Smolensk toward Moscow.

The Preliminary Plan (November–5 December 1940)

During November the Army High Command was primarily concerned with preparations for an attack on Gibraltar and armed intervention on the Balkan Peninsula. At the same time, the training and equipment of the newly activated divisions proceeded according to schedule. Molotov's visit in Berlin on 12–13 November aroused some hope that Hitler's intentions might be modified by a change in Soviet policy. When Admiral Raeder saw the Fuehrer on the day after Molotov's departure, he found that Hitler continued to plan for an attack on Russia. Raeder suggested that such a conflict be delayed until a victory had been won over Britain. His reasons were that a

war with the Soviet Union would involve too great an expenditure of German strength and that it was impossible to foretell where it would end. Raeder then explained that the Soviets were dependent on German assistance for building up their navy and would therefore not attack Germany for the next few years.

In November the Soviet Government made the first official inquiry at the German Embassy in Moscow with regard to German troop concentrations in the former Polish provinces adjacent to the Russian border. General Koestring, the German military attaché, was called to Berlin, where he was instructed to reply that the troop movements were incidental to the redeployment after the campaign in the West,

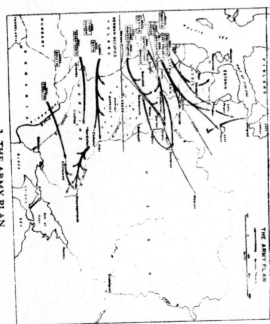

THE ARMY PLAN

3. THE ARMY PLAN

13

the requirements of the occupation, and the better training facilities available in this area.

While these demarches were being carried on, the Army prepared its preliminary plan on the basis of previous staff and concurrent General Staff exercises. On 5 December Brauchitsch and Halder presented their plan to Hitler at a conference during which the preparations for various future operations were examined. [See DA Pam No. 20-260, *The German Campaigns in the Balkans (Spring 1941)*, Map 2.] In his verbal report, Halder first explained the topographical features of the Russian theater and mentioned that the most important industrial centers were in the Ukraine, in Moscow, and around Leningrad. The Pripyat Marshes divided the theater into a northern and a southern part. The roads in the latter were poor; the best rail and road net was to be found in the region between Warsaw and Moscow. The northern part of the theater was therefore more favorable for large-scale maneuvers than the southern. For this reason the Russians were apparently concentrating more troops in the northern regions than in the south. Another remarkable feature in their distribution of forces was the massing of forces in the vicinity of areas in which Soviet and German spheres of interest overlapped. [See map 3.]

The course of the Dnepr and Dvina would be the easternmost limits to which the Russians could withdraw without exposing their industrial centers. German armored wedges would have to drive through the Russian lines and break up the enemy defense system west of these rivers. A particularly strong attack force would have to be assembled for the thrust from the Warsaw area toward Moscow. Three army groups were to launch the offensive: Army Group North was to thrust from East Prussia toward Leningrad, Army Group Center via Minsk toward Smolensk, and Army Group South toward Kiev. The third drive was to be executed by two armies jumping off from the Lublin and Jaroslav areas respectively, and by a third army thrusting from Moldavia toward the lower course of the Dnepr. The objective of the entire offensive was to reach the course of the Volga and the region around Archangel. The total assault force was to consist of 105 infantry and 32 armored and motorized infantry divisions, strong elements of which were to form the second wave.

Hitler agreed with Halder's plan and added that it was of the utmost importance to prevent the Russians from making a planned withdrawal. The Soviet military potential had to be eliminated and its regeneration made impossible. In planning the initial distribution of forces, every effort would have to be made to destroy the maximum number of Russian units near the border. For this purpose the armored and motorized divisions of the two army groups operating in the northern part of the theater would have to be committed on their adjoining wings. In the north, the enemy forces stationed in the Baltic States would have to be enveloped and cut off. Army Group Center would therefore have to be so strong that it could divert considerable forces northward to assist Army Group North if necessary. Army Group South would jump off later than the other two, with some elements advancing from Romania, while the main force, thrusting southeastward, was to envelop the enemy forces in the Ukraine. Finally, Hitler indicated that Romania and Finland would participate in the operation. A secondary attack in the far north was to be launched by three German divisions.

The Fuehrer did not consider the capture of Moscow as particularly important. He therefore did not want to commit himself whether the destruction of the bulk of the Russian forces in the northern and southern pockets was to be immediately followed by an advance toward and beyond Moscow. He also believed that 130-140 divisions would suffice for bringing the Russian campaign to a successful conclusion.

Upon resuming his report Halder pointed out that according to the most recent data the assembly would take 8 weeks and that the German preparations could not be concealed from the enemy after the beginning or the middle of April at the latest.

General Staff and Command Post Exercises
(November–December 1940)

The preliminary plan was tested in a General Staff exercise conducted by the Assistant Chief of Staff, Operations, General Paulus. General Staff officers responsible for the drafting of the plan acted as group leaders. Paulus divided the exercise into three phases: the first began 29 November with the invasion and the initial battles near the border; the second, beginning 3 December, continued the offensive operations to the line Kiev–Minsk–Lake Peipus; and the last, staged 7 December, dealt with reaching the potential objectives beyond this line.

After each phase Paulus indicated the premises for the start of the next part of the exercise by explaining the phase line that had been reached, the condition of the troops, the supply situation, intelligence estimate, etc. All participants thus based their ideas on the same data. During the third phase of the game it became evident that the German ground forces would hardly be sufficiently strong to fan out across the funnel-shaped Russian theater if—contrary to the generally prevailing opinion—the Red Army was capable of offering continued resistance. Paulus reported the results and the lessons learned to Halder.

Generalmajor (Brig. Gen.) Eduard Wagner, Chief, Supply and Administration Division, prepared logistical exercises, which were to take place in December and January. Wagner also worked on a logistical plan that was to serve as a counterpart to the strategic survey prepared by the Operations Division. Special emphasis was placed on establishing an efficient supply system in the assembly areas and drawing up a sound base-development plan to guarantee the flow of supplies during the execution of far-reaching operations in the Russian theater.

Concurrent with, but independent of, these exercises the chiefs of staff of the three army groups were asked to work on problems involved in a campaign against Russia. They were briefed by Halder

who limited the scope of their investigations to defeating the Russian forces in White Russia and the western Ukraine. Paulus provided them with all the necessary data, and each officer was instructed to arrive at a solution without consulting his fellow workers. The studies submitted at the beginning of December 1940 were carefully scrutinized by both Halder and Paulus. Ideas that were at great variance with those submitted in the preliminary plan were selected as topics of discussion for a conference of all chiefs of staff of any groups and armies which took place at Army High Command Headquarters on 13 and 14 December 1940. The discussions served to clarify a number of problems for which no solution had been found during the various exercises. It was also concluded that the Soviet Union would be defeated in a campaign not exceeding 8–10 weeks' duration.

Economic Survey

In November 1940 Reichs Marshal Hermann Goering ordered General der Infanterie (Lt. Gen.) Georg Thomas, Chief, Armed Forces Economic Office, to study the economic implications of a campaign against the Soviet Union. In the summary of his report Thomas arrived at the following conclusions:

a. During the initial months of an operation which would lead to the occupation of European Russia excluding the Urals, Germany would improve its food and raw material position, if the destruction of Soviet supplies could be prevented, if the Caucasus oil region was seized intact, and if the transportation problem was solved.

b. In the event that hostilities should continue for some time, Germany would benefit only if the transportation problem was solved and the civilian population induced to remain and cooperate. More specifically:

(1) The destruction of mechanized equipment would have to be prevented and the production of new farm machinery would have to be resumed without delay. Supplies of petroleum, oil, and lubricants (POL) would have to be allocated to agriculture.

15

(2) The industrial production would depend on the immediate availability of electric power plants and the delivery of raw materials generally unavailable in European Russia.

c. Until the establishment of a link with the Far East, Germany would be short of s'ch strategic materials as rubber, tungsten, copper, platinum, zinc, asb'tos, and jute.

d. The area sou... of the Volga and Don estuaries including the Caucasus would have to be included among the objectives of the operation. The oil produced in the Caucasus region would be essential for the exploitation of any territories occupied in Russia.

e. By occupying European Russia, Germany would seize 75 percent of the total Soviet armament potential and almost 100 percent of the precision-tool and optical industries.

The study was submitted to Hitler who, though recognizing its intrinsic value, failed to make any basic changes in his overall military-political plans.

Directive BARBAROSSA (18 December 1940)

On 6 December General Jodl requested General Warlimont to draw up a directive for the campaign against Russia on the basis of the preliminary plan that had been approved by Hitler. Six days later the draft of Directive No. 21 was submitted to Jodl who made a few insignificant changes and ordered a revised draft prepared. The same day the Navy submitted a report stressing the danger of starting a war on a second front while Germany's naval forces were fully engaged in the struggle against Britain. On 16 December Warlimont submitted the revised draft of the directive to Jodl who was to present it to Hitler the next day. During their conference Jodl and Warlimont discussed the dangers of a two-front war and the serious POL problems it would involve.

On 17 December Jodl presented the draft of Directive No. 21 to Hitler who made some basic changes with regard to the mission of the two army groups that were to be committed north of the Pripyat Marshes. First priority was to be given to the capture of Leningrad and Kronshtadt and to the destruction of the enemy forces in the Baltic States. The advance on Moscow would not be resumed until these objectives had been attained. Only if Russia's military machine collapsed earlier than anticipated would Army Group Center be permitted to drive simultaneously on Leningrad and Moscow.

After the necessary changes had been incorporated in the directive it was signed by Hitler on 18 December and distributed to the services under the new cover name Operation BARBAROSSA. The directive read as follows:

Directive No. 21

Operation BARBAROSSA   18 December 1940

The German Armed Forces must make preparations to crush *Soviet Russia in a lightning campaign*, even before the termination of hostilities with Great Britain (Operation BARBAROSSA).

For this purpose the *Army* will commit all available forces except those needed to safeguard the occupied territories against surprise attacks.

The *Air Force* will earmark sufficient forces in support of the ground operations to guarantee the rapid conclusion of this campaign and to minimize any potential damage eastern Germany might suffer through enemy air attacks. The concentration of air power in the East is, however, subject to certain limitations. First, all German-held military bases and war production centers must be adequately protected against enemy air raids. Second, the air offensive against Great Britain and against its life lines in particular must not be slowed down.

The *Navy* will continue to focus its attention on *Great Britain* while the campaign against Russia takes place.

In due time, i. e., at least eight weeks before the intended start of the operation, I shall issue a directive for the strategic concentration against Soviet Russia.

Any preparations which require more time and are not already under way will be initiated immediately and brought to a conclusion before 15 May 1941.

It is absolutely essential that the preparations for the attack remain unobserved.

The operational planning of the individual services should be based on the following premises:

I. Overall Plan

During the initial phase the bulk of the Russian *Army* stationed in western Russia is to be destroyed in a series of daring operations spearheaded by armored thrusts. The organized withdrawal of intact units into the vastness of interior Russia must be prevented.

During the next phase a fast pursuit will be launched up to a line from which the Russian air force will be incapable of attacking German territory. The ultimate objective of the operation is to screen European against Asiatic Russia along the course of the Volga and thence along a general line extending northward toward Archangel. Thus, if necessary, the German Air Force would be in a position to neutralize the last industrial region remaining in Russian hands, i. e. that situated in the Urals.

As a result of these ground operations the Russian *Baltic Fleet* will rapidly lose its bases and thus cease to be operational.

Any effective interference by the Russian *Air Force* will be eliminated by the delivery of decisive blows at the very beginning of the campaign.

II. Prospective Allies and their Mission

Romania's and Finland's active participation in the war against Soviet Russia is to be anticipated; they will provide contingents on either wing of our ground forces.

In due course the Armed Forces High Command will approach these two countries and make arrangements as to the manner in which their military contingents will be placed under German command at the time of their intervention.

Romania will employ elite forces to give at least initial support to the offensive launched by the German southern attack forces. In addition, Romania's mission will call for tying down enemy forces in the south, wherever no German units are committed, and lending assistance in maintaining the lines of communications.

Finland will cover the concentration of the German Force North (elements of Force XXI) which will be transferred from Norway, and the Finnish troops will operate in conjunction with this force. Moreover, Finland will have to neutralize Hanko.

It may be assumed that, by the start of the campaign at the latest, there will be a possibility of using the *Swedish* railroads and highways for the transfer of the German Force North.

III. The Campaign Plans

A. *Army* (in conformity with the plans submitted to me by the Army):

For the purpose of the campaign the theater of operations is divided into a southern and northern part by the Pripyat Marshes. The main effort is to be placed *north* of the Pripyat, where two army groups are to be committed. Of these two army groups the one on the right will be provided with especially powerful motorized infantry and armored forces. Its mission will be to thrust from the area around, but especially north, of Warsaw and to shatter the enemy forces in White Russia. This preliminary operation will set the stage for a pivoting movement performed by strong motorized elements that will drive northward in order to annihilate the enemy forces in the Baltic area in conjunction with the northern army group which will be driving from East Prussia in the general direction of Leningrad. After this most urgent mission has been successfully accomplished, the cities of Leningrad and Kronshtadt must be captured. Only then will the offensive operations leading to the seizure of Moscow, the important communications and armament production center, be continued. Simultaneous drives toward both objectives might be envisaged only in the event of an unexpectedly rapid collapse of the Russian resistance.

During the Russian campaign, Force XXI will continue to consider the protection of Norway as its primary mission. Any excess forces available beyond the scope of this mission will be committed primarily in the north (mountain corps) to secure the Petsamo region and its ore mines as well as the highway connecting Petsamo with Oulu (Arctic Highway). Together with Finnish contingents these forces will subsequently thrust toward the Murmansk railway in an attempt to prevent supplies from reaching the Murmansk area by land.

Whether an operation by a *stronger* German force—consisting of two to three divisions which would jump off from the region around and south of Rovaniemi—can be executed, will depend on Sweden's willingness to make its railroads available for such a concentration of German units.

The bulk of the Finnish Army will coordinate its operations with the advance of the German north wing. Its principal missions will be to tie down the maximum Russian forces by an attack west of or on both sides of Lake Ladoga and to seize Hanko.

The army group committed *south* of the Pripyat Marshes will also attempt a double envelopment. Strong forces concentrated on both wings are to achieve the complete annihilation of the Russian troops in the Ukraine west of the Dnepr. The *main attack* will be directed from the Lublin area toward Kiev, while the forces concentrated in Romania will cross the lower Pruth River and form the other arm of a wide envelopment. The Romanian Army will have the mission of tying down the Russian forces which are to be caught between the two pincers.

Once the battles south and north of the Pripyat Marshes have been brought to a successful conclusion, pursuits will be launched with the following objectives:

In the south the Donets Basin, highly important from a military-economic poln. J view, must be seized without delay. The political and economic significance of capturing this city is tremendous. Moreover, German possession of Moscow will deprive the enemy of the most important railway hub.

B. Air Force:

Its mission will be to paralyze and eliminate the Russian air force, and to support the Army's operations at the points of main effort, particularly in the Army Group Center area and along the north wing of Army Group South. According to their significance for the course of the campaign, the Russian railways will be severed by air attacks. In some instances most important railroad installations (river crossings!) will be seized by vertical envelopments performed by parachute and airborne troops.

In order to concentrate the entire striking power of the German Air Force on neutralizing the enemy air force and on providing direct support for the Army, the Russian armament industry will not be attacked during the initial phase of the campaign. Once the war of movement has come to a conclusion, such attacks might be considered, particularly against the industrial region in the Urals.

C. Navy:

In addition to defending the German coast, the Navy will have the mission of preventing the enemy naval forces from forcing their way out of the Baltic Sea. Once the Leningrad area has been seized, the Russian Baltic Fleet will have been deprived of all its bases. Since its situation will then be altogether hopeless, major naval engagements prior to that time must be avoided.

After the Russian fleet has been eliminated, it will be important to establish full-scale maritime traffic in the Baltic, including the logistical support of ground forces in the northern part of the Russian theater (mine sweeping!).

IV. All orders issued by the commanders in chief of the services on the basis of this directive are to be formulated in such a manner that they leave no doubt on the *precautionary nature of these measures* which are prepared for the event that Russia should change her present attitude toward us. The number of officers to be informed during the preliminary stage must be kept to a minimum. Additional personnel will be initiated as late as feasible, and then only to the extent necessary for the performance of their individual duties. This will minimize the risk of serious political and military consequences that might result from our preparations—for the implementation of which not even a deadline has been set—becoming known.

V. I request the commanders in chief of the services to report to me on their future plans which are to be based on this directive.

All services will submit to me progress reports on their projected preparations through the Armed Forces High Command.

ADOLF HITLER

The generally held opinion that the Russian campaign would be of short duration found its clearest expression in Section III B of Directive No. 21, pertaining to the Air Force. By giving the Luftwaffe primarily a ground-support mission and equipping it accordingly, Hitler and Goering expressed their belief that strategic bombing would be unnecessary. The Navy, however, did not anticipate the Russian campaign with so much optimism.

On 27 December Admiral Raeder tried once more to convince Hitler that Germany's most urgent task was to concentrate all its military power against Britain. That country was gaining strength as a result of the Italian reverses in the Mediterranean and the increasing support it received from the United States. On the other hand, Britain could be defeated if Germany turned its entire war potential to strengthening the Navy and Air Force. Any dissipation of strength would prolong the war and jeopardize the final success. In concluding, Raeder raised very strong objections against starting the Russian campaign before Britain was defeated.

In his reply Hitler agreed that greater stress would have to be placed on submarine construction. In general, however, he felt that the Soviet Union's expansionist policy in the Balkans made it mandatory that Germany eliminate its last opponent on the European continent before the final showdown with Britain. For this purpose, the Army would have to be built up first; as soon as the Russian campaign had been won, the needs of the Navy and Luftwaffe would have priority.

Critique of the German Plan

To understand campaign failures it is important that you know what the Barbarossa directive implied. Hitler had ordered that; "The armed forces of Germany must be prepared . . . to defeat Soviet Russia in one rapid campaign. . . The bulk of the Russian Army stationed in Western Russia is to be destroyed in a series of daring spearheaded armored thrusts. The organized withdrawal of intact units into the vastness of interior Russia must be prevented. . ."

The directive then divided the area of operations into southern and northern halves by the Pripet marshes. The main effort was to be in the northern half where two army groups were committed. The southern of these two army groups - in the center of the whole front - had the task of breaking out of the area around Warsaw with strong armored formations. The destruction the enemy forces in White Russia was to create a situation which would enable strong formations of mobile troops to swing north to cooperate with the northern army group in destroying the enemy forces in the area of the Baltic states. Only *after* the accomplishment of these offensive operations, which was to be followed by the capture of Leningrad were further offensive operations to be initiated against Moscow.

Only a surprisingly rapid collapse of the Russian ability to resist was to justify an attempt to achieve both objectives simultaneously. Only after winning the battles south and north of the Pripyat Marshes was the pursuit toward the Donetz Basin, and Moscow to begin. The capture of Moscow was recognized to be a decisive goal from both the political and the economic point of view. It would also neutralize the most vital Russian rail center.

The map on the right shows what the implied and stated objectives actually were. The Marcks plan envisaged heavy thrusts to Moscow and Kiev, later culminating in a large pincer from Moscow and Kiev to the Kharkov region. The plan was modified by the Army High Command by weakening the Kiev thrust and in favor of strengthening the subsidiary flank operation against Leningrad. The army plan involved three relatively equal drives, with a continuation of the thrust through Moscow to the East and North. Hitler's plan was essentially the same as that of the army with one important exception, perhaps based on Jodl's appraisal, or perhaps invented through "intuition". This change is represented by the arrow northwards from Smolensk. Leningrad's capture was to preceed a conclusive Moscow offensive! In principle, Hitler and his generals agreed on importance of Moscow, and there may have been little strategically wrong with the modification of the army plan. After all it would free the northern mobile units to participate in the Moscow drive.

In fact, the plan was flawed by timing and weather. It both assumed an unrealistically rapid advance and ignored climate trends (temperature table) which indicated that campaigning weather near Moscow ended in November. The Moscow area began freezing one month sooner than areas to the north and two months sooner in the south. Since the German army was unprepared for winter warfare it would have been more logical to complete the Moscow fighting before diverting either north or south. This was the fallacy of the planned Leningrad diversion.

In any case, no generals protested the changing of the original plans. The generals either trusted Hitler and shared his wild optimism or, more likely, held a completely opposite opinion - that the entire directive was merely precautionary and would not be implemented. In either case, on 22 June the commanders on the eastern front knew that their advance might temporarily be halted once Smolensk was reached. They were prepared for that contingency. What no one had prepared for, on the other hand, was a drive from Smolensk toward Kiev. Such diversion was not mentioned in the directive. The known weather trends definitely indicated a lack of urgency in the southern area versus need for haste in the Moscow drive. This unplanned diversion ultimately doomed the 1941 campaign to failure.

The Roads to Moscow

There are many roads to Moscow. Charles XII chose the road by Pultava. Napoleon went by way of Borodino. Hitler paused on the road through Smolensk and attempted a detour by way of Stalingrad. All three invading armies found the road home more difficult.

The importance of European Russia can only be understood in terms of the entire continent. The Soviet Union is the world's largest political unit, occupying about one-sixth of all inhabitable land. The Soviet Union is three times the size of the United States and it stretches about 6000 miles from Poland to the Pacific and some 3000 miles from the Arctic circle to Afghanistan.

The 200 million 1941 population was about ¾ Slavic but only ½ true Russian (Great Russian). About 37 million Ukrainians comprised the largest of the minority groups. The 8½ million White Russians (*Byello-russians*) who occupied much of the area from Brest Litovsk to Smolensk were a peasant people plagued by repeated invasions, with low literacy and little national identity.

European Russia, the most developed portion of the U.S.S.R., re-presented a fraction of the total Soviet landmass and yet was tremendous by European standards. It is about 600 miles from Warsaw to Moscow. The distance to Leningrad is about 100 miles closer to the West, and Stalingrad is some 300 miles further East. The lateral distance from Leningrad to Odessa is about 900 miles.

Most of European Russia (west of the Urals) consists of the East European plain - a series of plateaus with an average elevation of 500 feet. There are few abrupt topographical changes. Nevertheless, there is an impressive series of obstacles to shield the heart of the country. The largest is the great Pripyat marsh between White Russia and the Ukraine, consisting of about 150,000 square miles of densely forested swamps. A wide belt of forests and smaller swamps obstruct movement to the north. Deep woodlands near Gomel and Bryansk combine with these to blunt any thrust toward Moscow.

The natural barriers include a series of river lines-notably the Berezina, Dvina, Dnepr and Desna. These tributaries and swampy watersheds cut across invasion routes. The German invaders faced innumerable cross-ings and periodic flooding necessitated constructing approach roads which often was more difficult than actual bridging.) Only in the Vitebsk - Orsha - Smolensk triangle was the river net's defense value reduced - which explains its strategic importance as an invasion route. But even there, as throughout most of the central front, the soil and climatic con-ditions could void all schedules of military movements.

Bottlenecks blocked and delayed movement through the forests and mud stopped most wheeled, and even some tracked movement. Advances were often confined to a few narrow and unpaved roads. Normal col-umns could rarely be organized and more than a non-motorized pace was difficult to maintain. (Special road equipment and supporting tracked vehicles were scarce in 1941). Reliable travel calculations proved impossible and a motorized pace of 5-6 miles per hour was used as a rule of thumb. This type of movement required a much higher expen-diture of fuel, which averaged three or four times what was needed in Western Europe.

Such conditions naturally threw a heavy burden on the few decent roads and rail lines, thereby increasing their relative importance. In 1941 the Soviet Union had only about 60,000 miles of rail roads - mostly in European Russia. Less than 30% of these were double tracked. The rail density of European Russia was less than 21 miles per 1000 square miles, as compared to about 155 miles per 1000 square miles in Germany, for example. In addition to the scarcity, the track was also wider than the standard European (except in Lithuania and Latvia). This often made transshipment, and essential track replacement man-datory at the Soviet border. There was only one double track line in central Russia, from Warsaw to Brest to Minsk to Smolensk to Moscow. Some medium and low capacity lines offered alternate possibilities, but each of the three invading army groups had only one major rail line for logistical supply.

The road net was similarly poor. Of the total Soviet estimated mil-eage of about 65,000 miles, only about 4% was asphalted and just one stretch, from Moscow to Minsk, could be compared to an American superhighway. All but the few paved roads deteriorated rapidly during the muddy season, thereby limiting most movement to the rail system. Because of the many rivers, requiring innumerable bridges, most roads paralled the rail lines, so the transportation map also reflects the road system. Army Group Center had the best Russian transportation net. Even more so than in Napoleon's time the central road to Moscow offered the most direct and efficient means of reaching that city.

The Lightning War Concept

The German "operational" level corresponded to activities between "strategic" and "tactical" as used in the West. It pertains to mainly corps and division level maneuvers. This term is not commonly used by the American Army. The idea of *Blitzkrieg* or lightning war is best understood at the level.

Terms like "pincer", "point of main effort" and "double development" were mentioned in different portions of the Barbarossa directive and were essential to the plan. Schematic interpetations that do not reflect this are in error. The encirclement idea was integral to *Blitzkrieg* warfare.

German terms like *Keil und Kessel, Kesselschlaht* and *Schwerpunkt* capture the spirit of the concept if they are properly translated. The term *Blitzkrieg* - lightning war - is itself mostly a journalistic expression, referring to the brevity of a battle, with certain economic implications about the lack of total mobilization. *Keil und Kessel* has often been translated to mean "wedge and trap", and *kesselschlacht* to "encirclement battle". "Pierce and cauldron" and "cauldron battle" are closer to the actual meaning. Pierce implies the penetration on a narrow front by the *schwerpunkt* or "point of main effort." A cauldron holds something within. The idea was to mass combat power on narrow fronts, pierce through the enemy line, and cauldron-off enemy units. The encircled units were thus forced to fight at a disadvantage in order to survive.

The *schwerpunkt* was almost irresistable when adequately supported by artillery and air units. The first wave of Blitzkrieg consisted of the armored units - a mailed fist that punched across and around the defender's line. *Stukas*, artillery, and antitank units dealt with counterattacks and reduced strongpoints, while an infantry crust observed and absorbed the initial shocks of counter enemy reaction. The early German campaigns in Russia illustrate a *Blitzkrieg* warfare.

II

OPERATIONAL PLANNING

The Army's Operation Order (3 February 1941)

During January 1941 each army group was informed of its mission as stipulated in Directive No. 21 and ordered to carry out intracommand map maneuvers for the purpose of studying the operation plan in detail and examining the proposed courses of action. A number of command post exercises took place at each army group headquarters, and the ideas formulated on these occasions were discussed in great detail during meetings of Army High Command and army group representatives.

At a conference that took place in Berlin on 31 January, Field Marshal von Brauchitsch told the commanding generals of the army groups that his plans were based on the assumption that the Russians would give battle west of the Dnepr–Dvina line. Later on, when one of the army group commanders asked Halder whether this assumption was supported by facts, the latter replied: "It might easily turn out different."

Some of the ideas expressed during the exercises and meetings were incorporated into the operation order, which was the Army High Command's implementation of Directive No. 21. The order originated from the Operations Division and was eventually signed by Field Marshal von Brauchitsch after Hitler approved it on 3 February. In the introductory part of the order it was stated that preparations for defeating the Soviet Union in a lightning campaign had to be made in the event that the USSR should change its attitude toward Germany. For this purpose armored wedges would have to be driven deep into western Russia and the bulk of the Red Army would have to be destroyed before it had a chance to withdraw.

The Russians would probably try to stem the tide by defending prepared positions along the new and former borders as well as by holding the numerous river lines west of the Dnepr and Drina Rivers. It was to be expected that the Soviet command would make a special effort to hold the Baltic States and the coastal provinces along the Black Sea as long as possible in order to keep important air and naval bases in its possession. If the battles southeast and northeast of the Pripyat Marshes took an unfavorable turn for the Russians, the next attempt to stop the German offensives would probably be made along the Dnepr and Dvina.

After stating the overall mission of each army group, the order assigned the specific tasks as follows:

a. *Army Group South.* This army group was to assemble two strong attack forces, one along the Prut River in Romania, the other in the Lublin–Jaroslav area. [See *map 8.*] These two forces were to thrust in the direction of Kirovograd and Kiev respectively, and thus accomplish a double envelopment of Russian forces in the western Ukraine. The significance of Kiev as the capital of the Ukraine, the headquarters of one of the most important military districts of the Soviet Union and the site of vital bridges across the Dnepr, was unquestioned. Here, too, was the point from which, after the initial border engagements, Army Group South was to coordinate any further advance with the movements of Army Group Center.

The southern arm of the pincers was the Twelfth Army, consisting of German and Romanian divisions and including one motorized infantry and two armored divisions. It was to drive northeastward via Kirovograd toward the Dnepr. The connecting link between the two prongs was to be the relatively weak Seventeenth Army, which had no armored units. Since neutral Hungary's territory was not to be used, this army was to assemble southeast of Lublin and advance toward Vinnitsa and Berdichev, in order to pin down the front of the Russian forces that were threatened by a double envelopment.

was to jump off from Suwalki and drive toward Molodechno and Orsha. The objective of these two forces was the encirclement and destruction of all Russian forces between the border and Minsk. Second and Third Panzer Groups were then to move on Smolensk from the southwest and from the northwest respectively, thus preventing a reorganization of enemy forces along the upper Dnepr and Dvina Rivers. Fourth Army was to follow Second Panzer Group, advancing via Bobruysk and Borisov to Mogilev and the area north of that town. At the same time Ninth Army, taking advantage of the Third Panzer Group thrust, was to gain the Dvina at Polotsk and farther upstream.

c. *Army Group North.* The topography of the Baltic States favored the massing of power on the right of Army Group North. A powerful drive emanating from central East Prussia and directed via Kovno and Dvinsk into the area south of Pskov would cut off the Russian troops stationed in the Baltic States and squeeze them against the Baltic. Moreover, by establishing themselves in the vicinity of Lake Ilmen the German units would be in a favorable position for continuing their advance on Leningrad. The possibility that Army Group Center would support Army Group North was anticipated but was to be made contingent upon Army High Command approval.

At the outset of the operation Fourth Panzer Group, in conjunction with Sixteenth and Eighteenth Armies, was to break through the Russian border defenses in the area bordering on the Gumbinnen-Kovno highway. The armored units were to precede the infantry elements and cross the Dvina at Dvinsk and farther downstream. Their objective was to proceed to the area south of Pskov as quickly as possible, so that they could continue their drive to the north or the northeast in accordance with the overall situation.

After breaking through the Russian border positions, Sixteenth Army was to strengthen its right and follow Fourth Panzer Group in the direction of Pskov.

Forming the northern arm of the pincer, Sixth Army was to assemble in the Lublin area together with First Panzer Group. These two forces were given the most important as well as the most difficult task within the Army Group South mission. They would have to carry the main effort and, in addition to breaking through to Kiev and participating in the encirclement of the Russian forces in the western Ukraine, Sixth Army would have to screen the army group's north flank along the Pripyat Marsh region. In its distribution of attack forces the Army High Command had not allocated any combat elements of this region on the assumption that it was unsuitable for major operations and could therefore simply be kept under observation. In view of the unsatisfactory manpower situation, the Army High Command preferred to save forces for employment in more important attack zones.

After Sixth Army and First Panzer Group had succeeded in breaking through the enemy front, the latter was to speed toward Zhitomir, establish bridgeheads on the east bank of the Dnepr at Kiev and below, wheel southeastward to hit the enemy flank and rear, and link up with Twelfth Army. Covering the left flank of the advancing armor along the Pripyat Marshes, Sixth Army was to follow the First Panzer Group as quickly as possible, first to Zhitomir and then to Kiev.

During its direct thrust across the territory west of the Dnepr, Sixth Army was to earmark strong forces for a sudden southeastward diversion.

b. *Army Group Center.* In the Army Group Center area, immediately north of the Pripyat, the Russian salient west of Bialystok offered the possibility for a double envelopment. In this area the principal objective of rapidly destroying major Russian forces seemed more easily attainable than in the area of Army Group South. Exceedingly strong forces were to be massed on both extremities of the army group front while relatively weak ones were to be employed in the center. On the right, Fourth Army, including Second Panzer Group, was to advance along the main highway Baranovichi–Minsk–Orsha, while on the left, Ninth Army, including Third Panzer Group,

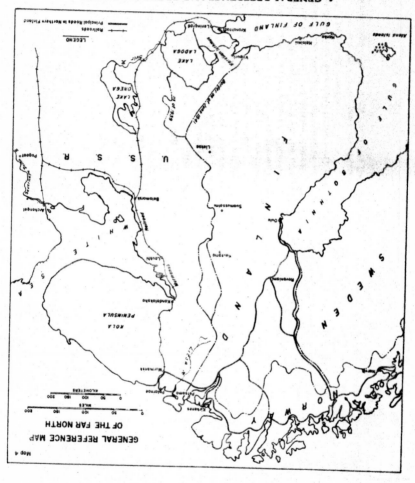

4. GENERAL REFERENCE MAP OF THE FAR NORTH

Eighteenth Army was to mass its forces along, and east of the Tilsit–Riga highway, break through the Russian lines, cross the Dvina in the vicinity of Yekabpils, and destroy the encircled Red Army forces southwest of Riga. By quickly driving on to Pskov, the army was to prevent the withdrawal of Russian forces from the area southwest of Lake Peipus and set the stage for a subsequent seizure of Estonia and the islands of Hiiumaa and Saaremaa.

At the beginning of the operation the Army High Command reserves were to be moved up to the areas west of Jaroslav and east of Warsaw, where relatively strong forces were to be assembled, and to the Lublin and East Prussian border areas, where weaker groups were to be stationed.

d. *Far North.* Finland was to coordinate its offensive across the southeastern border with the Army High Command. The Finnish forces could attack either to the east or to the west of Lake Ladoga, and they were to time their offensive to coincide with Army Group North's crossing of the Dvina River.

The Army of Norway was given a defensive and an offensive mission [See *map 4.*]:

1. To protect Norway against any landing attempt by the British, and, in particular, to strengthen the defense forces in the Kirkenes–Narvik area.

2. To seize the Petsamo area in Finland in order to secure the nickel mines and to bear down upon the Russian port of Murmansk with the intention of seizing it as soon as the overall situation would make sufficient troops available for this mission.

On 2 February Hitler received Field Marshal Fedor von Bock, the commanding general of Army Group Center, with whom he discussed the plans for Operation BARBAROSSA. Bock expressed his belief that the Germans would be able to defeat the Russians, if the latter chose to give battle. He was wondering, however, how they could be forced to make peace. The Fuehrer replied that the German Army's seizure of the Ukraine and capture of Moscow and Leningrad would surely compel the Russians to come to terms. If, however, the Soviets refused to abandon the struggle even then, German motorized forces

would have to advance as far as the Urals. He added: "In any event, I am happy that our war production is equal to any demand. We have such an abundance of materiel that we had to reconvert some of our war plants. The armed forces now have more trained manpower than at the beginning of the war, and our economy is in excellent condition." He rejected any possibility of conciliation by exclaiming: "I shall fight!"

At a conference the next day, when the campaign in the Balkans and the Army's operation order were being discussed, General Halder estimated that 100 infantry, 25 cavalry, and 30 mechanized Russian divisions would oppose the German invasion. The average Russian infantry division had direct armored support, but the tanks were of poor quality. In mechanized divisions the Red Army had quantitative superiority, the German Army qualitative. The Russian artillery, though numerically strong, was considered relatively ineffective. Among Russian leaders only Timoshenko was outstanding. But, on the other hand, the Soviet plans were unknown. Near the border were massed strong Red Army forces whose voluntary withdrawal would be limited if the Soviets wanted to keep the Baltic States and the Ukraine in their possession. And the Russians were constructing fortifications, particularly along the northern and southern sectors of the border.

Halder then summarized the instructions issued to the three army groups in the operation order. He added that Army Groups Center and North would jump off with 50 infantry, 9 motorized infantry, and 13 armored divisions, or a total of 72 divisions. Army Group South would have 30 infantry, 3 motorized infantry, and 5 armored divisions, or 38 divisions altogether. Most of the Army High Command reserves would be stationed in the northern part of the theater. Six armored divisions, which were to take part in the campaign in the Balkans, would be transferred to the Russian theater, provided the situation in the Balkans and particularly Turkey's attitude permitted such action.

Hitler interrupted by stating that once the die was cast Turkey would not budge, and that no special protection would be needed in the Balkans. He added that he had no basic objection to the Army's operation plan as presented by Halder: the theater of operations was tremendous; major elements of the Red Army could be trapped only if a tight noose was thrown around them; and he did not expect the Soviets to abandon Leningrad and the Ukraine without a struggle. On the other hand, it was quite possible that, after suffering their initial defeats and having perceived the German objectives, the Russians might stage a large-scale withdrawal to a defense line. In this event the Baltic States and the Leningrad area would have to be seized first because possession of these areas would greatly improve the logistical situation for the continuation of operations. If the center of the line was left in place until the enveloping wings began to apply pressure, the enemy forces would be unable to escape by withdrawing into the depth of the theater.

Halder continued his report by stating that one and one-half divisions of the Army of Norway were to advance toward Petsamo, while a force of approximately equal size was to be moved to northern Finland via Sweden. These two forces were to protect northern Finland and isolate the Russians around Murmansk. The Finns intended to commit 4 corps in southern Finland: 5 divisions were to advance on Leningrad, 3 toward Lake Onega, and 2 on Hanko. They would need strong German support since 15 Russian divisions stood on the other side of the Russo-Finnish border and approximately 1 division was stationed in the Murmansk area.

After Hitler observed that a rapid advance from Romanian territory was essential for safeguarding the oil fields, Halder broached the subject of Hungary. If that nation did not take an active part in the campaign, it should at least permit the use of its territory for detraining and staging purposes. Hitler felt that Hungary would consent to whatever Germany demanded, provided that proper compensation was offered. The necessary agreements would, however, have to be delayed until the last moment in order to maintain secrecy. Finland, Sweden, Hungary, and Slovakia were to be approached with regard to their cooperation only after the German intentions could no longer be concealed. The political leaders of Romania, whose participation in the campaign was certain, were the only ones to whom the German plans could be revealed. In accordance with Hitler's previous instructions, the concentration of forces in the East would be dissimulated as a large-scale deception preparatory to launching the invasion of England.

Halder then discussed matters pertaining to the other services and logistical problems. Flak protection would have to be provided by both the Army and the Luftwaffe. The Navy would have to open supply routes via the Baltic ports as rapidly as possible. The initial transport burden would fall upon truck transportation since the Russian rail lines would have to be converted to normal gauge. It was intended to organize long-distance truck transportation units to haul supplies to distribution points in the field. All transportation matters would have to be coordinated with the Luftwaffe so that no motor vehicle would remain unused. Even then, supply bases were being established in former eastern Poland, and similar installations were to be set up in Romania.

Halder also explained the plans for the strategic concentration of forces. The first echelon was then being moved into the theater. The second echelon was scheduled to begin its movement in mid-March, and these very substantial forces would be concentrated in rear areas away from the border. At the beginning of April Hungary would have to be approached regarding the transit of troops. The third echelon was to begin its movement in mid-April; from then on concealment would become difficult. The transfer of the fourth echelon was foreseen for the period from 25 April to 15 May.

Hitler approved the order as indicated, adding that "the world will hold its breath at the launching of Operation BARBAROSSA."

Initiation of Subordinate Staffs (February–March 1941)

Upon receiving the operation order from the Army High Command, the army group headquarters held map exercises and briefed the army and panzer group headquarters under their commands on their missions. Command post exercises were conducted at army and panzer group level, and special logistical problems were examined. The ideas expressed during these various exercises were incorporated into the drafts of the operation orders drawn up by each army group headquarters. Prior to being issued, these orders were submitted to the Army High Command for final approval.

A little later, corps and division headquarters were briefed on their missions. They then reexamined the tentative operation plans and orders and initiated personnel under their commands, using command post and map exercises for this purpose. The final step in this process of initiation, which actually did not take place until May or June, was to acquaint the lowest-echelon commanders with their future mission and to study the peculiarities of the terrain across which the initial attacks would have to be launched.

On 5 February for instance, General der Infanterie (Lt. Gen.) Georg von Sodenstern, Chief of Staff, Army Group South, conducted a command post exercise in which the operation plan, so far as it pertained to his army group, was put to the test. The participants were the chiefs of staff and operations officers of the armies and corps assigned to Army Group South. The outcome of the exercise revealed the difficulty of effecting an envelopment east of the Dnepr because the Russian forces remaining in the Pripyat area could easily interfere with the progress of the northern arm of the pincers. Another lesson learned was that a number of faulty assembly movements would impede the execution of the initial maneuver. The necessary changes in the plans were made on the spot. General Halder, who attended the exercise, expressed his satisfaction with the excellent presentation and fruitful discussion.

Changes in Plans (March–April 1941)

Army Group South

On 18 March Hitler decided that Sixth Army was to carry out the main thrust of Army Group South. The plan for a Twelfth Army advance from Moldavia toward the northeast was abandoned. The German and Romanian units assembling along the Pruth were to tie or more of the armed services. On 20 February Goering formed a small Luftwaffe planning staff and set it up under his own supervision near Berlin.

At the beginning of March logistical exercises took place at Army High Command headquarters, and Army Group South held a supply and administration game based on the lessons learned during Sodenstern's command post exercise of the preceding month. During the following weeks the Armed Forces and Army High Commands issued a series of directives and regulations pertaining mainly to supply and administration.

At this time the question of infantry-armor cooperation during the initial breakthrough was also the subject of particular attention. It was resolved by the decision of the Army High Command to place one infantry corps under the operational control of each panzer group during the initial assault phase. The infantry's mission was to open gaps for the armored forces which would emerge suddenly, thus achieving complete surprise. An additional advantage was that the armored units would thus be able to keep their full striking power for thrusting deep into the Russian theater. As soon as the panzer groups had advanced sufficiently, the infantry corps would revert to the control of their respective armies.

In February General Jodl and his associates in the Armed Forces High Command prepared propaganda material for the invasion, drafted special regulations pertaining to the administration of occupied Russian territories, drew up plans for military cooperation with those nations which had expressed their willingness to join Germany against the Soviet Union, and coordinated functions pertaining to two down the opposing forces and pursue them only in the event that they should withdraw. This change in plan had to be made because Hitler contended that the Dnestr was a formidable obstacle that could not be surmounted by a frontal attack without considerable delay. According to the new plan the powerful left of Army Group South was to punch its way to the Kiev area and approach the Dnestr line from the rear. The forces assembled in Moldavia would have to be sufficiently strong to prevent a Russian penetration into Romania, but this danger did not seem acute since Brauchitsch had expressed the opinion that the Russians would not attack Romania unless they were attacked from Romanian territory. According to Hitler, Hungary was to take no part in Operation BARBAROSSA, and Slovakia was to assist only in the concentration and supply of German troops.

The Yugoslav *coup d'état* on 26 March induced Hitler to expand the operations in the Balkans by attacking Yugoslavia in addition to Greece. The greater scope of the campaign in the Balkans necessitated that an army headquarters assume control of the occupied territories after the end of hostilities. Twelfth Army, which was in charge of the operations against Greece, was selected for this role, and Eleventh Army was designated as substitute headquarters for the forces assembled in Moldavia.

On 30 March 1941 the army group and army commanders reported to Hitler. During this conference the mission of Eleventh Army was discussed, and Hitler ordered the army forces divided into three separate groups, capable of backing up the Romanian divisions in case of need. Since Eleventh Army had thus been given a defensive mission, the motorized forces originally earmarked for that area were transferred to First Panzer Group. The encirclement of the Russian forces in the western Ukraine was to be effected by a single envelopment from the north, during which the armored forces were to thrust to the Dnepr at and south of Kiev, bear southeastward, and follow the bend of the river to its mouth, thus preventing the Russian forces in the western Ukraine from withdrawing across the river.

As a result of the foregoing changes, Directive No. 21 had mean-

while been amended as follows:

Section II, paragraph 3: In conjunction with the German troops assembled on Romanian territory, Romanian troops will tie down the enemy forces opposite their borders and will also lend assistance in maintaining the lines of communications.

Section III, A, paragraph 6: The army group committed south of the Pripyat Marshes will concentrate its main-effort forces in and to the south of the Lublin area for an attack in the general direction of Kiev. From there strong armored forces will thrust deep into enemy territory and envelop the Russian forces by following the course of the lower Dnepr.

The mixed German-Romanian force in the south will have two missions:

1. To secure Romania as a base and thus guarantee the continuity of operations in the southern part of the theater; and

2. To tie down the opposing enemy forces during the advance of the army group's north wing. In accordance with developments in the situation, the mixed force—supported by Air Force contingents—will launch a pursuit to prevent the Soviets from making an organized withdrawal across the Dnepr.

The corresponding changes were also incorporated into the Army's operation order. [See *map 5*.] Army Group South was no longer to concentrate its strength on both its wings; instead, it was to strengthen its left so that mobile forces could pace the drive on Kiev, where they were to bear southeastward and destroy—or at least cut off—all enemy forces still in the western Ukraine.

The missions of the individual armies were changed as follows:

Eleventh Army was to protect Romania against an invasion by Russian troops, tie down the forces opposite the Romanian border by tricking the enemy into believing that major forces were being assembled, and eventually launch a pursuit to prevent the Russians from making an organized withdrawal.

Seventeenth Army was to jab with its powerful left, push back the enemy southeastward, and pursue him via Vinnitsa and Berdichev.

First Panzer Group was to thrust via Berdichev and Zhitomir toward the Dnepr River at Kiev, and then immediately continue its southeastward drive in order to block the Russian routes of withdrawal.

Sixth Army was to screen the north flank of the army group along the Pripyat Marshes and follow First Panzer Group closely up to Zhitomir. Upon receiving specific orders from army group, Sixth Army was to shift strong forces southeastward along the west bank of the Dnepr and join First Panzer Group in the destruction of the Russian forces fighting in the western Ukraine.

The difficulties of such an operation, hinging on a single envelopment, were fully realized by the Army High Command. Its success depended essentially upon whether the Russian leaders would react swiftly to the situation. If they recognized the danger in time, major Russian forces would probably get across the Dnepr River—or at least those opposite the Romanian border. The outcome of the offensive in the south therefore seemed doubtful from the outset.

For North

In the far north Hitler wanted to close in on Murmansk and seize that port, if sufficient attack forces could be made available. The Russians would thus be unable to use Murmansk as a base for attacks against northern Finland and Norway, and British landings along the Kola Peninsula would not materialize. Another drive in the direction of Kandalaksha was planned in order to cut the lines of communications of the Russian troops stationed near Murmansk. Thus, two thrusts were to be staged in northern Finland in addition to the three in the southern part of that country: across the Karelian Isthmus, east of Lake Ladoga, and at Hanko. Initially, it was intended that the two German forces operating in northern Finland would be under the overall command of Field Marshal Carl Gustav Mannerheim, Commander in Chief, Finnish Armed Forces. When the latter refused to assume this additional responsibility, the German Army of Norway was put in charge of the northern and central Finnish theaters of operation. The Finnish Armed Forces Command was to exercise independent command authority over operations in southern Finland.

Delay in the Start

At the beginning of April, immediately after the start of the campaigns in the Balkans, the invasion of Russia was postponed by 4 to 6 weeks. On 30 April Hitler decided that the new D Day was to be 22 June. [See DA Pam 20-260, *The German Campaigns in the Balkans* (*Spring 1941*), pt. Five.]

The fighting in the Balkans ended with the withdrawal of the British at the end of April. During the second half of that month most of the German divisions engaged in the Balkans were being redeployed for rehabilitation so that they would be available for Operation BARBAROSSA. It was anticipated that, despite the planned invasion of Crete, all ground and air forces earmarked for the strategic concentration preceding the Russian campaign would be ready to jump off, with the possible exception of two panzer divisions that had advanced all the way to southern Greece.

The Draft of Directive No. 32 (11 June 1941)

Throughout this period of intensive planning and preparations Hitler and his military advisers believed in all seriousness that Germany could defeat the Soviet Union within 3 to 4 months. The Russo-Japanese pact of neutrality, concluded on 13 April, did not change any of the German dispositions. On the contrary, so convinced was Hitler of his future success that he made far-reaching adventurous plans even before the start of the Russian campaign. As early as 17 February 1941 he had asked Jodl to draw up a plan for the invasion of India from Afghan territory in order to permit closer German-Japanese cooperation. These and similar ideas met with no objection from the Army. But on 4 June 1941 the latter requested the Armed Forces Operations Staff to state which operations were to be conducted after the defeat of the Russian armed forces. Directive No. 32, "Preparations for the Period after BARBAROSSA" was drafted on 11 June and circulated among the three services for comments. It envisaged the following operations for the future:

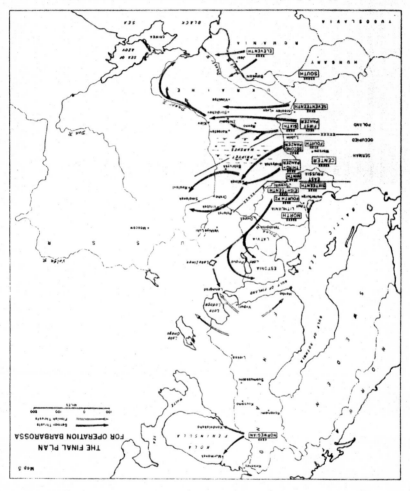

Map 5. THE FINAL PLAN FOR OPERATION BARBAROSSA

30

a. Seizure of British strongholds in the Mediterranean and the Near East by concentric drives from Libya toward Egypt, from Bulgaria across Turkey, and possibly from the Caucasus across Iran;

b. Seizure of Gibraltar, and the closing of the gate to the western Mediterranean; and

c. Intensification of the siege of Britain and eventually a landing on the British Isles for the *coup de grâce*.

Strategic Concentration (21 June 1941)

The Army High Command had 145 divisions—including 19 armored—available for the invasion of Russia. These divisions were distributed among the individual army groups and armies in conformity with their mission and with a view to rail transport facilities. [See *chart 2.*] The distribution was as follows:

a. *Army Group North* (Field Marshal Wilhelm von Leeb).
  (1) Sixteenth Army
  (2) Eighteenth Army, including Fourth Panzer Group
  (3) Army Group reserves

The total strength of Army Group North was 3 armored, 3 motorized infantry, 21 infantry, and 3 security divisions, for a grand total of 30 divisions.

b. *Army Group Center* (Field Marshal Fedor von Bock).
  (1) Fourth Army, including Second Panzer Group:
  (2) Ninth Army, including Third Panzer Group
  (3) Army group reserves

The total strength of Army Group Center was 9 armored, 7 motorized infantry, 31 infantry, 1 cavalry, and 3 security divisions, for a grand total of 51 divisions.

c. *Army Group South* (Field Marshal Gerd von Rundstedt).
  1. Eleventh Army
  2. Seventeenth Army

3. Sixth Army, including First Panzer Group
4. Army group reserves

The total strength of Army Group South was 5 armored, 3 motorized infantry, 26 infantry, 6 mountain and/or light infantry, and 3 security divisions, for a grand total of 43 German plus 14 Romanian divisions. After the start of the invasion Army Group South was reinforced by a gradually increasing number of Italian, Hungarian, and Slovak units.

d. *Army High Command Reserves* (as of D Day).
  (1) In transit and assigned to:
    Army Group South—4 infantry divisions, Army Group Center—6 infantry divisions, and Army Group North—2 infantry divisions.
  (2) In transit and unassigned: 2 armored, 1 motorized infantry, 9 infantry divisions.

The total Army High Command reserves were 2 armored, 1 motorized infantry, and 21 infantry divisions, for a grand total of 24 divisions.

e. *In Finland.*
  (1) Finnish Army High Command.
    a. Karelian Isthmus forces: 7 divisions west of Viipuri.
    b. Karelian Army: 5 divisions, 1 cavalry and 2 light infantry brigades in the area northeast of Lake Ladoga.
    c. Other forces: 1 division in the Lieksa area, 1 division blocking Hanko, 1 German division as reserve.
  (2) German Army of Norway.
    a. Finnish III Corps: 2 Finnish divisions in the Suomussalmi-Kuusamo area.
    b. German XXXVI Corps: 1 Finnish and 1½ German divisions in the area east of Rovaniemi.
    c. German Mountain Corps Norway: 2 German mountain divisions in the Kirkenes area.

f. *In Norway.* 5 infantry and 2 security divisions on occupation duty and guarding coastal areas.

Air Support

Each army group was to be supported by one air force, so that the Fourth, Second, and First Air Forces were to operate in conjunction with Army Group South, Center, and North respectively. Second Air Force was the strongest, whereas First Air Force actually consisted of only one corps. This deficiency was partly compensated for by committing the Fifth Air Force in the far north, where the Luftwaffe contingents were given the threefold mission of guarding the Norwegian coastal waters, striking at the naval base of Murmansk and the convoys heading for that port, and supporting the Army of Norway's operations in northern Finland.

4. LUFTWAFFE STRENGTH FIGURES (June 1941).)

Unit	Total	Bombers and dive bombers	Fighter planes	Reconnaissance planes
Totals	2,000	1,160	720	120
Fourth Air Force (A Gp South)	600	360	210	30
Second Air Force (A Gp Center)	910	490	390	30
First Air Force (A Gp North)	430	270	110	50
Fifth Air Force (Finland)	60	40	10	10

Other Factors

Perhaps the most striking feature of the distribution of forces for the invasion of Russia was the small number of reserve divisions assigned to the army groups. The Army High Command, however, was in a quandary: the reserve divisions could either be assigned to the Army groups, leaving hardly any strategic reserves, or the Army High Command could retain them under its control. The latter solution was given preference because it offered Hitler a possibility of exercising closer control over the course of operations. In view of the 900-mile width of the attack front, the total reserves were too small to give a safe margin of depth to the strategic concentration and the invasion proper.

The main attack groupings were in the Sixth, Fourth, and Ninth Army areas where, within narrow zones of action, deeply echeloned wedges were to be driven across enemy lines. By contrast, the Carpathian border and the central sector of the Bialystok salient were screened by only weak security units.

The strategic concentration of forces was carried out over a period of several weeks. The rate of troop transfers, moderate in order to maintain secrecy, was not stepped up until the final phase. Most of the divisions of Eleventh Army moved up from Greece, covering up to 500 miles on foot and arriving just before D Day. The initial concentration of forces took place away from the border. From the assembly areas most of the troops reached their jump off positions in a few night marches.

German Army Personnel and Equipment Assembled for the Invasion of Russia (20 June 1941)

Officer and Enlisted Personnel	3,050,000
Horses	625,000
Motor Vehicles (incl. armd. recon. cars)	600,000
Tanks	3,350
Artillery Pieces	7,184

Estimate of Soviet Strength (June 1941)

Sources of Information

Radio intercepts were the only reliable source of intelligence available to the Germans before the outbreak of hostilities. Intercept stations had been set up in Bulgaria, Romania, Hungary, Bohemia, Moravia, western Poland, East Prussia, and Finland. Because of insufficient personnel and inadequate equipment these stations did not reach very deeply into the interior of the Soviet Union, their range being limited to the territories west of the Desna and Dnepr, the Baltic States, and some of the border area near the Finnish frontier.

Reports from agents in Finland and Turkey proved valuable in tracing Russian troops movements.

5. ORDER OF BATTLE, 21 June 1941

Army groups	Subordinate panzer groups and armies	Assembly areas	Planned direction of attack
North: Field Marshal Wilhelm von Leeb (Attached: First Air Force: General Alfred Keller)	Eighteenth Army: General Georg von Kuechler	3 armored, 3 motorized infantry, 1 security, and 10 infantry/divisions north, south, and east of Tilsit.	North of Tilsit	Estonia
	Fourth Panzer Group: General Erich Hoepner		South and East of Tilsit	Thrust toward Leningrad
	Sixteenth Army: General Ernst Busch	10 infantry and 2 security divisions east of Insterburg.	East of Insterburg	Leningrad via Lovat, to follow Fourth Panzer Group
Center: Field Marshal Fedor von Bock (Attached: Second Air Force: Field Marshal Albert Kesselring)	Third Panzer Group: General Hermann Hoth	1 infantry division.		
	Ninth Army: General Adolf Strauss	4 armored, 3 motorized infantry, 1 security, and 12 infantry divisions in and south of the Suwalki area.	North and East of Suwalki	Northern arm of pincers
			Southeast and Southwest of Suwalki	Polotsk, Vitebsk
	Fourth Army: Field Marshal Guenther von Kluge	5 armored, 4 motorized infantry, 18 infantry, 1 cavalry, and 2 security, divisions northeast and east of Warsaw.	Northeast and East of Warsaw	Mogilev area, to follow Second Panzer Group
	Second Panzer Group: General Heinz Guderian	1 infantry division.	Southeast of Warsaw	Southern arm of pincers
South: Field Marshal Gerd von Rundstedt (Attached: Fourth Air Force: General Alexander Loehr)	First Panzer Group: General Ewald von Kleist	11 infantry, 1 security, 3 motorized infantry, and 5 armored divisions southeast of Lublin	Southeast of Lublin	Enveloping maneuver toward Kiev
	Sixth Army: Field Marshal Walter von Reichenau		Southeast of Lublin	North of Kiev, to follow First Panzer Group
	Seventeenth Army: General Karl Heinrich von Stuelpnagel	7 infantry, 4 mountain or light infantry, and 2 security divisions west of Jaroslav.	West of Jaroslav	Vinnitsa
	Eleventh Army: General Eugen von Schobert	7 German and 14 Romanian infantry divisions in north eastern Romania.	East and Southeast of Botosani	Lower Dnepr
		1 infantry and 2 mountain or light infantry divisions.		

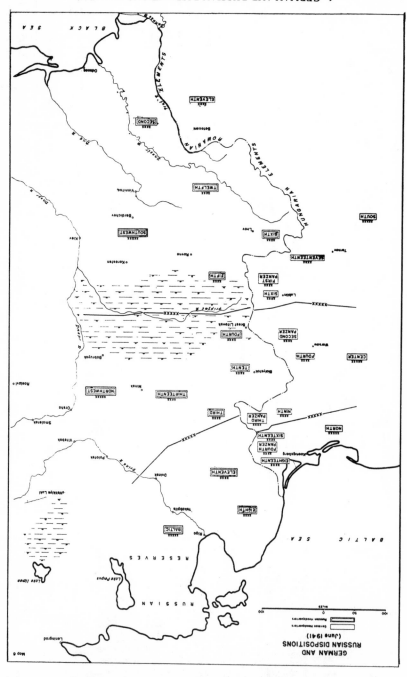

GERMAN AND
RUSSIAN DISPOSITIONS
(June 1941)

German Headquarters

Russian Headquarters

MILES

100   50   0   100

Reconnaissance missions were flown by special high-altitude, long-range planes from bases in the Balkans, western Poland, and East Prussia. The picture obtained by air reconnaissance remained incomplete because of strong Soviet protests against such Luftwaffe activities.

6. ESTIMATE OF RED ARMY DISPOSITIONS

	Total Army Strength	Western Border Regions	Rest of European Russia	Far East
Infantry Divisions	170	118	27	25
Cavalry Divisions	33½	20	5½	8
Motorized and Armored Brigades	46	40	1	5

[For the distribution of the Red Army forces in the western border regions, see *map 6.*]

Estimate of Soviet Air Force Strength

The total strength of the Soviet Air Force was estimated at 8,000 planes, 6,000 of which were in Europe and the rest in Asia. The composition of the air forces in Europe was believed to be as follows:

800 obsolete close reconnaissance planes.
2,000 fighters, including 250–300 modern planes.
1,800 bombers, including approximately 800 up-to-date planes.
700 fighter-bombers, consisting of Stormoviks and obsolete planes.
700 naval planes of obsolete designs.

In the spring of 1941 a few Luftwaffe experts received permission to visit some airplane factories in the Urals. They saw six plants and reported that a large-scale aircraft production program was under way. These reports—just like all other warnings—were not heeded: Operation BARBAROSSA started according to plan.

GERMAN PONTON BRIDGE, 1941

PART TWO
OPERATIONS IN 1941

III

THE INITIAL OPERATIONS (22 JUNE - 31 JULY 1941)

D Day

The German invasion of Russia began at 0300 on 22 June 1941. In some places the Germans achieved complete tactical surprise. The Russians were caught asleep in their billets, and in many instances Russian commanders proved helpless before the onslaught. In general, however, the Russian troops recovered quickly and offered strong local resistance.

The Situation on 30 June 1941

In the Army Group South area, the First Panzer Group had fought its way into the area east of Rovno, its advance having been repeatedly held up by counterattacks of skillfully led Russian units. Further to the south the Seventeenth Army advance had progressed to the area around and especially south of Lvov but against strong resistance. The general impression was that the Russians facing Army Group South had recovered from their initial shock and, having realized the seriousness of the situation, were showing considerable skill in blocking the advance. Developments in the southern part of the theater were therefore not up to expectation.

In the Army Group Center area, the ring of encirclement around the Russian forces west of Minsk had been completely closed. The Second and Third Panzer Groups had linked up near Minsk according to plan. The Russians had been unable to prevent this maneuver or coordinate any countermoves. By the end of June the encircled units made uncoordinated efforts to break out of the pocket. Eventually, some 20 Russian divisions were destroyed in the Minsk pocket, and the Germans captured 290,000 prisoners, 2,500 tanks, and 1,400 guns. The situation in this area was so satisfactory that Hitler considered diverting forces to Army Group South to intercept and destroy the Red Army reserves being brought up from the rear.

In the Army Group North area the situation developed according to plan. The Dvina had been crossed at Dvinsk and Yekabpils, and the crucial step toward implementing the army group plan had thus been taken. In Lithuania and Latvia, the Russians were offering strong resistance in a series of delaying actions. By this time 12 to 15 Russian divisions had virtually been wiped out during the fighting west of the Dvina.

In general, the Germans had every reason to be satisfied with the progress of the first nine days. The Luftwaffe had gained complete air supremacy. The Russians had been forced to give battle on all fronts. An organized withdrawal opposite Army Groups Center and North was no longer to be feared, whereas in the Army Group South area the Russians could still evade the German envelopment. In view of the heavy losses suffered by the Soviet forces, the overall success of the German operation seemed assured. In a conference on 29 June Hitler stated that, instead of driving straight toward Moscow, he would prefer to divert forces for a thrust on Leningrad. The capture of Leningrad would drive the Russians from the Baltic and thus secure German shipments of ore across that body of water, enable the Finns to seize the initiative, and disengage the German left for a thrust on Moscow. Jodl interjected that the detour to Moscow via Leningrad would be beyond the capabilities of the panzer formations. After some discussion it was decided that the question would be reexamined at a later date.

Developments in Early July 1941

In a diary entry of 3 July General Halder expressed the justifiable optimism, shared at that time by most Germany military leaders, that the mission of destroying the Red Army west of the Dvina and Dnepr had been accomplished. He did not doubt the word of a captured Russian corps commander that east of these two rivers the Germans would encounter only isolated forces whose strength would be insufficient to hamper operations decisively. It therefore seemed to him no exaggeration to state that the Russian campaign had been won in less than two weeks. Of course, this did not imply that the campaign was completely terminated. It would take many more weeks to occupy the vast Russian theater and overcome the stubbornness with which the Soviets would continue to offer resistance.

Hitler's opinion on the same subject, as expressed on 4 July, ran as follows: "I constantly try to put myself in the enemy's position. For all practical purposes the enemy has lost this campaign. It is a good thing that we have destroyed the Russian armored and air forces right at the beginning. The Russians will be unable to replace them." At the same time the Fuehrer was preoccupied with the question of what was to happen after crossing the Dnepr-Dvina line. "Are we to turn north or south? This will probably be the most difficult decision of the entire campaign." He obviously did not consider driving straight on to Moscow.

The next day Jodl asked Halder to submit his plans and ideas for the continuation of the offensive to Hitler. In Jodl's opinion the significance of the next movements of the panzer groups was so great that Halder should consult Hitler before definitely committing these forces. Jodl added that two important questions preoccupied Hitler:

1. Would Army Group North be sufficiently strong to accomplish its mission singlehandedly or would the Third Panzer Group have to lend its assistance? In the latter case, should this panzer group be diverted northeastward immediately after crossing the Dnepr-Dvina line?

2. Should Second Panzer Group be diverted southward immediately after having crossed the Dnepr?

Brauchitsch and Halder reported to Hitler on 8 July. They indicated that out of 164 Russian rifle divisions so far identified by the Germans, 89 had been destroyed, 46 were still capable of commitment, 18 were employed in secondary theaters such as Finland, and the whereabouts of 11 divisions were unknown.

Brauchitsch then suggested that First Panzer Group immediately turn southward for a close-in envelopment and that a protective screen be built up west of Kiev. Hitler, however, preferred to capture Kiev first and then launch a wide envelopment along the east bank of the Dnepr with the assistance of strong Army Group Center forces. Brauchitsch objected to this plan, indicating that the logistical problems it involved seemed insuperable at that time. He did advocate, however, that the wide envelopment be carried out after the close-in one had met with success. No immediate decision was taken.

At that time the Army Group South operations hinged upon the progress made by Sixth Army and First Panzer Group. To achieve a decisive success the latter would have to penetrate the Red Army defenses that blocked the German axis of advance in the direction of Vinnitsa and Korosten. The mounting pressure, exerted by the Russian *Fifth Army* which was threatening the German north flank from the Pripyat Marshes, had to be eliminated at the same time. Moreover, the Eleventh Army would have to join the offensive and move northeastward toward Vinnitsa, where—despite its relative weakness—it was to assist First Panzer Group. This maneuver might pave the way to the encirclement of Russian forces southwest of Berdichev.

The next objective of Army Group Center was to bring about the collapse of the Russian defensive triangle anchored on Orsha, Smolensk, and Vitebsk. There, between the Dnepr and the Dvina, was the corridor that was vital for the continuation of the German thrust on Moscow. The Russians were apparently preparing an all-out defense along this same corridor, using not only whatever forces had escaped from the Minsk pocket but also fresh ones then being moved up. Another Soviet concentration was being built up near Velikiye Luki for future commitment against Army Group North.

To accomplish its next mission Army Group Center would have to make a sweeping double envelopment in the course of which Second Panzer Group was to advance in the general direction of Bobruysk-Roslavl and Third Panzer Group along the upper Dvina via Polotsk and Vitebsk. The infantry divisions of the Fourth and Ninth Armies would have to close up and constantly support the armor if the Orsha corridor was to be enveloped.

Army Group North was to drive toward Lake Ilmen, with Fourth Panzer Group in the lead, and then turn northward in the direction of Leningrad. Strong Russian resistance was to be expected at the former Russian-Estonian border, and Estonia proper would have to be mopped up by infantry divisions brought up in the rear.

At this stage the crucial problem confronting all three army groups was to keep the infantry from falling too far behind the armor. The infantry divisions with their horse-drawn vehicles could not help being delayed whenever they were engaged in completing encirclements or in mopping up pockets. To overextend the distance between the onrushing armor and the temporarily stalled infantry meant courting danger. The Army's low strength in motorized infantry divisions (because of the constant POL and materiel shortage, Germany had but 14 such divisions) proved to be a handicap. It is true that this deficiency was somewhat compensated for by the almost unbelievable march performances of the infantry divisions, which time and again succeeded in closing up even though they were denied the use of the few good roads reserved for the motorized units.

The question of determining the proper size for a ring of encirclement also preoccupied the Army. The lesson learned from the battle that had raged between Bialystok and Minsk was that it was unsound to try to envelop too much at one time; if the ring of encirclement was too large it would not be sufficiently strong to prevent a breakout of Russian forces.

For the time being, supply was no problem since the precautionary measures of establishing forward depots and new base sections guaranteed a satisfactory support of the projected operations.

The railroads functioned surprisingly well. By 3 July, for instance, the tracks from Brest Litovsk half-way to Minsk had been converted to European gauge, with the remaining section being reopened two days later for trains using captured Russian rolling stock. A few days later this section also had to be converted because the Germans had not captured any Russian tank cars. Fleets of German tank cars moved up the large quantities of POL needed to feed the offensive.

The Luftwaffe had achieved air superiority despite the surprising numerical strength of the Russian Air Force. An Armed Forces High Command communiqué, issued on 12 July, mentioned that 6,233 Russian planes had been destroyed against very minor Luftwaffe losses. Soviet communiqués covering the same period spoke of 1,900 Russian planes lost against 2,300 German planes destroyed—300 more than the of the First Panzer Group. The latter was thrusting southeastward toward Uman in an attempt to envelop the Russian forces in front of Seventeenth Army. Despite stubborn Russian resistance and unexpectedly heavy rainfall, the Seventeenth Army had meanwhile penetrated into the Vinnitsa area, while the Eleventh Army had advanced as far as the Dnestr. Some German elements had pushed to Kishinev for the purpose of getting the Romanians started on the road to Odessa.

The Russians opposing Army Group South continued to fight a stubborn and skillful delaying action, meanwhile avoiding most German enveloping maneuvers. Marshal Semen Budyenny who commanded the Russian *Army Group Southwest* was Rundstedt's opponent.

Brauchitsch, Halder, and Rundstedt agreed that First Panzer Group would have to launch a wider envelopment than originally intended. The thrust toward Uman no longer complied with the total number of German planes committed in the Russian theater. Even though these figures are obviously exaggerated and differ so greatly, they do convey an idea of the impact of the initial air battles.

The Mid-July Estimate

On 14 July Hitler mentioned that Moscow would have to be bombed from the air if the center of Communist resistance was to be hit and the orderly evacuation of the Soviet Government prevented.

Three days later Hitler considered once against the diversion of Hoth's Third Panzer Group to the northeast and Guderian's Second Panzer Group to the southeast. For the latter maneuver, to be initiated immediately after the liquidation of the Smolensk pocket, Guderian's panzer forces were to be reinforced by strong infantry units of the Second Army.

In the Army Group South area, the efforts of Sixth Army and First Panzer Group were in danger of being dissipated. The pressure exerted by the Russian *Fifth Army* from the Pripyat Marshes

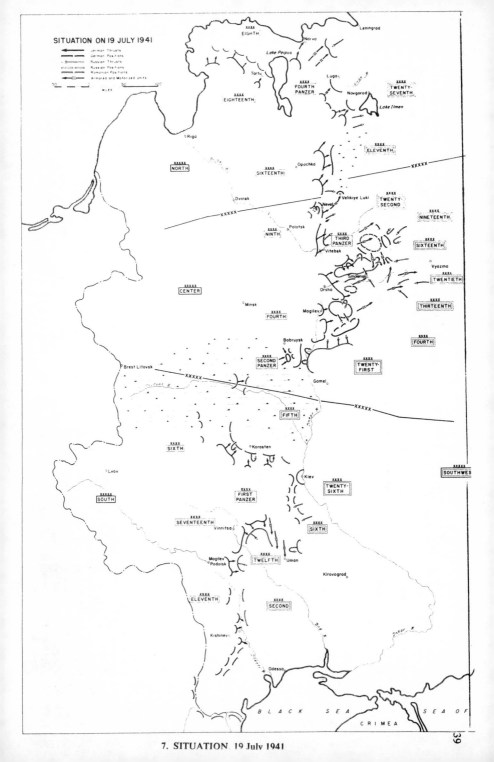

SITUATION ON 19 JULY 1941

German Thrusts
German Positions
Russian Thrusts
Russian Positions
Romanian Positions
Armored and Motorized Units

50   50   100
MILES

EIGHTH

Narva

Leningrad

Lake Peipus

Tartu

Luga

FOURTH
PANZER

Novgorod

TWENTY-
SEVENTH

EIGHTEENTH

Lake Ilmen

Riga

ELEVENTH

NORTH

Opochka

SIXTEENTH

XXXXX

Dvinsk

XXXXX

Velikiye Luki

TWENTY-
SECOND

Nevel

NINETEENTH

NINTH

Polotsk

THIRD
PANZER

SIXTEENTH

Vitebsk

Vyazma

Smolensk

TWENTIETH

CENTER

Orsha

Minsk

FOURTH

Mogilev

THIRTEENTH

Bobruysk

FOURTH

SECOND
PANZER

Brest Litovsk

XXXXX

TWENTY-
FIRST

Gomel

XXXXX

FIFTH

SIXTH

Korosten

Lvov

Kiev

TWENTY-
SIXTH

SOUTHWES

FIRST
PANZER

SOUTH

SEVENTEENTH

Vinnitsa

SIXTH

Mogilev
Podolsk

TWELFTH

Uman

Kirovograd

ELEVENTH

SECOND

Kishinev

Odessa

B L A C K   S E A

S E A   O F

C R I M E A

39

7. SITUATION 19 July 1941

against the army group's flank diverted more and more Sixth Army troops from their original mission. [See *map 7.*] Armored elements were arriving in the vicinity of Kiev where they protected the flank existing situation, and the armored forces were therefore to drive deeper into the Dnepr bend and attempt to establish a bridgehead south of Kiev. At the same time Rundstedt stressed the necessity for offensive action to eliminate Russian forces threatening his left flank from the Pripyat region. While Halder agreed in principle, he did not believe that combing out the Pripyat Marshes could be accomplished effectively without employing the proper forces. He felt that it would be more expedient to cut the lines of communication of the Russian *Fifth Army* between the Pripyat and the Dnepr and let the army perish in the swamps.

The situation of Army Group Center was far more favorable. The Orsha–Smolensk–Vitebsk barrier had been pried open and the ring of encirclement near Smolensk closed. Another 100,000 prisoners, 2,000 tanks, and 1,900 guns had fallen into German hands. Russian attempts to build up a new front and to extend it to the north and south had failed. The Russians, although split into isolated and more or less encircled groups, continued to stubbornly resist east of Mogilev, between Orsha and Smolensk, northeast of Vitebsk, and near Nevel.

There was a certain amount of Russian pressure from the Gomel area, but in general the Red Army had been badly shaken; two weeks would be needed for mopping-up operations. Marshal Semen Timoshenko's *Army Group West* was receiving a constant flow of reinforcements, improvised units were arriving from Moscow, and the Soviet Government was obviously using every possible means to stop the German advance on the Russian capital.

In the Army Group North area Sixteenth Army had fought its way eastward against stubborn resistance in the difficult terrain east of Opochka, while Fourth Panzer Group had turned northward, advancing between Lakes Ilmen and Peipus toward Leningrad. Marshal Klementi Voroshilov, who commanded *Army Group Northwest*, was strongly resisting this German drive. The two armored corps of Fourth Panzer Group became separated during the course of their

advance. While the corps on the right was driving toward Novgorod to isolate Leningrad from the east, the other corps moved up the east shore of Lake Peipus, because the more direct route to Leningrad via Luga led through extremely difficult terrain that was unsuitable for armor. The latter corps was to capture Narva, thereby closing the corridor between Lake Peipus and the Baltic, and then resume the advance on Leningrad from the west. The splitting of this armored force was a totally undesirable development since the Army High Command had planned to keep the Fourth Panzer Group intact until it reached the area southeast of Leningrad. The city would thus be cut off from the east, and the way paved for the advance of the Finns approaching along the shores of Lake Ladoga. Leeb was reminded of the necessity of implementing this plan and was given specific instructions to move up infantry forces behind the panzer corps which had turned northward.

For the first time in the campaign the flow of supplies became unsatisfactory. Delays occurred in the Army Group Center area and to some extent also in the north. Increasing difficulties in rail transportation affected operations accordingly.

Directive No. 33 (19 July 1941)

The introductory paragraph of this directive, which carried the subtitle "Continuation of the Russian Campaign," enumerated the successes hitherto achieved. It also mentioned that Army Group Center would need some time to mop up the remaining Russian pockets and that the progress of Army Group South was hampered by Fortress Kiev in front and the Russian *Fifth Army* in the rear.

The twofold objective of future operations was to prevent the withdrawal of strong Soviet forces and to annihilate them. The measures to be taken for this purpose were as follows:

a. South. A concentric attack on the Russian *Twelfth* and *Sixth Armies* was to lead to their destruction west of the Dnepr. [*See map 7.*] The Russian *Fifth Army* was also to be destroyed through a joint effort of Army Group South and Center forces. The Second Panzer Group and strong infantry forces of Army Group Center were to be diverted to the southeast to cut off those Russian units trying to escape across the river.

b. Center. Army Group Center was to mop up the numerous pockets in its area and then continue its advance on Moscow with a force exclusively composed of infantry divisions. The Third Panzer Group was to thrust northeastward to cut the communications between Moscow and Leningrad and simultaneously protect the right flank of Army Group North during its advance on Leningrad.

c. North. The drive on Leningrad was to continue as soon as the infantry divisions of Eighteenth Army had closed with Third Panzer Group and the Sixteenth Army had made contact with Third Panzer Group.

d. Finland. The Finnish forces in the south, reinforced by the German 163d Infantry Division, were to place their main effort east of Lake Ladoga and coordinate their offensive with Army Group North. This mission of the German units committed in northern Finland remained unchanged.

e. Air Support. The Luftwaffe was to support the diversion to the southeast with all its available forces. The Second Air Force, temporarily reinforced by the transfer of forces from the West, was to bomb Moscow as retribution for Soviet air attacks on Bucharest and Helsinki.

f. Naval Support. The Navy was to safeguard supply convoys and prevent the escape of Russian naval units to neutral ports in Sweden. After the Baltic had been cleared of the Soviet forces, some elements of the German Baltic Fleet were to be transferred to the Mediterranean. A few submarines were to be dispatched to the Norwegian Sea to support the operations in Finland.

The last paragraph of the directive dealt with the redistribution of forces in western and northern Europe.

Two days after signing the directive Hitler visited Army Group North headquarters, where he discussed the implications of his orders with Leeb and his staff. He pointed out that the capture of Leningrad—a symbol of Bolshevism since 1917—might lead to a complete collapse of the already badly shaken Soviet regime. Because of the significance of the city it was to be expected that the advancing German troops would encounter strong resistance. The Third Panzer

Group was still engaged in liquidating the pockets near Smolensk, but the decision would have to be made within the next five days whether this force was to be diverted from the drive on Moscow. Despite having issued the directive, Hitler was still undecided as to its implementation. During the conference Hitler also stated that, to him, Moscow was simply a place name.

On 23 July Hitler attended a conference at Army High Command headquarters. General Halder reported the most recent information on Russian and German strength figures, as follows:

Russian Strength	Divisions			
	Total	Rifle	Armored	Cavalry
Opposite German Army Group:				
North	23½	20	3½	
Center	35½	32	3½	
South	34	26	6	2
Totals	93	78	13	2

After one month of fighting, the effective strength of the German infantry divisions had been reduced by approximately 20 percent and that of the panzer and motorized infantry divisions by 50 percent.

For future planning, Halder estimated that Army Group South would be able to cross the Dnepr by the middle of August, but that Army Group Center could not possibly resume its advance before 5 August. The pockets would have to be mopped up, supplies moved up and distributed, etc. Very strong resistance was to be expected west of Moscow where the Russians were building up strength, including a formidable antiaircraft defense system. The Army Group North forces would probably have to be regrouped before the final drive on Leningrad could be launched.

Hitler emphasized that the basic principle in conducting the operations was to destroy enemy forces wherever they were encountered. In addition the three principal objectives to be attained were as follows:

1. The Leningrad region because of its industrial, naval, and political importance;

2. The Moscow area because of its war production facilities; and

3. The Ukraine because of its natural resources and industry. He repeated that after the fighting around Smolensk had subsided the Second and Third Panzer Groups would have to turn right and left respectively to support the adjoining army groups. Army Group Center would have to carry out its advance on Moscow without armored support.

As a result of this conference the Supplement to Directive No. 33 was issued on 23 July. This order specified the scope of future operations as follows:

a. South. All enemy forces remaining west of the Dnepr were to be defeated and destroyed. As soon as circumstances permitted, First and Second Panzer Groups were to be put under the command of Fourth Army and assembled west of the Dnepr. Reinforced by infantry and mountain divisions, this army was to seize the industrial region of Kharkov, cross the Don, and drive into the Caucasus.

b. Center. After having mopped up around Smolensk and stabilized the situation along its southern flank, Army Group Center was to defeat the Russian forces still remaining between Smolensk and Moscow and seize their capital, "using the infantry units of its two armies, which were sufficiently strong for this purpose."

The Third Panzer Group was to be temporarily attached to Army Group North, but would revert to Army Group Center as soon as its mission was accomplished. The armored forces would then take part in the subsequent drive from Moscow to the Volga River.

c. North. Receiving the support of Third Panzer Group, Army Group North would be able to commit its infantry in a direct assault on Leningrad while the mobile units would attempt enveloping maneuvers.

d. Redeployment. The Army High Command was to plan organizational measures for the transfer and reassignment of Army Group North forces after their mission to seize Leningrad had been accomplished.

The last two paragraphs of the Supplement dealt with air and naval reinforcements for the Finnish theater and with rear area security measures in occupied Russian territories. Greater security was to be achieved by "applying appropriate Draconian measures, not by requesting more security forces."

The Army vigorously protested against the contents of the Supplement to Directive No. 33, and Brauchitsch claimed that for the time being its implementation was impossible, particularly in the Army Group Center area. On 23 July he asked Keitel, who had signed the Supplement, to defer its application until current operations had been brought to a more conclusive point. After Keitel refused this request, Brauchitsch asked for another conference with Hitler, this time on the subject of the contents of the Supplement.

This conference apparently took place on the same day. Hitler listened to Brauchitsch's objections, then stressed that certain lessons on the conduct of mobile operations could be learned from the experience of the five weeks'-old Russian campaign. Because of the Soviet forces' stiff resistance, operations with far-reaching objectives would have to be deferred until the Russians no longer had the strength to counterattack. Close-in envelopments would have to be attempted instead, thus giving the infantry divisions an opportunity to directly support the spearhead units, which in turn would become available for their proper mission.

The Army's Letter to the Armed Forces High Command

The Army's ideas on the further conduct of operations were explained in a letter drafted by the Operations Division of the Army High Command and approved by Halder on 30 June. The letter was never sent because its contents were partly superseded by Directive No. 33 and because the entire Armed Forces High Command—with the possible exception of Keitel—seemed to share the Army's point of view.

After dealing with secondary problems in the initial paragraphs, the letter stated the Army's case as follows:

a. The Offensive against Moscow. After the transfer of the forces that were to be diverted to the north and south, the two remaining armies of Army Group Center would be composed of 20–22 divisions, including all reserves in rear areas. These forces would have to suffice for launching an offensive along an approximately 150-mile front against an estimated force of 19 Soviet divisions, of which 3 were armored and 2 motorized. The Russians could probably move up reinforcements from the immediate vicinity of Moscow.

The German attack forces would have to penetrate a fortified position behind which there would surely be some additional field fortifications. Such a maze of defensive positions could be overcome only by a proper massing of forces. The forces for the main effort in the south would have to be assembled near Yelnya, those in the north around Bely. The southern axis of advance would have to run somewhere between the Roslavl–Moscow and Smolensk–Moscow roads, and the northern one would lead from Bely via Rzhev to Moscow.

No quick advance toward Moscow could be expected without costly and painstaking, and it might bog down altogether.

b. Critique.

1. According to present plans Army Group Center would be composed of three different forces. The Second Panzer Group would attack in the direction of Gomel and the Third Panzer Group northeastward to the Valdai Hills; by eliminating any possible threat to the flanks these two movements would pave the way for a third force thrusting toward Moscow.

2. A decisive offensive against Moscow could not get under way before the beginning of September, when the two panzer groups would become available to participate in the drive.

3. The Russians would thus have one extra month to organize and strengthen their defenses while warding off the weak German attacks launched with insufficient forces. They would have achieved their objective of splitting up the German forces by continually jabbing at their flanks. At the same time the immediate danger to Moscow would subside for several weeks. Aside from the political significance of this success, the Soviets would benefit from remaining in control of the industrial and communications facilities of their capital.

4. The effectiveness of air attacks on Moscow remained doubtful because of the long distance separating the German airfields from the target area. No immediate improvement was in sight.

c. General Suggestions. A reexamination of the plans regarding the redistribution of the Army Group Center forces therefore seemed warranted. Being unable to evaluate the political and economic factors that might have motivated the decisions of the Armed Forces High Command, the Army could base its suggestions only on military factors. These were as follows:

1. The Russians would probably try to build up a defense line between the Baltic and Black Seas, along which they would attempt to stop the German advance before the onset of winter. They would no doubt try to establish this line west of their major industrial centers. If the present war of movement developed into position warfare, the Russians would probably be able to organize and train strong units by next spring. This in turn would force the Germans to divert even more forces to the Russian theater. Such a course of events would, however, be contrary to the military objective of the Russian campaign, which was to quickly knock out one adversary and then turn all the power against the other one—Great Britain.

2. To forestall the Russian intentions, the Germans would have to keep their adversaries off balance. This could best be achieved by smashing the Russian resistance by a direct thrust on Moscow. Since possession of the Russian capital was vital from a military, political, and economic standpoint, the Soviet leaders would commit every available soldier to defend the

43

city. By attacking Moscow the German Army could therefore destroy the bulk of the Red Army, split the Russian theater in two parts, and seriously impair the Soviet unity of command.

3. All secondary operations, having as the objective the destruction of individual Russian groupings, would have to be abandoned unless such operations could be integrated into the overall plan for a powerful offensive against Moscow.

d. Specific Suggestions.

1. Two armies composed of infantry divisions would launch a frontal attack on Moscow. The axis of advance of the southern army would be the Roslavl-Moscow road, that of the northern the line Bely-Rzhev-Dmitrov.

2. On the right of these two armies Second Panzer Group would thrust into the area south of Moscow, cut the railroads leading to the capital from the south, and support the right wing of the southern army. On the left Third Panzer Group would drive in the direction of Kalinin, cut the lines of communications between Moscow and Leningrad, seize the area north of Moscow, and support the left wing of the northern army.

3. Another army composed of infantry divisions would move up behind the Second Panzer Group, dislodge the Russian forces north of Gomel, and establish flank security along the line Bryansk-Pogost.

4. The offensive could probably begin on 12 August after the rehabilitation of the armored and motorized units. If the operations proceeded at all well, it could be assumed that Moscow would be reached by the beginning of September.

5. The essential difference between this and the previous plans was that the Russian forces around Gomel would not be encircled and destroyed by the Second Panzer Group but simply driven southeastward by an infantry army. Moreover, the Third Panzer Group would not be diverted to Army Group

North; on the other hand, the principal mission it was supposed to accomplish during its temporary attachment to Army Group North—that of cutting the lines of communications between Moscow and Leningrad—would also be achieved according to this plan.

6. By assembling Second Panzer Group west of Roslavl and Third Panzer Group southwest of Bely, this or any alternate plan could be carried out without delay.

7. The decision on which the plan of operation for Army Group Center was to be adopted would not have to be made until 4 August; this delay would make it possible to take into account any further developments in the enemy situation.

This letter expressed the Army's anxiety over Hitler's plans, the implementation of which would be the first step toward dissipating the momentum of the powerful German offensive. Involvement in a series of local operations would eventually lead to a loss of initiative. Instead of applying the principles of grand strategy, the Army would be using grand tactics; and attempts to eliminate a local threat here and close a gap there, without considering strategic factors, would inevitably lead to position warfare.

During a visit to Army Group Center headquarters on 25 July, Keitel explained Hitler's contrasting viewpoint as follows: Instead of the sweeping enveloping maneuvers that had been successful during the preceding campaigns, the Germans would have to conduct small-scale battles of annihilation leading to the complete destruction of the encircled forces. In Russia the execution of too far-reaching envelopments had invariably resulted in the escape of major Soviet elements, which eventually were reintegrated into the opposing forces. This tactic also had the disadvantage that the precious armor was being decimated by Russian flank attacks. The distance between the armored and infantry units would have to be shortened, both to protect the armor and to tighten the rings of encirclement. The latter improvement was all the more necessary because air reconnaissance reports indicated that streams of Russian columns had been escaping for days from the Smolensk pocket through a gap on the eastern side.

Keitel continued by enumerating Hitler's plans for future operations which corresponded to the contents of the Supplement to Directive No. 33.

On 27 July Jodl asked Hitler to reconsider his plans. The drive on Moscow ought to be envisaged after all, he stated, not because the city was the Soviet capital, but because the Russians would scrape together their last forces for the defense of Moscow. Moreover, the plan to attack Moscow was in conformity with Hitler's own concept of destroying the main Soviet forces. Hitler replied that the Germans would have to seize the Donets Basin as soon as possible to deprive the Russians of their armament production facilities and cut off their oil supplies. The next day Hitler gave another reason for his refusal to drive straight toward the Soviet capital—that the industrial region around Kharkov was more important to him than Moscow. Finally, on 29 July, he suddenly explained that the successes hitherto attained in Russia went far beyond his most optimistic expectations, so far as both territorial acquisitions and the destruction of Russian forces were concerned. He had believed that the question of diverting the two panzer groups from the drive on Moscow would arise much sooner in the campaign. In the case of Army Group North, for instance, he had thought that the first major delay would occur along the Dvina and that the Third Panzer Group would have to be diverted at that time. By this last utterance Hitler made it obvious that the idea of diverting forces from the center to the wings went back to the early planning stage and had found expression in the first changes to Directive No. 21, Operation BARBAROSSA, made on 17 December 1940.

The Situation Toward the End of July 1941

No radical changes in the situation occurred during the second half of July. In the Army Group South area, First Panzer Group had finally succeeded in breaking through the Russian front and driving to Pervomaysk. [See map 8.] It was therefore to be hoped that large Soviet forces would eventually be encircled in the Uman area.

On the other hand, Sixth Army was still unable to make headway against the Russian *Fifth Army* in the Pripyat Marshes and was stalled west of Kiev. It was to be assumed, however, that the threat to the army group flank would be eliminated as soon as all the elements of Sixth Army had closed up. Then, a main effort could be built on the army's right and the Russians could be driven out of the Dnepr area. Bad weather marked by cloudbursts and torrential rains hampered all movements. Although the Russians continued to defend stubbornly, the general impression was that they were weakening.

Army Group Center had practically completed the mopping up of the numerous pockets with the exception of one near Smolensk. The disposition of forces was revised so that the armored divisions could be pulled out and sent to the rear for rehabilitation. The Russians continued to exert considerable pressure against both army group wings, from the area north of Gomel on the right and from the region northeast of Vitebsk on the left. Opposite the central portion of the army group front the Russians made strenuous efforts to build up a new defense line, moving up a steady flow of reinforcements via Moscow.

Army Group North had made progress on the right, while most of the infantry divisions had succeeded in closing with the two panzer corps along the Luga River and near Novgorod. Taking advantage of the delay in the German advance, the Russians had worked feverishly at strengthening the defenses of Leningrad.

Offensive operations had meanwhile also begun in Finland. The northernmost attack force of the Army of Norway had occupied Petsamo, but had bogged down near the Litsa River upon encountering superior Russian opposition during its advance on Murmansk. The other forces which were driving toward the Murmansk railroad made very slow progress in the primeval forests and swamps of central Finland. In the southern part of the theater of operations, which was under the Finnish Army High Command, the Karelian Army, advancing along the eastern shore of Lake Ladoga, had reached

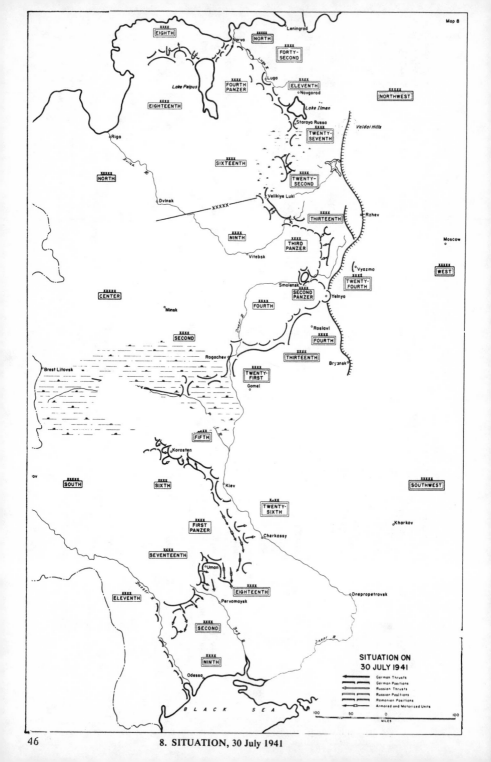

SITUATION ON
30 JULY 1941

8. SITUATION, 30 July 1941

the pre-1940 Russo-Finnish border. However, the Finns were unable to comply with a German request to resume their advance in the direction of the Svir River without delay, because Russian forces massed in the Lake Onega area threatened their flank. The Finnish forces on the Karelian Isthmus launched their offensive against

GERMAN ASSAULT GUN attacks behind smoke screen.

Viipuri on 31 July, after the Russian contingents in that area had been weakened by the withdrawal of units needed for the defense of Leningrad.

The supply situation of Army Group Center, far from having improved, began to hamper the progress of current operations.

IV

PLANNING FOR FUTURE OPERATIONS

The conflict over the continuation of operations became acute when Hitler overrode all his advisers—except Keitel—and imposed Directive No. 33 and the Supplement upon the Army. Once Hitler made a decision, its execution was mandatory: therefore on 28 July the Army High Command issued an order implementing the Fuehrer's directives. By that time, however, Hitler apparently felt less sure of himself and drafted another directive which was actually a compromise between his viewpoint and that of his military advisers. Whereas in the Supplement to Directive No. 33, dated 23 July, Hitler had envisaged drives into the Caucasus and beyond Moscow to the Volga River, in Directive No. 34, issued seven days later, he set aside these operations with their distant objectives. Actually, these were secondary issues compared with the basic problem: was the drive on Moscow to be continued or not?

At this moment Hitler was at the zenith of his military triumphs. Starting with the remilitarization of the Rhineland in 1935, an uninterrupted series of successes seemed to have vindicated his intuition whenever he had come into conflict with his military advisers. More than logic or strength of character was needed to make a successful stand against a man who had been so consistently lucky.

If on this occasion Hitler was vacillating and inclined to adopt some of the Army's suggestions, this would simply imply that he realized the importance of his decisions for the future course of the Russian campaign. The following steps, reconstructed and juxtaposed, led to Hitler's final decision.

The Army's Order of 28 July 1941

In the first part of this order the Operations Division of the Army General Staff analyzed the Russian capabilities, arriving at the conclusion that the bulk of the regular Red Army forces had been destroyed. The Russians were trying to obstruct the German advance by throwing in strong reinforcements and even improperly trained personnel, but it was believed that their military strength would prove insufficient. In continuing the operation, the Germans would have to take advantage of every opportunity for isolating and destroying individual Soviet groupings. These tactics were to be employed to (1) prevent the Russians from building up a continuous defense line; (2) safeguard the German forces' freedom of maneuver; and (3) seize the Soviet armament production centers.

All plans for conducting far-reaching operations would have to be abandoned. The immediate objective was to destroy the Russian forces west of the Dnepr, north of Gomel, and south of Leningrad. In addition, Army Group South would employ the armored and infantry forces that were to be transferred from Army Group Center for a thrust into the Donets Basin. Army Group Center was to commit its remaining forces for an advance in the direction of Moscow; and Army Group North was to encircle Leningrad, establish contact with the Finns, and occupy the remainder of the coastal areas of the Baltic States.

The contents of the order then defined the mission of each army group, outlining such details as assembly areas, direction of attack, coordination with adjacent units, etc. Because of the Russian combat methods, particular attention was drawn to forming points of main effort, protecting flanks by mine fields, and maintaining contact between armored and infantry units. Rear areas and the lines of communications leading through them would have to be properly secured.

Attached to this order was an intelligence summary dated 27 July. The 150 infantry, 25 armored, and 5 cavalry divisions identified along the German front to date were estimated to have suffered an average

48

reduction in strength of 50 per cent. The 25 newly organized Soviet divisions were understrength and were short of artillery and heavy weapons. Their personnel were barely trained and the shortage of cadre, drivers, and radio operators was particularly noticeable. Because of the inadequacy of the corps commanders, the Soviet army group staffs had to rely more and more on army command staffs composed of a nucleus of trustworthy and experienced individuals.

The estimate of Russian strength given in this report differed with the figures of 23 July only insofar as it mentioned the presence of 10 newly formed divisions in the area around Moscow. Another major body of troops stood west of Vyazma where 10 divisions blocked the road to Moscow. A Soviet force of 9 infantry and 2 armored divisions was attacking the southern flank of Army Group Center northwest of Gomel. Out of 20 divisions defending Leningrad, 6 were facing the Finns and 14 stood opposite Army Group North.

In summary, the Red Army command was making every effort to stabilize the situation. Russian morale was far from broken, and no signs of internal disintegration had so far appeared.

Directive No. 34 (30 July 1941)

In this new directive Hitler stated that the distant objectives designated in Directive No. 33 of 19 July and in the Supplement, dated 23 July, would be temporarily set aside because of recent developments: the appearance of strong Soviet forces in front of and along the flanks of Army Group Center, the precarious supply situation, and the panzer groups' urgent need for rehabilitation, which would take about 10 days. Instead he ordered:

a. *Army Group North* to continue its offensive against Leningrad while taking the necessary precautions to protect its flank south of Lake Ilmen.

b. *Army Group Center* to switch to the defensive so that its two panzer groups could be withdrawn and rehabilitated; the Third Panzer Group thrust toward the Valdai Hills to be deferred for the time being.

c. *Army Group South* to receive no additional forces for accomplishing its previously designated missions of destroying the Russian forces west of the Dnepr, establishing bridgeheads near Kiev, and neutralizing the Russian *Fifth Army*.

d. In *Finland* the German attack in the direction of Kandalaksha to be stopped, but attempts to sever the Murmansk railroad to be continued, especially at Loukhi.

e. *Air Support:* The Luftwaffe to shift its main effort from Army Group Center to Army Group North by 6 August at the latest; bombing attacks on Moscow to continue; essential air support to be given to ground operations in all other parts of the theater.

On 31 July the Army issued an order implementing Directive No. 34, in which special emphasis was put on the rehabilitation of Second and Third Panzer Groups and their eventual commitment in the direction of Gomel and the Valdai Hills respectively.

Hitler's Vacillation Over Strategy

Directive No. 33, the Supplement, and Directive No. 34 may be considered as manifestations of Hitler's hesitancy with regard to the continuation of operations. Feeling none too sure about the advisability of diverting forces from Army Group Center, Hitler made strenuous efforts to inform himself on the subject by personal visits to two army group headquarters. The first of these conferences took place on 4 August, when Hitler and his staff visited Army Group Center headquarters. The Army group commander, Field Marshal von Bock, began the conference by reporting on personnel and equipment matters. Then both Generals Guderian and Hoth, his subordinate panzer group commanders, emphasized that major operations would be feasible only if an adequate number of spare engines could be delivered in time to replace the wornout ones.

Hitler replied that the bulk of the current production of tank engines was needed for equipping newly formed armored divisions. Nevertheless, 400 new engines might be made available to the two panzer groups. Guderian immediately objected that this number would prove unsatisfactory because he alone needed 300 engines for the Second Panzer Group. Hitler thereupon quickly changed the subject to the future conduct of operations. Going into great detail, he reemphasized how important it would be to capture Leningrad, the Donets Basin, and the Crimea. To him, all these objectives had priority over Moscow.

Before the conference was brought to a conclusion, Guderian and Hoth stated that, if withdrawn from the line by 8 August, their panzer groups would be operational by 15 and 18 August respectively. Whether they would be capable of executing far-reaching maneuvers or only operations with limited objectives would depend on the number of tank engines that could meanwhile be made available.

In concluding Hitler stated that the Soviets rated the Moscow area third in importance after Leningrad and the industrial regions of the south. Reports by experts on Russian weather tended to prove the soundness of his plans, since in southern Russia the rainy period in autumn usually started in mid-September, whereas in the Moscow area it did not begin until one month later. Hitler continued that he had also "briefly considered" the possibility of a limited thrust toward Moscow. Bock interjected that such an offensive could have decisive results, if it were properly staged and supported. But Hitler needed more time to arrive at a definite decision.

On 6 August during a conference at Army Group South headquarters Rundstedt emphasized the significance of the possession of Moscow in achieving a quick victory over the Soviet Union. Hitler, however, refused to listen to his arguments, enumerating the most important objectives of the campaign in their former priority: Leningrad, eastern Ukraine, and Moscow.

On the next day Halder asked Jodl whether Hitler's primary objective was to defeat the Soviet Union or to acquire economic assets in the Ukraine and the Caucasus. Jodl expressed the opinion that Hitler was attempting to attain both objectives simultaneously. Halder then stated that Leningrad could be seized without diverting any forces from Army Group Center that would be needed for the drive on

Moscow. If the Russians were to be defeated by autumn, the offensives against Moscow and the Ukraine would have to be conducted simultaneously.

Halder also stressed that German strategy should not be influenced by Russian tactics. By trying to eliminate threats to their flanks the Germans would dissipate forces instead of concentrating them for decisive operations. Jodl seemed impressed by these arguments and submitted them to Hitler on 10 August in an Armed Forces Operations Staff memorandum.

This document restated that according to all available intelligence the bulk of the Russian forces were massed in front of Moscow. Their destruction and the seizure of the Russian capital were therefore the primary objectives for the German Army. Tempting diversions to the north or south would have to be ignored for the time being. On the other hand, the flanks of Army Group Center would have to be secured by limited-objective attacks—some of which were already underway—before the army group committed its forces to an all-out drive on Moscow.

If the maneuvers to secure the flanks could be successfully concluded within the next two weeks, the Moscow offensive could be launched by the end of August. During the initial stage of the offensive Army Groups South and North would have to get along as best they could, but would be certain of support from Army Group Center as soon as the latter launched its pursuit.

The memorandum continued by outlining the missions of the different armies operating in the north and south of the theater and stressed that the VIII Air Corps would support Army Group North only until around 20 August, by which time the forces of Army Group Center would be concentrated.

In summarizing, the Armed Forces Operations Staff recommended that Army Group Center prepare an offensive against Moscow for the end of August. Once the advance had reached the pursuit stage, Guderian's panzer forces could be diverted southeastward in the direction of the Don bend.

Halder noted in his diary on 11 August that the Germans had reckoned with 200 Russian divisions at the start of the campaign, but that by 10 August 360 Russian divisions had already been identified. Even though these divisions were not as well organized, equipped, and led as the German ones, they nevertheless existed and had to be defeated. Each time the Germans destroyed a dozen of them, the Soviets simply moved up 12 more. The German frontline was overextended, and there were no reserves. As a result, German troops were exposed to Russian counterattacks, some of which were successful because the Germans were unable to close all the gaps in their lines in so vast a theater of operations.

The Supplement to Directive No. 34 (12 August 1941)

The effect of the Armed Forces Operations Staff memorandum and the personal impressions gathered by Hitler during his visits in the field were reflected in the contents of the Supplement to Directive No. 34, issued on 12 August. The latter defined the missions of Army Group South as follows:

1. To prevent the establishment of a continuous Russian defense line along the Dnepr;

2. To seize the Crimea; and

3. To capture the Donets region and the industrial area around Kharkov.

The attack on the city of Kiev proper was to be stopped; instead the city was to be annihilated by fire bombs and artillery shells as soon as a sufficient quantity of these means of destruction would become available. The Luftwaffe was to give every possible support to the ground forces.

Army Group Center's primary mission was to eliminate the Russian salients that were protruding far into its flanks. After this had been successfully accomplished and the armored groups had been rehabilitated, the army group forces were to jump off for the Moscow offensive on a wide front. However, the operation against Leningrad had to be brought to a conclusion and VIII Air Corps had to revert to Second Air Force before the offensive against Moscow could be undertaken.

The current attacks in the Army Group North area were to lead to the encirclement of Leningrad and a link-up with the Finnish forces. Air support units were to pinpoint their missions on selected targets to achieve maximum effectiveness.

The Supplement did not mention any diversion of Army Group Center forces to the south and made only a very indefinite reference to shifting of divisions to strengthen Army Group North. On the other hand, the launching of the offensive authorized an offensive against Moscow, the launching of the offensive was to be contingent upon the success of the Leningrad drive.

This priority was even more clearly expressed in a conference note signed by Jodl and dated 15 August. It referred to Brauchitsch's verbal report of the same date, following which Hitler had ordered that all further attacks in the direction of Moscow be stopped. Army Group Center was to switch to the defensive and hold the line without major air support. The Army Group North attacks would have to be brought to a successful conclusion with a minimum of delay. As many Third Panzer Group divisions as could be employed and supplied by Army Group North were to be transferred from Army Group Center to eliminate the threat to Army Group North's flank. Moreover, a breakthrough achieved by several Russian divisions south of Staraya Russa prompted Hitler to issue a direct order for the transfer of one armored corps to Army Group North.

Developments to Mid-August 1941

During the first half of August Army Group South partially succeeded in destroying the Russian forces that were left west of the Dnepr. By 5 August, First Panzer and Seventeenth Armies encircled 16 to 20 Russian divisions near Uman and destroyed them despite repeated delays caused by bad weather. Subsequently, the entire Dnepr bend was cleared of Russian forces, their remnants withdrawing across the river wherever they were able to do so. The Sixth Army was in a less favorable situation, since it had been unable to seize Kiev or score a decisive success against the Russian Fifth Army. On the contrary, several relatively strong Russian counterattacks had led to critical situations, particularly around Kiev and south of that city.

b. *The Next Objective.* Whereas the objective of a German offensive in the north or south would be either to eliminate the Russian Baltic Fleet or to seize important industrial areas in the Donets Basin, an offensive in the center would lead to the destruction of strong Soviet forces and the laceration of the Russian front. That in turn would result in the German seizure of Moscow which, together with the losses suffered in the north and south, would prevent the Soviets from offering any further coordinated resistance.

The decision of selecting Moscow as the next objective of Army Group Center was based on the following considerations:

(1) *The Time Element.* Because of Russian weather conditions the offensive against Moscow would have to be carried out during September and October. In view of the distances to be covered and the strong resistance the Russians were bound to offer, two months would be the minimum time requirement for executing the operation.

(2) *Combat Efficiency.* After emergency rehabilitation, the armored and motorized infantry units would be capable of covering only limited distances. Because of their reduced combat efficiency, these units would have to be reserved for decisive actions exclusively.

(3) *Massing of Forces.* The offensive against Moscow could meet with success only if the forces of Army Group Center were properly massed to attain this one objective to which all other operations would have to be subordinated. Otherwise, Army Group Center could not achieve a decisive success during the current year. In any event, the two other army groups would be sufficiently strong to accomplish their missions without outside assistance.

c. *Plan of Operations.* The main effort should be placed on both extremities of the Army Group Center front. There, strong forces would carry out enveloping attacks while the center of the front tied down the opposing forces. The southern attack force would advance via Bryansk and Roslavl toward Kaluga, and the northern one from southwest of Bely and west of Toropez via Rzhev to the east. An entire army—including some motorized units capable of smashing any

On the whole, Army Group South had concluded the initial phase of the operation without fully attaining its objective. The weather had seriously hampered operations. Rundstedt next intended to establish bridgeheads at Dnepropetrovsk, Kremenchug, and Cherkassy.

In the Army Group Center area the first days of August were characterized by furious Russian local attacks. Strong Soviet counterthrusts near Yelnya were held off during heavy fighting lasting until 8 August. At the same time German local attacks near Rogachev and Roslavl eliminated immediate threats and relieved the pressure against the southern flank of the army group and against Yelnya. The entire Second Panzer Group was pulled out of the line by 8 August, and the Third Panzer Group followed two days later. It was anticipated that the rehabilitation of these armored units would be completed between 15 and 20 August.

Up to 8 August the Russians seemed intent upon forcing a withdrawal of Army Group Center; at that time they apparently decided to switch to the defensive with the intention of preparing the line Bryansk–Vyazma–Rzhev for an all-out defense.

The Army Group North drive began on 10 August with a three-pronged attack on Leningrad. One force thrust northward from Lake Ilmen, a second one from the Luga area, and a third one approached Leningrad from the west. All three forces encountered stubborn resistance, and their progress was therefore slow.

The Army Memorandum of 18 August 1941

On 18 August General Halder sent Hitler a memorandum that presented the viewpoint of the Army as follows:

a. *Summary of the Enemy Situation.* The Russians were massing their forces opposite Army Group Center in anticipation of a German drive on Moscow. They were exploring every possible method of strengthening the Moscow sector. Russian forces then stationed in salients protruding into the German lines, such as those near Gomel, would probably be withdrawn to shorten the lines in view of the noticeable shortage of Soviet units. [See *map 9.*]

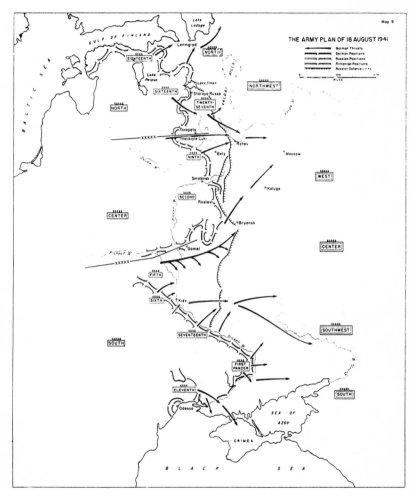

Map 9. THE ARMY PLAN, 18 August 1941

threat from enemy forces without delay—would have to cover the south flank of Army Group Center. A similar flank cover would be provided for the northern force once the situation south of Lake Ilman had been cleared up. Both attack forces would have to break through the Russian defense lines because any effort to envelop the Russian positions would involve too great a detour. Whether the attack groups were to continue their advance north and south of Moscow or initiate enveloping maneuvers immediately after having broken through would depend on the situation and the punch they would be able to deliver at that time.

d. *Distribution of Forces.* For the execution of the operation Army Group Center would have 42 infantry, 1 cavalry, and 12½ armored and/or motorized infantry divisions. After both army group flanks had been secured by preliminary operations, the Red Army forces opposing the German drive would number approximately 42 divisions to which should be added about 20 divisions that were in the process of activation. Russian numerical superiority would be outmatched by German combat efficiency and excellence of equipment. The suggested distribution of forces was as follows:

(1) *Southern Attack Force.* This force would be composed of 12 infantry and 6 armored and/or motorized infantry divisions deployed along an 80-mile front extending from Bryansk to Roslavl.

(2) *Central Front.* East of Smolensk, 10 infantry divisions would cover a defensive sector 95 miles wide.

(3) *Northern Attack Force.* This force would consist of a southern group composed of 6 infantry and 2 armored and/or motorized infantry divisions jumping off from the area southwest of Bely and a northern group assembled west of Toropez and composed of 7 infantry and 2 armored and/or motorized infantry divisions. The latter group would have to eliminate the Russian salient around Velikye Luki in a preliminary move.

(4) *Flank Protection Army.* An army consisting of 1 cavalry, 5 infantry, and 2 armored and/or motorized infantry divi-

sions would advance into the area east of Gomel and leave 2 additional divisions to cover the Pripyat flank.

e. *Assembly of Forces.*

(1) The assembly of the southern attack force by the beginning of September would present no major difficulties, if the fighting around Gomel were brought to a successful conclusion by 23 August.

(2) The attack group assembling west of Toropez would also be ready to jump off by the beginning of September if the attack on Velikye Luki started no later than 21 August.

(3) Regrouping of the other army group forces could also be accomplished by the beginning of September.

(4) The armored and/or motorized infantry divisions assigned to the attack forces would be rehabilitated by the end of August at the latest. The two divisions that might not be ready in time could be used for flank protection.

f. *Projected Course of Events*

(1) Army Group Center would be ready to jump off at the beginning of September to carry out the operations outlined above.

(2) Army Group South would begin its attack against the Russian *Fifth Army* by 23 August. By early September elements of *Sixth Army* were to reach the Dnepr north of Kiev and *Seventeenth Army* was to force river crossings farther to the south. With these operations in full swing, it would be unlikely that the Russians could shift forces to the north.

(3) Army Group North was to complete the encirclement of Leningrad by the end of August, and its forces would then attempt to establish contact with the Finns. The Army group forces south of Lake Ilmen were to eliminate the Russian penetration south of Staraya Russa and start their advance to the Valdai Hills simultaneous with the offensive of Army Group Center. If these forces could advance far enough toward the southeast, it might be possible to integrate their advance into the drive of the northern attack force.

The operations of all three army groups would therefore be coordinated. To assure the success of the offensive, the necessary orders would have to be issued without delay.

On 18 August General Warlimont wrote an Armed Forces Operations Staff estimate that fully endorsed the Army memorandum of the same date. He stated that to attain the objectives of the Russian campaign before the outbreak of winter the forces operating in the north had only 8 weeks at their disposal and those in the south just 13. Because of the long distances, the relatively short time, and the high attrition of automotive vehicles, the operations conducted during the coming months would have to be driven straight toward the primary objective without any deviation. In determining whether the Army Group Center forces—less the panzer corps recently transferred to Army Group North—were to be kept together for the thrust on Moscow or whether the Second Panzer Group was to be diverted to the southeast to take advantage of the very favorable opportunities in that area, Warlimont arrived at the same conclusion as the Army: Army Groups North and South were sufficiently strong to accomplish their missions with their own forces while Army Group Center conducted the offensive against Moscow. In summarizing he restated that, to guarantee the success of the latter operation, no forces should be diverted to such secondary operations as the southeastern thrust of Second Panzer Group. Moreover, if necessary, critical situations along the flanks or in the rear should be ignored so that the attack forces could concentrate on the essential drive toward Moscow.

Hitler's Decision (20 August 1941)

On 20 August Hitler declared that he disagreed with the contents of the Army memorandum. He was not interested in Moscow and the forces assembled in the vicinity of the Soviet capital. His ideas found their expression in an order issued to the Commander in Chief of the Army on 21 August which ended the controversy over the continuation of the operations. Among the significant points were the following:

a. The most important objective was not the capture of Moscow; top priority was to be given to seizing the Crimea and the industrial region in the Donets Basin, to cutting off the Russian oil supply from the Caucasus in the south, and to encircling Leningrad and linking up with the Finnish forces in the north.

b. The situation was favorable for a concentric attack executed by the contiguous fronts of Army Groups South and Center against the Russian Fifth Army to prevent the latter from withdrawing. Regardless of subsequent operations Army Group Center was to assign to this mission all the forces necessary for the destruction of the Russian Fifth Army, because the liquidation of this force was the only means of assuring that Army Group South could resume its advance toward Rostov and Kharkov.

c. The seizure of the Crimea was of utmost importance for safeguarding the German oil supply from Romania against air attacks. A rapid advance into the Caucasus would be desirable to exercise pressure on Iran.

d. Only after a and b had been accomplished would the necessary forces be available to attack and defeat the Russians defending Moscow in accordance with the instructions issued in the Supplement to Directive No. 34.

General Guderian, the commander of Second Panzer Group, made one last attempt to change Hitler's mind by explaining the difficulties involved in pivoting his force southeastward. His arguments failed to impress the Fuehrer, and the Army High Command was forced to implement Hitler's order.

A Russian general, captured by the Germans in the spring of 1942, stated that the German failure to drive home the offensive against Moscow in the early fall of 1941 impressed the Soviet High Command as being a second "miracle of the Marne," which saved the Soviet capital in 1941 in much the same way the first one had spared Paris in 1914.

V

THE DIVERSION AND REASSEMBLY

The Personnel Situation (End of August 1941)

The German Army suffered a total of 409,998 losses, or 11.05 per cent of the average strength figure of 3.78 million men employed in the Russian theater, from 22 June–31 August, 1941.

To compensate for these losses, the Army High Command assigned 317,000 replacements from the Zone of Interior to the Russian theater, distributing them as follows:

8. GERMAN ARMY LOSSES AND REPLACEMENTS

German Army Losses	(22 June–31 August 1941)		
	Total	Officers	EM
Totals	409,998	14,457	395,541
Killed in Action	87,489	4,006	83,483
Wounded in Action	302,821	10,080	292,741
Missing in Action	19,688	371	19,317

Replacements Transferred to the Russian Theater				
Period	Total	Army Groups		
		South	Center	North
Totals	317,000	119,000	131,000	67,000
22 Jun–25 Aug 41	146,000	52,000	66,000	28,000
25–31 Aug	71,000	27,000	25,000	19,000
Expected to arrive after 31 Aug	100,000	40,000	40,000	20,000

As of 31 August, however, only 217,000 men had arrived in the Russian theater to compensate for the 409,998 losses, and the personnel shortage in the theater therefore amounted to about 193,000 men.

A total of 21 out of 24 divisions, constituting the Army High Command reserves at the beginning of the campaign, had reached the front by the end of August and had been distributed as follows:

9. DISTRIBUTION OF GERMAN FORCES, September 1941

Type	Total Divisions	Divisions assigned to Army Groups		
		South	Center	North
Totals	21	10	8	3
Infantry	20	9	8	3
Motorized Infantry	1	1		

Only three divisions were left in the hands of the Army High Command.

Increasing Logistical Difficulties (Early September 1941)

POL

The POL shortage was serious except in the Army Group North area. Stock piles were exhausted and newly arriving shipments were immediately distributed to the front-line units, particularly those of Army Group South, where occasional shortages hampered operations. In calculating the requirements for the offensive in the direction of Moscow the planners found that the daily rate of POL trains arriving in the theater would have to be stepped up from 22 to 27 for the period 17 September to 2 October and to 29 as of 3 October.

Track-Laying and Wheeled Vehicles

On 4 September the following breakdown of tank strength in the Russian theater was given by the Army High Command:

Available for employment _____ 47 percent
Deadlined for repair _____ 23 percent
Disabled _____ 30 percent

Compared with the tank status report of 4 August, the percentage of disabled tanks had increased from 20 to 30 percent. On the other hand, the percentage of deadlined vehicles had been reduced from 30 to 23 percent because of the arrival of spare parts and the possibility of allocating time for maintenance and repair. However, the repair facilities were inadequate and the shortage of tank engines continued. Moreover, the repaired tanks had been so overtaxed by previous employment that their future usefulness was bound to be short. It was estimated that the percentage of tanks available for employment at the start of the Moscow offensive could be increased to 60.5 of T/E strength if all new tanks then in the hands of the Army High Command were distributed to the field forces.

The number of trucks in operating condition had dropped to 77.85 percent of T/E strength, that of prime movers to 67.90 percent, including repaired vehicles. Only emergency repairs were being performed so that the complete loss of the vehicles after 200–250 additional miles had to be anticipated. The combat efficiency and mobility of the ground forces would therefore be greatly reduced at the decisive moment of the offensive—when they were approaching Moscow.

Halder suggested that all newly produced tanks and trucks be allocated to the Russian theater as replacements, instead of being used to equip new divisions. He believed that under such conditions the situation could be remedied. Immediate steps would have to be taken since the arrival of the vehicles could not be expected before three to four weeks. All possible disadvantages that might result from this suggestion would be of far less consequence than a sudden bogging down of the Moscow offensive at the beginning of winter.

Developments to Mid-September 1941

The implementation of the order issued by Hitler on 20 August resulted in the following developments:

Army Group South had succeeded in carrying out its enveloping maneuver with the assistance of Second Army and Second Panzer Group, even though the pivoting movement of the latter had encoun-

tered some difficulty. Several Russian armies, among them the *Fifth* which had finally been forced to withdraw to the east bank of the Dnepr, were facing annihilation east of Kiev. [See *map 10*.] When this gigantic pocket was finally mopped up, the Germans took 665,000 prisoners and a tremendous amount of booty. The original strategic objective in the Army Group South area had thus been attained, but only by diverting strong forces from Army Group Center. In any event, the way was open for a sustained eastward drive in the southern part of the Russian theater. At the same time the advance in the direction of the Crimea had made good progress and German forces were approaching the gateway to the peninsula.

In early September Army Group Center had been engaged in heavy defensive battles during which a number of critical situations had arisen in the central sector of the army group front. At the same time, the northern attack force of Army Group Center operating in conjunction with Army Group North had penetrated into the area east of Toropets. Bock was greatly weakened by heavy transfers of forces to the adjoining army groups. His front was overextended, and he had almost no reserves.

Army Group North had completed the encirclement of Leningrad. A direct attack on the city proper was expressly forbidden by Hitler, who wanted to avoid the heavy casualties of house-to-house fighting and who refused to assume the responsibility for feeding the city's millions. He considered throwing a ring around the city sufficient. One of the difficulties in carrying out this plan was that the flank protection forces along the Volkhov were very weak. South of Lake Ilmen, the Sixteenth Army was spread over a wide area in the difficult terrain at the foot of the Valdai Hills and was making little headway.

For the time being, Army Group North could not continue to advance into the area east of Lake Ladoga since it was forced to employ large bodies of troops to close the ring of encirclement around Leningrad. The planned linkup between German and Finnish forces east of Lake Ladoga could therefore not be realized. This in turn compelled the Finns to commit sizeable forces on the Karelian Isthmus so that Leningrad could be sealed off from the north.

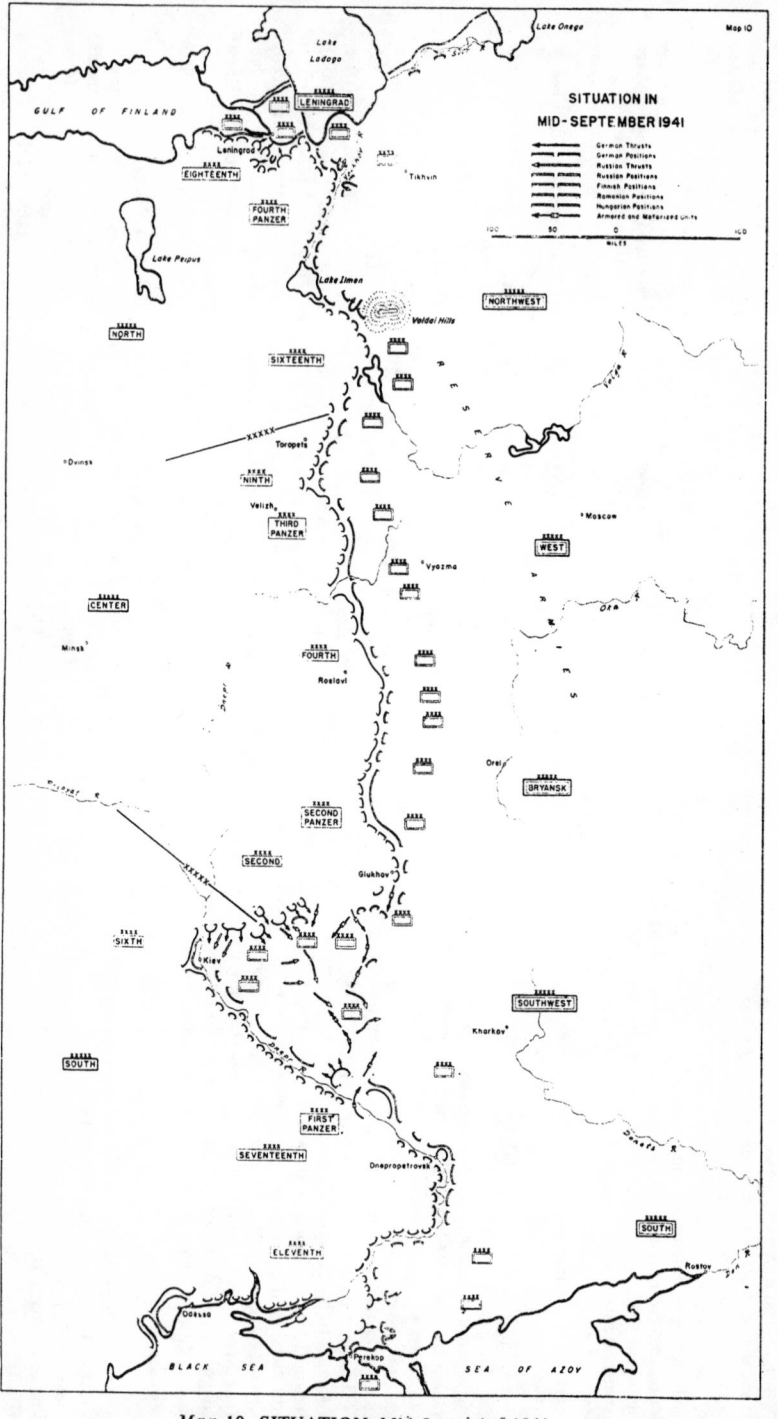

Map 10. SITUATION, Mid-September 1941.

In the north the war of movement had degenerated into position warfare. The Army of Norway, stopped or bogged down in all three attack zones, had failed to reach its objectives. At the request of its government, the Finnish High Command had limited the advance of its troops to a line approximating the Russo-Finnish border of 1939 on the Karelian Isthmus, and to the Svir River east of Lake Ladoga. The uncertainty regarding further developments around Leningrad induced Finnish political leaders to prosecute the war against Russia with restraint.

Directive No. 35 (6 September 1941)

On 6 September Hitler issued a new directive based on recommendations made by the Army High Command. The prerequisites for a decisive offensive existed in the Army Group Center area now that Leningrad was encircled and the early destruction of the Russian forces facing Army Group South could be anticipated. The plan called for the envelopment of the Soviet units west of Vyazma by a pincers attack that was to be launched at the end of September. For this purpose two armored forces were to be concentrated near Roslavl and east of Velizh. Only after the bulk of Timoshenko's forces had been annihilated were the attack forces to launch a pursuit in the direction of Moscow along a front extending from the Oka River on the right to the upper Volga on the left. Army Group South was to conclude the battle east of Kiev as soon as possible so that Second Panzer Group and Second Army would revert to Army Group Center without delay. Similarly, as soon as Leningrad had been cut off from the east, Army Group North was to return those air force and armored units which had previously been detached from Army Group Center. The Navy was to concentrate a sizeable fleet near the Aaland Islands to prevent the Russian Baltic Fleet from escaping. Mine fields were to be laid in the Gulf of Finland.

The directive conformed to the recommendations of the Army High Command, except for the deadline. The Army felt doubtful whether the mobile elements of Second Panzer Group could be moved up by the end of September. To avoid any delay, it was decided that the armored force whose assembly was near Roslavl would be controlled by Fourth Panzer Group headquarters, which was to be transferred from Army Group North. This attack force was to consist of the 10th Panzer Division, in the Roslavl area, the 2d and 5th Panzer Divisions, to be transferred from the Army High Command reserve, the 11th Panzer Division, to be transferred from Army Group South, and the 19th and 20th Panzer Divisions, to be transferred from Army Group North.

The armored force, to be concentrated near Velizh, was to be led by Third Panzer Group, whose headquarters had already been established in the area. This force was to be composed of the 7th Panzer Division, in the Velizh area, and the 1st and 6th Panzer Divisions, to be transferred from Army Group North.

Many difficulties were encountered in performing the lateral displacements necessitated by the assembly of the Third and Fourth Panzer Groups, some elements of which had to be moved several hundred miles.

As soon as it reverted to Army Group Center, Guderian's Second Panzer Group, composed of the 3d, 4th, 9th, 17th, and 18th Panzer Divisions, was to make a wide enveloping sweep from Glukhov toward Orel. If this maneuver proved successful, the Second Panzer Group would be well placed to continue its advance in the direction of Moscow.

To the uninitiated, the halt and diversion of strength, imposed upon Army Group Center at a decisive moment, appeared of little significance. In reality, however, and entirely apart from the time consumed in shifting the armored units, the Germans had lost six precious weeks, and this loss could be decisive in view of the advanced season. The Second Panzer Group had to march 400 miles before it could reestablish contact with Army Group Center. Its equipment was heavily overtaxed, and it was doubtful that it could withstand the wear and tear of another 300-mile thrust before reaching Moscow.

The mission of Army Group South was clear cut: after the battle at Kiev, it was to advance toward Rostov and Kharkov. During this drive the northern wing had to be so strengthened that it could provide flank protection for the advancing Army Group Center.

Army Group North was to tighten its grip on Leningrad and at the same time reinforce its flank along the Volkhov River and south of Lake Ilmen. The latter flank was particularly important in that its reinforcement provided simultaneous protection for Army Group Center.

The Situation at the End of September 1941

Army Group South continued its operations according to plan. On 26 September a breakthrough into the Crimea was attempted across the Perekop Isthmus. Toward the end of the month the armies that had participated in the battle of Kiev resumed their drives in the direction of Rostov and Kharkov respectively. The mopping up of the various pockets east of Kiev had caused considerable delay. Behind the army group front Odessa alone remained in Russian hands, and German forces had to be moved up to assist the Romanians besieging the city.

On 20 September Second Panzer Group began to regroup its forces for their next mission, the thrust on Orel. After overcoming the manifold difficulties involved in turning its axis of advance almost 180°, the panzer group jumped off 10 days later.

An estimate of the Russian intentions indicated that in the southern part of the theater the Russians were improvising a new defense line and moving up reinforcements, particularly west of the Donets salient and around Kharkov. The supply situation of Army Group South was considered serious because all railroad bridges across the Dnepr had been demolished.

Army Group Center had to overcome many obstacles in preparing for the new offensive. In order to meet the deadline, the Army High Command had to assume control over the movement of those armored divisions that were to be transferred from Army Group North. Deceptive measures were to be taken to conceal the shifting of ground and air force units. Whenever possible, movements were to take place during the hours of darkness.

West of Moscow the Russians were strengthening their defensive preparations, channeling reinforcements through their capital and building one defensive position behind another. Partisan activities against the road and rail nets in the rear areas became more and more effective, forcing the Germans to divert a large number of troops to security missions. The German supply situation was becoming precarious, but Bock's chief of supply was able to issue fairly adequate quantities of gasoline and ammunition to the spearhead divisions. It was evident, however, that the consumption of large quantities of POL would create a serious problem and lead to drastic rationing in other parts of the theater.

After Army Group North had transferred the armored forces, its offensive slowly ground to a halt. Having attained his immediate objective, Leeb had only to tighten the ring around Leningrad, strengthen his eastern flank near the Valdai Hills and along the Volkhov River, and close in on Leningrad by a series of local attacks. An attack via Tikhvin, for the purpose of linking up with the Finnish forces east of Lake Ladoga, was planned for a later date. By mid-September the first bad-weather period set in, hampering all operations.

The Russians appeared to be moving reinforcements into the Valdai Hills and toward the Volkhov River with the obvious intention of relieving Leningrad in the near future. It was therefore to be expected that they would exert pressure in these two areas, where relatively weak German forces were thinly spread and critical situations might easily arise. This threat had to be watched the more carefully because it could develop into an acute danger for the left flank of Army Group Center as the latter gradually became exposed during the eastward drive on Moscow. The Valdai Hills region therefore assumed a primary strategic importance and was kept under constant observation by the Army High Command.

To the rear, the struggle for the islands in the Gulf of Riga continued. Despite local shortages caused by the high rate of ammunition expenditure in the fighting around Leningrad, the overall supply situation of Army Group North was satisfactory.

In general, however, the German lines of communications had become very strained during the first three months of the campaign. Despite considerable effort less than 10,000 of the 15,000 miles of rail lines in use had been converted to normal European gauge. Army Group North was in the most favorable position because it also received supplies via Baltic sea transport.

In summary, no major surprise had occurred during the month of September. An analysis of Russian combat methods revealed that the Red Army continued to offer strong resistance and exploit every opportunity to counterattack. What did astound the Germans was the strength still displayed by the Russians, their ability to improvise quickly in any given situation, the apparently inexhaustible flow of new divisions arriving at the front, and the absence of any true symptoms of disintegration.

Despite the tremendous losses it had suffered, the Red Army was still a powerful adversary. The early collapse expected by the German military leaders had not materialized, and the elements of space and time thus assumed increasing strategic significance. Whether the Germans would be able to reach their objectives before the onset of winter remained to be seen.

Military-Economic Survey (2 October 1941)

On 2 October General Thomas submitted a survey of the military-economic situation of the Soviet Union for the following four hypothetical cases:

1. If all territory west of the line Crimea–Dnepr–Kharkov–Tula–Moscow–Leningrad–Kandalaksha (including the cities proper) were seized by the Germans, the Soviets would lose approximately two-thirds of their steel and aluminum production facilities. Such a loss would preclude any increase in the industrial capacity still available to the Soviet Government, probably making its full utilization impossible. As a result, the Red Army would be incapable of fully equipping its forces during a winter lull in operations; the Russians might, however, be able to produce the most urgently needed equipment, enabling them to continue resistance in the spring of 1942.

2. If, in addition, the Soviet Union lost the Maikop oil fields and the Donets Basin, its economic potential would be so greatly impaired that by the summer of 1942 the Red Army would lack the necessary equipment to resume the struggle west of the Urals.

3. Assuming that the USSR would suffer the above losses plus that of the industrial area of Gorki, the effect would be the almost complete stoppage of truck and passenger vehicle production. The aircraft industry would lose one of its key fuselage construction plants which in turn would lead to a further reduction in airplane output. In general, however, the military-economic situation would be no worse than predicted in Case 2.

4. In the event that all territory west of the Volga was seized by the Germans, the Soviet armament potential would be greatly weakened without necessarily collapsing. A complete economic breakdown of the Soviet system was not to be expected unless the industrial area of the Urals was occupied by the Germans.

In General Thomas' opinion the military-economic potential of the Soviet Union had not been decisively affected by the German operations conducted up to the end of September. Moreover, his analysis indicated that the seizure of Moscow and Leningrad, even if achieved before the onset of winter, would by no means guarantee the collapse of Soviet resistance. Hitler and his military advisers failed to draw the proper conclusions from this survey.

The Muddy Period and Its Effect on Operations (October 1941)

In compliance with Directive No. 35 Bock launched the Army Group Center offensive on 30 September when Second Panzer Group jumped off, followed two days later by the two enveloping forces from Roslavl and Velizh. By the beginning of October Bock attained his immediate tactical objective. The rings of encirclement around the Russian forces southwest of Moscow were closed near Vyazma and Bryansk. [See map 11.] The liquidation of these two pockets was time-consuming (but it yielded another 658,000 prisoners) and Bock grew anxious to prevent his armored forces from losing their mo-

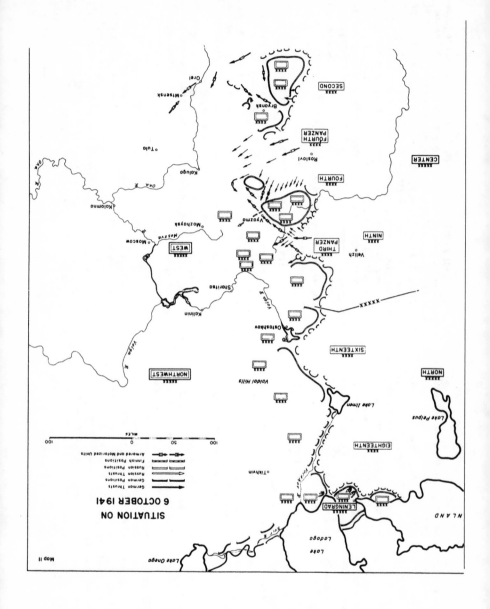

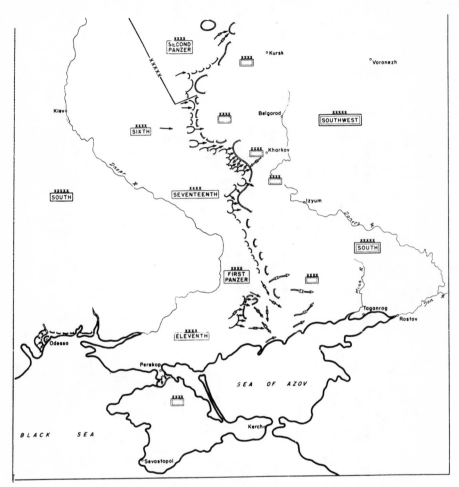

Map 11. **SITUATION, 6 October 1941**

mentum or getting bogged down. To this end it was important that Second Panzer Army (First and Second Panzer Groups had been redesignated panzer armies as of 5 October), whose lead elements were approaching Mtsensk against light opposition, advance rapidly toward Tula in order to break through to Moscow from the southwest. The Third Panzer Group was to cut off the main railroad connecting Moscow with Leningrad, drive to the Volga River, and thence descend upon the capital from the northwest. These two enveloping drives would simultaneously protect the flanks of those army group elements which were to launch the secondary frontal attack in the center. Army Group North was to support the offensive by seizing the area east of Ostashkov, while Army Group South was to assist by advancing into the region west of Voronezh.

Moscow, the final objective, seemed close at hand. Then, on 7 October, the autumn rains began turning the ground into a sea of mud. While it handicapped every movement in the Army Group Center area and slowed down Guderian's vital thrust, some of the latter's forces were able to push eastward. By 20 October Fourth Panzer and Fourth Panzer Group reached the area east of Kaluga and Mozhaysk, and Ninth Army and elements of Third Panzer Group captured Kalinin and Staritsa; but Guderian's Second Panzer Army remained bogged down. Closing with Second Panzer was Second Army whose mission it was to provide flank protection along the upper Don River and maintain contact with Army Group South.

In general, the period from 7 to 20 October was marked by heavy fighting; hot pursuit of a defeated enemy gradually turned into a desperate effort to make headway in rain, snow, and mud. Realizing the imminent threat to their capital the Soviet leaders threw all available resources into the battle.

Up to the beginning of November the situation was generally unchanged. Only Second Panzer Army had gained some ground and, advancing into the Tula area, had reached its designated jump off area for the thrust on Moscow. Its exposed east flank practically invited counterattack, if the Russians were still strong enough to make one. For the time being there was no indication that such an

attack was being prepared by the Soviets. The other elements of Army Group Center had made a few local gains; the area west of Kalinin seemed sufficiently secure, and the northern flank thus appeared protected.

During October Army Group South steadily gained ground in the direction of Rostov. Encountering only sporadic Soviet resistance, First Panzer Army had advanced into the Taganrog area by 20 October. Stronger Russian resistance, coupled with the effects of the mud, delayed Seventeenth Army and, even more, Sixth Army. In the Crimea, the struggle to force the Perekop Isthmus went on, the weak German forces meeting stubborn resistance. By 8 November the Russian defenders were split into two groups and thrown back toward Sevastopol and the Kerch Peninsula. At the same time First Panzer Army reached the western edge of the industrial Donets Basin, Seventeenth Army stood astride the Donets River at Izyum, and Sixth Army captured Kharkov and Belgorod. Sixth Army reported a particularly high materiel attrition rate and a lowering of its combat efficiency.

During the same period Army Group North had succeeded in establishing contact with Army Group Center at Ostashkov as planned. The ring around Leningrad had been strengthened and the islands in the Gulf of Riga had been seized by the Germans. By 20 October, all preparations were made for a thrust on Tikhvin. There, German forces were to link up with the Finns, who by the beginning of September had reached the Svir River east of Lake Ladoga. Tikhvin was also important to the Germans because of the bauxite deposits located in the vicinity. The attack, started on 21 October, led through difficult terrain where there was but a single road. On 8 November, after overcoming great difficulties, the German forces penetrated into the Tikhvin area.

In summary, the muddy season of October 1941 did more than deprive the Germans of the fruits of victory after the battle of Vyazma. The change in ground conditions eventually proved to be one of the major reasons for the German failure to capture Moscow.

Hitler's Plan for the Seizure of Moscow (12 October 1941)

Hitler's ideas on the future destiny of Moscow and its population were explained in an order issued on 12 October. According to this order the capitulation of Moscow was not to be accepted if the Russians decided to surrender the city. Time bombs and booby traps had endangered German lives during the seizure of Kiev, and no risks were to be taken at Moscow or Leningrad. Another reason for caution was the serious danger of epidemics that might break out in these two cities. The lives of German soldiers were not to be sacrificed for the sake of preserving Russian cities. For these reasons no German soldier was to enter Moscow or Leningrad.

Russian civilians trying to escape toward the German lines were to be turned back with fire. Their mass migration into the interior of Russia was considered desirable. No Russian civilians were to be fed at the expense of the German economy. As a general rule, Russian cities under siege were to be softened up by artillery fire and air attacks, and their civilian population was to be put to flight. The greater the chaos in unoccupied Russia, the easier the exploitation of German-occupied territories.

In the letter of transmittal to Army Group Center, the Army High Command added that every effort was to be made to close the ring around Moscow without delay.

Four days later, on 16 October, the Operations Branch of the Army High Command sent to the three army groups a memorandum containing an estimate of the situation. Apparently, a certain number of sources seemed to indicate that the Russians had decided to make a large-scale withdrawal preceded by thorough destruction of industrial facilities. According to this information the Soviets planned to withdraw the maximum number of their remaining units in order to use them as cadres for new divisions that were to be activated during the winter, thus improving their chances for successfully continuing the war in the spring of 1942.

In addition to their previously designated missions the three army groups were to tie down as many Soviet units as possible and destroy them. Wherever Russian units attempted to retreat, improvised pursuit forces—amply provided with gasoline—would have to follow and envelop them. The rest of the memorandum defined specific missions based on the above premises.

The contents of this memorandum indicated that the German estimate of Soviet strength and intentions was faulty at the crucial moment, when decisions regarding the continuation of the Moscow offensive had to be made.

GERMAN MOTORIZED COLUMN takes a break on the road to Minsk, July 1941.

65

VI

THE GERMAN ATTACK ON MOSCOW

Strategic Factors

At the beginning of November 1941 the question of whether the offensive on Moscow was to be resumed at the close of the muddy season was submitted to a thorough examination. The principal arguments against such an offensive were as follows:

1. *Weather Conditions.* A relatively short period of suitable weather with only light frosts could be expected immediately after the muddy season. The Russian winter was close at hand. Around Moscow it usually set in by mid-December at the latest, and its full impact would make itself felt by the end of the year. By then the German forces would have to be redistributed and billeted in such a manner that they could withstand the rigors of winter.

2. *The Condition of the Combat Forces.* The combat efficiency of the infantry divisions had dropped by 35 percent, that of the armored divisions by 40 to 50 percent. The tank attrition rate varied from 65 to 75 percent. The high percentage of officer losses—1 to 25—was striking. Approximately one-third of the officer casualties had been killed in action. On the basis of the above figures it was estimated that the real combat value of the 136 divisions employed in the Russian theater was equivalent to that of only 83 full-strength divisions.

3. *The Rail Transport and Supply Situation.* The flow of supplies was disrupted and only the most urgently needed rations, ammunition, and gasoline could be moved forward, and then only with difficulty. The situation could hardly be expected to improve soon. It would require considerable time to overcome the obstacles caused by the destruction of rail lines and installations, to change the gauge of the tracks, and to repair the damage resulting from various causes. Meanwhile, the German forces would have to live a hand-to-month existence that was not conducive to launching an all-out offensive. Because of the transportation difficulties practically no winter clothing and equipment for Army units would become available for distribution before early January.

4. *Flank Protection.* The southeast flank of Army Group Center in the area east of Kursk and Orel was very exposed. Here weak forces of Second Army were scattered over a wide area, having only occasional contact with Army Group South. If the Russians were still capable of exploiting such an opportunity, this latent threat might develop into an acute danger.

5. *Change in Tactics.* All the forces of Army Group Center were deployed along the front without any units being held in reserve. Any major reverse could have disastrous consequences, and launching an offensive under such circumstances would be a desperate gamble. Far more promising would be a temporary switch to elastic defensive tactics allowing even for major withdrawals, if necessary. By adopting such tactics, the front line could be held with relatively small forces. Meanwhile, such strong reserves of manpower and materiel would gradually be built up that a decisive offensive could be launched as soon as there was a favorable opportunity.

By contrast, the proponents of the offensive advanced the following arguments:

1. *Russian Exhaustion.* The Russians had apparently exhausted their strength. The Soviet Government was scraping together every man and machine and throwing them into the defense of Moscow. The Red Army had uncovered wide sectors of the front and, having run short of trained combat troops, was using hastily improvised units on a large scale.

2. *The Knock-Out Blow.* There seemed a good chance that an all-out effort before the winter would knock the Soviets out of the war. On the other hand, if the attack was postponed until spring, the Russians would be given time to reorganize their forces.

3. *The Missed Chance.* This last offensive would have to be risked, if only because one could not possibly give up within sight of the goal.

In any event the German mistake at the Marne in 1914, when victory was conceded although the battle was far from lost, was not to be repeated.

4. *The Closeness of the Objective.* Moscow was but 40 miles away. Thus, even though there were only a few weeks of relatively favorable weather ahead, the objective was so close that it seemed within reach. Under these circumstances there was no doubt that the troops would once again make every effort to take Moscow.

5. *Political Significance.* The political effect would be resounding if the German Army succeeded in capturing Moscow despite all obstacles.

After carefully weighing the pros and cons, the Army High Command decided that the offensive had to be risked. However justified this decision may have been on the basis of the estimate of the situation and available intelligence, it did not take into account the demands which the offensive would make upon the German troops and the shortage of manpower and equipment that beset Army Group Center. To make matters worse, more and more fresh and well-trained Russian divisions were arriving at the front from Siberia, apparently unobserved by German air or ground reconnaissance.

Before the decision to launch the offensive was made, Gen. Friedrich Fromm, Commander, Replacement Army, suggested to Brauchitsch that a peace offer be extended to the Soviets. Since the plan "to crush the Soviet Union in a lightning campaign" had not materialized, he urged that the opportunity of extricating Germany from the risk of a two-front war be exploited—now that the fortunes of the Wehrmacht looked most promising and the threat of losing Moscow loomed large before the Soviet Government. Whether such a peace proposal would have had any chance of success will have to remain a point of conjecture. There is little doubt, however, that Hitler would have sharply rejected such a recommendation.

Last-Minute Planning and Operations to 13 November 1941

The offensive was to start with another attempt at double envelopment as soon as the weather and the supply situation permitted. The immediate objectives were to be the Moskva River and the Volga Canal, and the continuation of the operation would depend upon the prevailing situation. Second Panzer Army was to drive northward from Tula, enveloping Moscow from the southwest. The enemy situation in front of Guderian's armor was obscure, but it seemed probable that the Germans would eventually be faced by strong Russian forces. Guderian's right flank grew longer and longer so that more and more forces had to be diverted from the main thrust to cover the flank. The frontal attack from the west was to be delivered by Fourth Panzer Group as well as by Fourth and Ninth Armies, and the enveloping thrust from the northwest by Third Panzer Group. With its left anchored on the Volga River, the latter was to drive on Moscow from the north. Fierce resistance, mostly by improvised units, could be expected.

On 13 November General Halder presided over a meeting of the chiefs of the army group and army staffs which was held at Orsha. The discussions covered intelligence information, organization matters, and tactical and logistical problems on the theater and army group level. A review of current operations showed that the situation had meanwhile developed as follows:

Army Group South. In the Crimea, the Kerch Peninsula had been almost cleared of Soviet forces. First Panzer Army was slowly closing in on Rostov. Seventeenth Army had consolidated its front along the Donets, while Sixth Army, despite repeated orders to do so, was unable to resume its advance. This delay was particularly inopportune because Russian intentions at the army group boundary were obscure; in this area the Soviets appeared to be withdrawing forces to bolster the defense of Moscow.

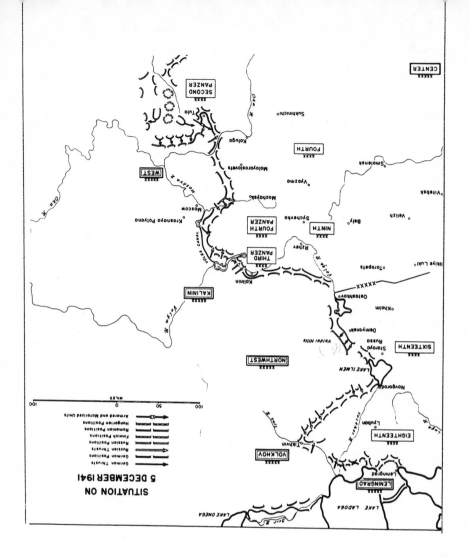

SITUATION ON
5 DECEMBER 1941

German Thrusts
German Positions
Russian Thrusts
Russian Positions
Finnish Positions
Romanian Positions
Hungarian Positions
Armored and Motorized Units

MILES
100   50   0   100

LENINGRAD
VOLKHOV
EIGHTEENTH
SIXTEENTH
NORTHWEST
CENTER
WEST
KALININ
FOURTH PANZER
THIRD PANZER
NINTH
FOURTH
SECOND PANZER

LAKE ONEGA
LAKE LADOGA
Lake Ilmen
Novgorod
Lyuban
Tikhvin
Staraya Russa
Demyansk
Valdai Hills
Ostashkov
Okholm
Toropets
Velikiye Luki
Rzhev
Sychevka
Bely
Velizh
Vitebsk
Smolensk
Sukhinichi
Kalinin
Moscow
Krasnaya Polyana
Klin
Mozhaysk
Vyazma
Maloyaroslavets
Kaluga
Tula
Svir R.
Volkhov R.
Lovat R.
Volga R.
Oka R.
Dnepr R.
Moskva R.
Oka R.
Volga Canal

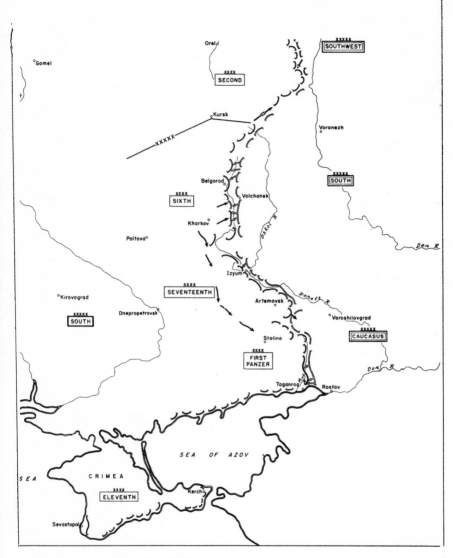

Map 12. SITUATION, 5 December 1941

Army Group Center: Few changes had occurred on the Second Army front, which extended over a wide area between Kursk and Orel. Here, too, the Russian intentions were unclear. Major troop movements in the direction of the Soviet capital were apparently under way. Seven concentric rings of antiaircraft defenses, established two to three miles from one another, surrounded Moscow and made the city almost invulnerable from the air. For the first time since the early days of the invasion the Soviet Air Force intervened actively.

Army Group North: Tikhvin was captured on 11 November after a hard struggle; at the same time other forces drove a wedge across the Volkhov River toward Lake Ladoga. The Finns were expected to exploit the German thrust on Tikhvin by launching an offensive during which the Karelian Army was to link up with Army Group North. But this hope was not fulfilled because political considerations modified the Finnish military plans. One German division, reinforced by Finnish troops, attempted to advance on Tikhvin from the lower course of the Svir River, but was stopped by numerically superior Russian forces.

The Course of the Offensive (14 November–5 December 1941)

The three weeks from 14 November to 5 December 1941 marked the turning point in the Russian campaign. The German offensive ground to a halt along the entire front. At the same time the Russians began to seize the initiative.

The first warning came in the south, where Kleist's First Panzer Army attempted to seize Rostov by a *coup de main* and succeeded in entering that city from the east on 20 November. [See *map 12.*] The German propaganda agencies celebrated this success in such enthusiastic terms that Kleist felt obliged to hold Rostov despite mounting Russian pressure. His position, however, became so precarious that Rundstedt requested the authorization for Kleist's evacuation of Rostov. When Hitler refused, Rundstedt asked to be relieved of his command. His successor, Field Marshal Walter von Reichenau, was forced to abandon Rostov, when the Soviet forces began to assault the city from three sides on 28 November. (Halder noted in his diary

that the people at the Fuehrer's headquarters had no idea of the true condition of the German troops, their plans being conceived in a vacuum.) On 1 December Hitler finally agreed to a withdrawal to the Mius, where the German troops were able to dig in. They had to summon all their strength to stop the Russian counterattack and stabilize the front. The other sectors of Army Group South remained quiet during this period, but it became obvious that the Russians were ready to stop any German advance toward the Caucasus or Stalingrad with every means in their power, and that they had concentrated strong forces for this purpose.

In the Army Group North area no gains could be made beyond Tikhvin or in the direction of Lake Ladoga. Here, too, the Russians were pouring in reinforcements for a series of counterattacks which started in early December. Along the front south of Lake Ilmen the Soviet forces had been counterattacking intermittently since the end of November. Similar attacks were also launched by the Leningrad garrison in an attempt to relieve the pressure on the Moscow front.

In the all-important zone of Army Group Center, Third Panzer Group and Ninth Army had jumped off on 15 November, with Second Panzer Army following shortly afterward. While the Russians offered stubborn resistance in front of Ninth Army, they seemed to give way opposite Guderian's forces in the south. This also appeared to be the case in front of Second Army whose eastward drive began to gain momentum, thereby removing any immediate threat to the exposed right flank of the army group. The Russians apparently lacked the strength to exploit their opportunity for a counterthrust. On the central portion of the army group front, however, the Russians began to launch heavy attacks as early as 16 November, thus preventing Fourth Army from joining the offensive.

Despite these inauspicious developments the Army High Command and Bock, feeling confident that the greater stamina of the Germans would carry the day, agreed that the offensive had to be continued. By the end of November the two enveloping forces had scored further successes, even though they advanced but slowly against stiff opposition. The Fourth Army, however, was engaged in a defensive see-saw battle which greatly sapped its strength. Newly organized and freshly equipped Russian forces, such as an armored brigade almost exclusively equipped with British tanks, appeared unexpectedly all along the army group front. Not until 1 December could the divisions forming the center of Fourth Army switch to the offensive, and then they scored only local gains. From 1 to 5 December the entire offensive gradually bogged down. Winter came suddenly with temperatures down to −40° F. The German troops were in a state of almost complete exhaustion. Orders to halt the offensive had to be issued—first to Fourth Army, then to the spearhead units. The Fourth Panzer Group came to within 25 miles of Moscow when it was stopped at Krasnaya Polyana. Frostbite casualties were more numerous than those resulting from enemy action. To continue was beyond human endurance. Thus the last German all-out effort to force a decision in 1941 ended in failure.

The Personnel Situation (End of November 1941)

At the end of November the German ground forces in the Russian theater were short 340,000 replacements. With infantry companies at half strength, the average number of men available for combat duty varied from 50 to 60 per company. Day-to-day losses were about equal to the number of convalescents returning to duty. The shortage of replacements could not be compensated for by transfers from the Zone of Interior, where only 33,000 trained replacements were available. The only possible solution was to disband a number of units and use their personnel as replacements. Hitler, however, refused any such suggestion.

The official casualty reports as of 26 November 1941 read as follows:

10. GERMAN CASUALTIES

	German Losses (From German Sources)	Russian Losses (From Russian Sources)
Killed in Action	156,475	490,000
Wounded in Action	555,885	1,112,000
Missing in Action	30,952	**520,000
Totals	*743,112	2,122,000

*23.3 per cent of the average strength (3.2 million men) employed in the Russian theater from 22 June to 26 November 1941.

**Against 3,000,000 prisoners of war claimed by the Germans as of 1 December 1941.

Critique

The German objectives for the Russian campaign in 1941 had not been attained. The Soviet military forces had not been destroyed and the Communist government had not collapsed. The danger of another two-front war loomed larger than ever. Instead of eliminating this threat, the invasion of Russia had actually brought it about.

Some of the basic mistakes that caused the German failure seemed to be the following:

a. *Political Mistakes.* Hitler had underestimated the internal political stability of the Communist regime. The average citizen's innate readiness to defend Mother Russia against any invader was stronger than his assumed aversion to the Communist dictatorship. Moreover, German failure to formulate and apply a satisfactory policy in the occupied territories, particularly in the Ukraine and the Baltic States, had intensified the spirit of resistance.

b. *Underestimation of Russian Strength.* The Soviet Union's economic foundations were more solid than Hitler had anticipated. The Germans were surprised by the Russians' ability to transfer and decentralize war plants. As to the Soviet armed forces, their unwavering determination, their unwillingness to admit defeat, and their capability to improvise astounded the Germans. Time and again these qualities compensated for the ineptitude of the Russian intermediate command.

c. *Faulty Strategy.* The change in German strategy decided upon in August 1941, when the main effort was shifted from Army Group Center to Army Group South and—to some extent—to Army Group North, was a crucial mistake. By making this decision the Germans may have lost their opportunity of knocking the Russians out of the war by a direct thrust on Moscow. There is, however, no way of proving the validity of this hypothesis, especially since a number of other, equally fundamental mistakes have to be considered in this connection.

d. *Inadequate Mobility.* The German Army did not have sufficient motor vehicles, planes, and POL reserves for operations in so vast a theater as European Russia. Instead of being able to take full advantage of their maneuverability, the panzer divisions were forced to halt time and again to permit the infantry to close up. Moreover, the inadequacy of the roads and the shortage of suitable air fields made the logistical support almost completely dependent on the damaged railroads, the operation of which was so difficult in Russia.

e. Wrong Space Calculations. During the planning stage the vastness of the Russian theater had not been fully taken into consideration. When the German Army failed to destroy the Russian armed forces in the initial onslaught, the space factor gave rise to problems which the Germans with their limited resources were not able to master.

f. Bad Timing. The time element became an increasingly important factor once the operation got under way. The initial delay in launching the offensive, the month lost in vacillating over the continuation of the offensive, and finally the diversion of forces to the south and north cost the Germans dearly.

g. The "Russian" Weather. The Germans did not make proper use of the information on Russian weather conditions that was available to them. The effect of the weather on the conduct of military operations in Russia was no secret, and the German military leaders should not have been surprised by muddy terrain in the autumn or low temperatures in the winter. It seems almost inconceivable that the German troops in Russia were caught unprepared by the sudden outbreak of winter. The explanation is that Hitler and his military advisers were convinced that the campaign would end before the onset of bad weather; winter clothing had been ordered for only those 60 divisions that were to remain in Russia and form the military occupation force after Germany's victory.

h. Erroneous Air Warfare Concepts. The faulty concept of a short war was also the reason why the Luftwaffe's mission was mainly to lend tactical ground support. Strategic bombing was to be envisaged only after the war of movement had been brought to its conclusion, i. e. after the campaign in European Russia had been won. Hitler and his military advisers deemed it unnecessary to smash the Soviet

armament potential or even interfere with production schedules. Nor was it considered important to disrupt rail communications to the Urals and Central Asia, a course of action that might have prevented the subsequent evacuation of Soviet war industries and the moving up of reinforcements.

The fact that the Luftwaffe had no specific strategic air force probably contributed to these crucial decisions. Whatever strategic air units the Germans had left after the Battle of Britain were eventually dissipated in tactical fighting, probably because both strategic and tactical units operated under the same tactical headquarters.

i. Lack of Self-Restraint. As stated in the various plans prepared for the invasion of Russia, German strategy was based on the assumption that the bulk of the Red Army would be destroyed in western Russia. The decisive initial blows were to be delivered west of the Dnepr–Dvina line. The pursuit to the Volga, which was to be launched during the following phases, was to be contingent upon the successful accomplishment of the initial maneuvers.

In their attempt to implement those plans, the Germans realized by the end of July that they had been unable to destroy the bulk of the Red Army in western Russia. They had captured a great number of prisoners and booty, but the Soviets had been able to withdraw sufficient forces to continue active resistance. Instead of revising their plans, the Germans plunged into the depth of the Russian theater as if the prerequisites for the initial phase had been entirely fulfilled. It was therefore not really surprising that in December 1941 the Red Army succeeded in stopping the Germans short of their principal objectives—Moscow and Leningrad.

PART THREE

THE YEAR OF INDECISION

VII

THE RUSSIAN COUNTEROFFENSIVE (DEC. 1941 - FEB. 1942)

The First German Reverses

The true situation of the German troops in front of Moscow was not understood at Hitler's headquarters, where victories had been the order of the day for more than two years of war. It took a great number of oral and written reports to bring home the dimensions of the German reverses along the entire Russian front.

One of the first sober notes was struck in the intelligence summary of 1 December 1941 originating from the Eastern Intelligence Division of the Army High Command. The mobilization of so many divisions by the Soviet Government was considered less surprising than the tremendous quantity of material encountered—especially tanks and guns—which exceeded anything hitherto known. Contrary to previous estimates it was now believed that Russian war production capacity had been expanded so much that the output of materiel would remain sizeable even after the loss of many important areas.

In November 1941, the report continued, the Soviets had launched their first coordinated offensive, involving as many as 20 divisions in the successful recapture of Rostov. Up to that time Soviet tactics had consisted of simply contesting every inch of ground.

Among the unexpected qualities demonstrated by the Red Army leaders during the first months of fighting was their organizing ability in the spheres of supply, activation and rehabilitation of units, and rapid construction of rear area defense lines with mass employment of civilian labor. The Russians had also shown great skill in using rail communications for troop transfers, efficiently repairing tracks, and evacuating the bulk of the rolling stock without too greatly impairing the capacity of the remaining net. The infantry excelled in defensive fighting. The Russian soldier was naturally gifted in using favorable terrain features, skillfully digging in and constructing fortifications, and camouflaging himself. His willingness to hold out to the bitter end seemed to be a natural trait. This estimate differed considerably from the somewhat disdainful opinion of the Russian soldier held before the start of the campaign.

On 6 December Halder reported to Hitler that the troops committed in Russia had to be rehabilitated. Hitler agreed on principle, but immediately changed the subject, pointing out that the objective in the south remained the Donets bend, which was a stepping stone toward Maikop and the oil fields. In the north a linkup with the Finns would have to be achieved during the winter. Manpower requirements would have to be met by combing out the Zone of Interior and all German-occupied territories. No divisions stationed in France were to be disbanded for the time being.

Hitler's Directive No. 39 (8 December 1941)

On 8 December Hitler issued a directive to the three services in which he acknowledged that the surprisingly early start of severe winter weather and the supply difficulties caused thereby called for immediate cessation of all major offensive operations and a switch to the defensive. The conduct of the defense would depend on the strategic and military-economic value of each specific area that would come under Russian attack. Another important consideration was the availability of rest and rehabilitation facilities, the use of which would enable the Germans to resume major offensive operations in 1942.

The specific points of this directive made it even more obvious that Hitler did not consider making any major withdrawal. They read essentially as follows:

a. Army.

1. Most of the Army units in Russia were to switch to the defensive to save manpower. Once the front was consolidated, the armored and motorized infantry divisions would be withdrawn for rehabilitation.

2. Prior to any withdrawal not caused by enemy pressure a rear position would have to be prepared, offering better billeting and defense facilities than the hitherto occupied position. Lateral lines of communications would have to be held open for troop transfers.

3. Army Group South was to seize Sevastopol as soon as possible so that Eleventh Army would become available for another, not yet formulated mission. An advance leading to the seizure of the lower Don-Donets line would facilitate the spring offensive into the Caucasus.

4. Army Group North was to shorten its lines north of Lake Ilmen so that, after the arrival of reinforcements, the situation south of Lake Ladoga could be resolved. This maneuver alone could assure the isolation of Leningrad and permit the establishment of contact with the Finns in Karelia.

b. Luftwaffe.

The Air Force was to disrupt the rehabilitation of the Soviet armed forces by bombing such centers as Leningrad, Moscow, Gorki, Stalingrad, etc. The disruption of the Soviet lines of communications was particularly important. In addition, routine fighter protection and air reconnaissance missions were to be flown by the Air Force.

c. Navy.

Naval vessels were to secure supply and commercial shipping in the Gulf of Finland. The number of supply vessels to be constructed in Germany as well as in allied and occupied countries would have to be increased.

d. Personnel.

Sufficient replacements would have to be provided in 1942 to take care of any emergency. All armed forces agencies would have to be combed for young men who might in certain cases be replaced by older soldiers, presently serving at the front. Combat-ready divisions stationed in western Europe were to be exchanged against particularly worn-out divisions from the Russian theater. Contrary to previous orders, a temporary weakening of the forces in France would have to be taken into account. The Atlantic coast of western Europe, however, would have to be safeguarded in any event.

Young men in essential jobs who had been deferred from the draft were to be gradually replaced by prisoners of war and Russian civilians.

In the last paragraph of the directive the three services were requested to inform the Fuehrer of the measures taken toward its implementation.

The attack on Pearl Harbor, which had taken place the day before Directive No. 39 was issued, was not reflected in its contents. The Japanese move apparently took the Germans by surprise; they had not prepared any joint plans or military agreements. In fact, they had no clear concept of what Japan's entry into war really meant. Characteristic of this German unpreparedness was Jodl's request for a staff study on the question of whether the United States would give priority to the European or Far Eastern theater which was made only after Hitler had declared war on 11 December 1941.

At that time most German military men felt that the Axis had gained more strength than its opponents. Few, if any, Germans were able to visualize the extraordinary proportions the military conflict had suddenly assumed or the preponderance that the United States would eventually achieve. It was also believed that Japan's entry would greatly relieve the pressure borne by the Germans in different theaters of war, particularly in Russia. Even if Japan remained neutral, strong Soviet forces would be tied down in the Far

East. Siberian troops then pouring in opposite Army Group Center, would no longer be moved to Europe. On the contrary, Soviet reinforcements from central Russia would probably be diverted from Europe to the Far East.

In addition, the Germans began to make careful attempts to influence the Japanese policy toward the Soviet Union. Although the divergence of Germany's and Japan's military objectives soon became obvious, the Germans continued to exert diplomatic pressure on the Japanese. But even the fact that the Soviets had withdrawn practically all their forces from the Far East failed to induce the Japanese to abandon their neutrality. The only Japanese military effort that eventually was to have an indirect influence on German operations in the Russian theater was the promised intervention of Japanese submarines against the Allied supply lines leading through the Persian Gulf.

The Army High Command Order of 8 December 1941

The Operations Division of the Army High Command implemented Directive No. 39 on the day it was issued by disseminating an order pertaining to the mission of the German troops in Russia during the winter of 1941–42. Though more subdued in tone than preceding orders, these instructions must have struck the field commanders in front of Moscow as being singularly unrealistic. The introductory paragraph stated that with increasing cold and snow the operations of 1941 had generally come to an end; a few maneuvers that had not yet been concluded would be terminated as soon as possible. After the great victories of September and October the troops had reached the objectives designated at the beginning of the campaign against an opponent who had tremendous superiority in numbers and equipment. Moreover, the Russians had been deprived of vital economic resources and armament production centers. On the whole, German troops had destroyed the bulk of the Red Army before it could withdraw, and losses in men and materiel had decisively weakened the Soviet capacity to resist. The mission of completely eliminating Russian military power still remained to be accomplished after the winter.

Intelligence Estimate

The combat efficiency of the Soviet units was low, and they were insufficiently equipped with heavy weapons and guns. (This statement was in flagrant contradiction with the intelligence summary of the Eastern Intelligence Branch.) The Soviet tactical air force still had approximately 900 serviceable planes; in view of the production facilities remaining in Soviet hands, a steady increase in the number of planes was to be expected.

The ski training given to all Russian troops would enable the latter to carry out attacks during the winter months. The partisans and sabotage units could be expected to resume their activities with great vigor. The total strength of the Red Army was estimated as follows:

II. RED ARMY STRENGTH ON 1 December 1941

	Divisions		Armored Brigades
	Rifle	Cavalry	
Totals*	263	41½	51
Facing the Germans	b 200	35	40
In the Caucasus	17	2	3
In Finland	23	---	1
In Asia	5	3½	2
In the Far East	18	1	5

* Additional units, including the Polish Legion, were being activated in the Urals, Siberia, etc.

b Including rifle, naval, and NKVD brigades.

Plans

The Army High Command intended to safeguard German territorial gains achieved during the 1941 campaign along the most favorable defensive lines, behind which the ground forces were to be reinforced, rehabilitated, and reorganized. In establishing such lines the following factors were to be considered:

1. Retention of the industrial and communications facilities which the Russians had lost since the beginning of the campaign;

2. Safeguarding of supply and communications lines, including the lateral ones needed for shifting units behind the front;

3. Conservation of strength; and

4. Bringing of German units up to strength and giving them some rest.

The Mission of the Army Groups

The army group headquarters were to direct their subordinate units in accordance with the following instructions:

1. Army Group South was to prevent Russian attempts to break through between the Sea of Azov and the Donets. Kharkov was to be held and the rail line Belgorod-Kursk secured with the assistance of Army Group Center. Special attention would have to be devoted to safeguarding the Crimea, even after Sevastopol had been captured. If possible, Army Group South was to prepare for the seizure of the Maikop oil fields by the capture of Rostov and the Donets basin northeast of that city.

2. Army Group Center was to bring the Moscow offensive to its conclusion and then establish a defensive front against enemy counterattacks in the direction of the capital. Mobile divisions were to be rehabilitated behind the southern army group wing; they would have to be ready to intervene in the event of a Soviet thrust from the Voronezh area.

3. Army Group North was to continue its current operation south of Lake Ladoga, establish contact with the Finns, and thus cut off Leningrad from all sides. This objective had to be attained to avoid any waste of manpower and materiel in establishing a defensive front.

Conduct of Operations

It was realized that German strength had dropped to a new low. To keep the initiative and to deceive the Russians as to the true German intentions, the conduct of operations would have to remain as mobile as possible. The forces employed directly up front would have to be spread thinly so that troops could be rotated and reserves formed. Mobile reserve forces would have to be kept on the alert to intervene whenever necessary.

Desirable as a development in depth would be, it could not be effected because of the insufficiency of forces. The front line defenses would therefore have to be improved, strong points and obstacles constructed, etc. Rear area installations and billets would have to be prepared for all-around defense against enemy raids. Because of the weakness of the rear area security units, divisions withdrawn from the line for rehabilitation would have to form emergency combat groups to secure lines of communications, important terrain features, and boundary areas near the front. Effective air reconnaissance would be desirable to permit early recognition of enemy attack preparations and timely counteraction.

Organization

Replacements. Current losses would be compensated for by convalescents returned to duty. No decision had so far been made regarding the number of units that would have to be deactivated to obtain essential replacements for the remaining divisions. The army group headquarters would have to channel replacements to those divisions whose rehabilitation would produce the best results.

Equipment. Drastic measures would have to be imposed to remedy the shortage of motor vehicles and POL. Some of the infantry divisions and GHQ troops would have to be stripped of their motor vehicles, and all motorized supply units would have to be put under centralized control. Since future operations would largely depend upon the combat readiness of the armored divisions, the latter would have to be withdrawn from the front as soon as possible. Because of difficulties in transportation, their rehabilitation would have to take place in the theater of operations. The army group headquarters would have to find suitable locations for billeting, maintenance, and repair installations, etc.

The subsequent paragraphs of the order dealt with training and morale as well as supply for current operations during the winter, stressing particularly the importance of living off the land. Tactical air support was to be severely curtailed during the winter months. According to the instruction pertaining to signal communications, wire lines were to be improved, whereas radio traffic was to be reduced to a minimum. Intercept units were to keep partisan and enemy agent radio traffic under observation.

A survey of the transportation capacity indicated that no major troop movements could be executed, the rail lines being capable of supporting only very minor unit transfers involving the shipment of materiel and immobilized vehicles exclusively. Leave trains could be dispatched only at the expense of supply shipments.

This order did not take into account that the Russians would attack relentlessly at different points all along the front, defying cold and snow. No major German unit could be pulled out for rehabilitation during the winter months. And with the Russians holding the initiative, most of the German withdrawals took place under such heavy pressure that the field commanders had little latitude in selecting suitable defense lines.

The Red Army Seizes the Initiative

Beginning with the recapture of Rostov in November 1941 the Russians gradually seized the initiative, first opposite Army Group Center, then along the entire front. The moment was well chosen: the critical situation of the German forces was only too obvious. Standing deep in the heartland of Russia without sizeable reserves, the German Army was deployed in linear defense along an overextended front. Defective lines of communications to the rear caused continuous disruption in the flow of supplies. Lacking suitable winter clothing, the German troops were exhausted and disheartened. To make matters worse, the most severe winter imaginable suddenly set in with temperatures as low as -50° F. The fate that overtook Napoleon's army in 1812 obsessed the German leaders whose troops stood near the gates of Moscow.

By contrast, the Russians held all the trumps. Their lines of communications had grown progressively shorter, and they had remained in possession of Moscow, their supply and transportation center. They were accustomed to the Russian winter weather and were prepared for it. They had a vast reservoir of manpower which—though poorly

trained—could be thrown into battle. Russian morale was bolstered by the almost miraculous turning of the tide that had taken place at the time of greatest stress and by the conviction that the Germans would meet the same fate which through the centuries had been the lot of those who dared to invade the vast reaches of European Russia.

The Red Army initially concentrated on pushing back the Germans before Moscow by a series of local attacks launched at all suitable points. Since this process was continuous, it became more and more likely that the cumulative effect of Russian local penetrations would assume strategic proportions. By the same token the wider scope of the Russian operations seemed to indicate that Army Group Center was in danger of being crushed in a huge pincers whose northern one via would swing via Ostashkov toward Vitebsk, and the southern one via Orel and Bryansk toward Smolensk. If this plan succeeded, the Russians would be free to strike at the rear of the other army groups. The German armies in Russia were thus faced by a very dangerous situation.

To meet this threat, two courses appeared to be open:

1. To execute a major withdrawal and to try and consolidate the crumbling Army Group Center front. Such a maneuver would shorten and strengthen the front and obviate the danger of a double envelopment; or

2. To hold in place, fight for every inch of ground, disregard local enemy penetrations, and hope to master the situation by sheer staying power.

Hitler decided to hold fast. For reasons of prestige alone he considered that any major withdrawal would be out of the question. He also feared that mobile warfare under winter conditions would have disastrous consequences because the troops had little mobility, their winter equipment was deficient, and no defensive positions existed in the rear.

The Fuehrer therefore ordered Army Group South to stay in place and assemble reserves behind the contiguous wings of Seventeenth and Sixth Armies. Army Group Center was to move up all its reserves to close the gaps north of Livny and west of Tula. The Fourth Army was not to retreat one inch. If they had no other choice, Third and Fourth Panzer Armies could gradually withdraw to a shorter line along the Rusa River–Volokolamsk–Staritsa, and Ninth Army would link up with the Third Panzer Army.

Army Group North was permitted to withdraw its armored units behind the Volkhov, but any other withdrawal movements could be executed only in the face of acute danger to the entire front. A definite line along which this army group was to hold would be determined in due course. Reinforcements totaling 13½ divisions were to be transferred from western Europe and Germany. Every effort was to be made to improve the transportation system of occupied Russia.

This order was disseminated by the Armed Forces Operations Staff on 15 December. During the following weeks the Russians kept the Germans off balance and held the initiative. Having committed their fresh troops for the relief of Moscow, they found it more expedient to push back the Germans through local attacks at many different points instead of concentrating their forces on all-out efforts directed at breaking the siege of Leningrad, recapturing Smolensk, or liberating the Donets Basin.

The Russian successes west of Moscow had been achieved against German local air superiority over the Army Group Center area as shown by the following comparison of strength made on 12 December:

12. AIRCRAFT STRENGTH COMPARISON ON 12 December 1941

Army Groups	Number of Airplanes	
	German	Russian
Totals	1,050	1,060
South	310	600
Center	490	210
North	250	250

Analysis of radio intercepts had given the Germans a clear picture of the Russian order of battle. The entire theater was divided into eight "fronts," which corresponded approximately to German army group headquarters. Reading from south to north these were the *Caucasus, South, Southwest, West, Kalinin, Northwest, Volkhov,* and *Leningrad Fronts.* A number of armies were subordinate to each front. Corps-type headquarters were used exclusively to command mechanized units. Armored divisions were equivalent to German brigades, and in German reports and estimates they were therefore designated armored brigades for statistical purposes.

Developments to 25 December 1941

By 25 December the Russians had eliminated the threat to Moscow. Their counterattacks had pushed Army Group Center to the line from which it had launched its offensive on 15 November. The continuity of the German front was threatened when the Russians opened a gap between Second Panzer Army and Fourth Army to the north and south of Kaluga. A critical situation began to develop in this area, because the Germans, whose movements were restricted to major roads, were unable to seal off the Russian penetration.

The Army Group South area remained quiet. Local Russian attacks seemed to be of a probing nature. In mid-December Eleventh Army began its assault on Sevastopol.

In the Army Group North area the Russians were able to avert the threat posed by the German advance toward Lake Ladoga and to press the Germans back to the Volkhov. This was a bitter disappointment to the Finns who had been induced to believe in a swift victory and now saw themselves faced with a long war.

In the Finnish theater proper, no decisive result had been attained anywhere. Murmansk had not been taken and the Murmansk railroad had not been cut. The attempt at linking up with Army Group North had not been successful. Instead, the bulk of the Finnish forces were tied down in wasteful position warfare.

In his Directive No. 39 and the subsequent order of 15 December Hitler had allowed the army commanders a certain freedom of action within the framework of their overall mission of holding fast. A few local withdrawals executed in mid-December led to such losses of heavy weapons and equipment that Hitler decided to change his methods. On 18 December he ordered that no further large-scale withdrawal movements would be tolerated because of recent prohibitive losses. If the tide was to be stemmed, every inch of ground would have to be contested. The Fuehrer held the field commanders personally responsible for leading their troops in such a manner that they would offer fanatic resistance and hold their positions, even if Soviet forces should break through and attack from all sides. Only thus could sufficient time be gained to move up the reinforcements transferred from the West. After the reserves had arrived and taken up positions in the rear, the troops defending exposed salients might consider withdrawing to shorter lines.

Army Group South was to hold its positions and shift forces to Sixth Army so that they would be available south of Kursk for commitment near the boundary of Second Army.

Army Group Center was to receive the maximum number of reinforcements by all available means of transportation, including airlift. The most urgent need was for infantry replacements to reinforce some of the very weak divisions.

As an additional measure to strengthen Army Group Center, the Fuehrer had approved the transfer of five divisions which were scheduled to **arrive** at Vitebsk in January 1942. On 18 December the first airlifted replacements were flown in from East Prussia via **Orsha** to **Staraya Russa**. These replacements were transferred so hastily that they apparently **arrived without weapons or winter** clothing. When it turned out that no more German rifles were available and all captured ones had been issued, Hitler authorized an increase in rifle production. There were other shortages; the officer personnel, for instance, had been so decimated that all reserves were exhausted, with no replacements scheduled to become available before

April 1942. The total casualties suffered by the German Army in Russia from 22 June to 31 December 1941 were 830,903, including 26,755 officers.

On 19 December Field Marshal von Brauchitsch resigned for reasons of health. Since 7 December his position had become more and more untenable until he was nothing more than a messenger. His departure was followed by that of Field Marshal von Bock; on 20 December Field Marshal von Kluge replaced the latter as commander in chief of Army Group Center. The two other army group commanders were also replaced within the next month. [See *chart 3.*] When Guderian withdrew his Second Panzer Army to the Oka-Shusa line without informing army group headquarters, Kluge requested Guderian's dismissal which Hitler approved immediately as of 25 December. Two weeks later Generaloberst (Gen.) Erich Hoepner, the commander of Fourth Panzer Army, was dismissed under ignominious circumstances.

In summary, during the first three weeks of the counteroffensive the Russians had achieved important tactical victories. The divisions of Army Group Center had suffered very heavy casualties, particularly from frostbite, and their effective strength was declining steadily. The supply situation was critical. At the front, German apprehension was general because Russian aggressiveness showed no signs of diminishing. In the Zone of Interior signs of discouragement among the people were mostly to be attributed to the discrepancy between the official propaganda releases and the letters that soldiers sent from the front. Some of the military leaders felt that it would have been preferable to tell the truth. A dramatic Nazi appeal to the public, launched a few days before Christmas in which the people were urged to donate furs and winter clothing for the soldiers at the Russian front, contributed to the general lassitude.

The German Crisis in Mid-January 1942

The three weeks following Christmas of 1941 led to a major German crisis, the first one in World War II.

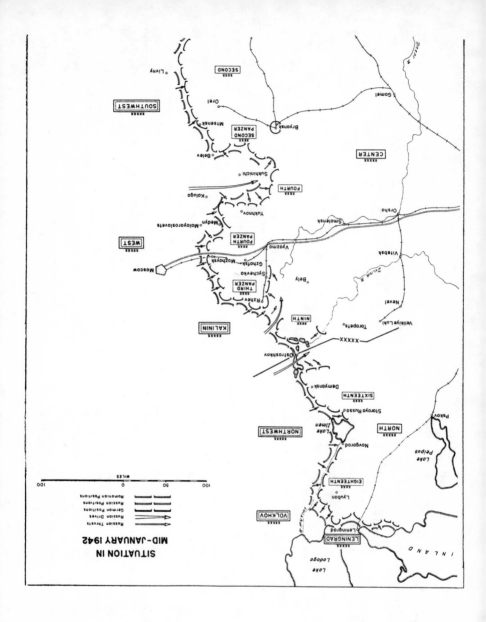

SITUATION IN
MID-JANUARY 1942

MILES
100   50   0   100

Russian Thrusts
Russian Drives
German Positions
Russian Positions
Romanian Positions

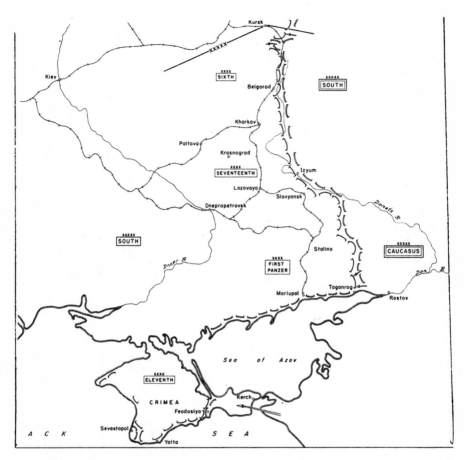

Map 13. SITUATION, Mid-January 1942

EASTERN FRONT GERMAN STRENGTH

FIELD ARMIES: 11, including 4 Panzer Armies

CORPS: 46, including 11 Motorized Corps, 2 Allied Corps, and 4
Rear Area Commands

DIVISIONS: 156, including 42 Panzer or Motorized Divisions, and 8
Mountain or Light Divisions

(see page 83 for a specific unit listing)

81

into battle, improvised units were brought from Germany by air or priority rail transportation. Winter clothing began to arrive. All these measures only served to aggravate the transportation problem. In every respect the crisis approached its climax. Whether this situation could be overcome preoccupied every headquarters, and the tension was extreme. In the Zone of Interior special military police measures were enforced against deserters and men who were absent without leave.

Hitler discussed every aspect of the military situation in endless conferences and staff meetings, but refused to make a decision. Halder observed in his diary on 14 January that this type of leadership would result in the destruction of the Army.

As usual, the critical situation at the front found its expression in some changes in the command positions. On 16 January Leeb requested to be relieved from the command of Army Group North and was replaced by Generaloberst (Gen.) Georg von Kuechler. On the following day Field Marshal von Reichenau, the recently appointed commander of Army Group South, had a stroke and was replaced by Field Marshal Fedor von Bock whose retirement had lasted less than one month. General Strauss, who had commanded Ninth Army since the beginning of the campaign, was unable to continue in his duties and had to be relieved by General der Panzer (Lt. Gen.) Walter Model. By making this appointment Hitler disregarded all seniority rules and introduced new criteria into the personnel policy of the Army. [See *Appendix A.*]

On 15 January Hitler issued his first order of a large-scale withdrawal in World War II. He expected that his men would execute the movement "in a dignified manner" and inflict maximum damage on the Russians. He continued by stating that since the gaps north of Medyn and west of Rzhev could not be closed, he authorized the commander of Army Group Center to withdraw to a line extending from east of Yukhnov-east of Gzhatsk-northeast of Rzhev. The road connecting these localities would have to remain in German hands. The Russian advance was to be definitely stopped along this line. The order then defined the methods to be used in closing the two gaps.

In the Army Group Center area the gap between Second Panzer Army and Fourth Army had been widened by a Russian breakthrough in depth, which extended far beyond Sukhinichi. [See *map 13.*] Farther to the north, the front was ripped open northwest of Maloyaroslavets. The Russians achieved a second major breakthrough at the boundary between Army Groups Center and North, where they drove via Ostashkov toward Toropets. These two thrusts seemed to indicate that the Russians intended to attempt a double envelopment of Army Group Center with the objective of squeezing the army group forces into the Vyazma area. At the same time the Rzhev–Sychevka railroad—the only supply line of the Third Panzer and Ninth Armies—was cut off by partisans.

Russian attacks directly south of Lake Ilmen indicated that the Soviets also intended to open a wide gap in the Army Group North area. By attacking along the Volkhov the Russians attempted to crack the Army Group North front at the same time as they pursued their offensive against Army Group Center. The Russians were also building a railroad on the ice of Lake Ladoga. Luftwaffe reports indicated that the Ladoga ice road and railroad had better flak protection than London or any other British city.

The Army Group South area was the only one in which the Russian intentions were not yet apparent. Local counterattacks, however, continued without letup. In the Crimea the Russians recaptured the Kerch Peninsula, forcing the Germans to abandon the siege of Sevastopol.

The overall situation had definitely taken a turn for the worse. The unpreparedness of the German Army was manifest. During the evacuation of positions, for instance, many wounded froze to death because of a shortage of blankets. The care for the wounded was improved on 13 January, when 133 medical officers and 290 enlisted men were airlifted into the Army Group Center area. In the Zone of Interior the number of hospital beds proved insufficient, and schools had to be used as emergency hospitals.

An all-out effort was necessary to avert disaster. The Army High Command introduced all sorts of expedients that would strengthen the front of Army Group Center. Rear echelon troops were thrown

14. GERMAN ORDER OF BATTLE-RUSSIAN THEATER (January 1942)

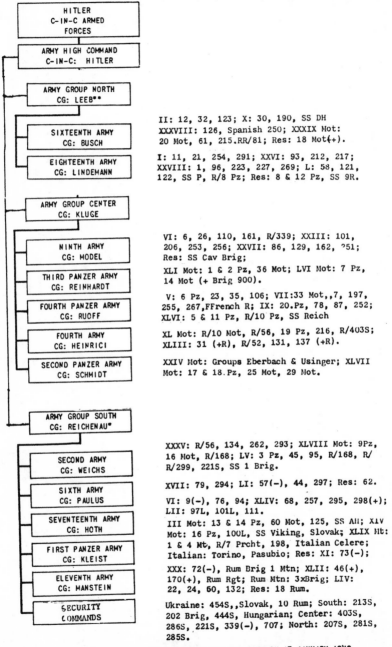

HITLER **C-IN-C ARMED** **FORCES**	
ARMY HIGH COMMAND **C-IN-C: HITLER**	
ARMY GROUP NORTH **CG: LEEB****	
SIXTEENTH ARMY **CG: BUSCH**	II: 12, 32, 123; X: 30, 190, SS DH XXXVIII: 126, Spanish 250; XXXIX Mot: 20 Mot, 61, 215.RR/81; Res: 18 Mot(+).
EIGHTEENTH ARMY **CG: LINDEMANN**	I: 11, 21, 254, 291; XXVI: 93, 212, 217; XXVIII: 1, 96, 223, 227, 269; L: 58, 121, 122, SS P, R/8 Pz; Res: 8 & 12 Pz, SS 9R.
ARMY GROUP CENTER **CG: KLUGE**	
NINTH ARMY **CG: MODEL**	VI: 6, 26, 110, 161, R/339; XXIII: 101, 206, 253, 256; XXVII: 86, 129, 162, ?51; Res: SS Cav Brig;
THIRD PANZER ARMY **CG: REINHARDT**	XLI Mot: 1 & 2 Pz, 36 Mot; LVI Mot: 7 Pz, 14 Mot (+ Brig 900).
FOURTH PANZER ARMY **CG: RUOFF**	V: 6 Pz, 23, 35, 106; VII:33 Mot,,7, 197, 255, 267,FFrench R; IX: 20.Pz, 78, 87, 252; XLVI: 5 & 11 Pz, R/10 Pz, SS Reich
FOURTH ARMY **CG: HEINRICI**	XL Mot: R/10 Mot, R/56, 19 Pz, 216, R/403S; XLIII: 31 (+R), R/52, 131, 137 (+R).
SECOND PANZER ARMY **CG: SCHMIDT**	XXIV Mot: Groups Eberbach & Usinger; XLVII Mot: 17 & 18.Pz, 25 Mot, 29 Mot.
ARMY GROUP SOUTH **CG: REICHENAU***	
SECOND ARMY **CG: WEICHS**	XXXV: R/56, 134, 262, 293; XLVIII Mot: 9Pz, 16 Mot, R/168; LV: 3 Pz, 45, 95, R/168, R/ R/299, 221S, SS 1 Brig.
SIXTH ARMY **CG: PAULUS**	XVII: 79, 294; LI: 57(-), 44, 297; Res: 62.
SEVENTEENTH ARMY **CG: HOTH**	VI: 9(-), 76, 94; XLIV: 68, 257, 295, 298(+); LII: 97L, 101L, 111.
FIRST PANZER ARMY **CG: KLEIST**	III Mot: 13 & 14 Pz, 60 Mot, 125, SS AH; XIV Mot: 16 Pz, 100L, SS Viking, Slovak; XLIX Mt: 1 & 4 Mt, R/7 Prcht, 198, Italian Celere; Italian: Torino, Pasubio; Res: XI: 73(-);
ELEVENTH ARMY **CG: MANSTEIN**	XXX: 72(-), Rum Brig 1 Mtn; XLII: 46(+), 170(+), Rum Rgt; Rum Mtn: 3xBrig; LIV: 22, 24, 60, 132; Res: 18 Rum.
SECURITY **COMMANDS**	Ukraine: 454S,,Slovak, 10 Rum; South: 213S, 202 Brig, 444S, Hungarian; Center: 403S, 286S, 221S, 339(-), 707; North: 207S, 281S, 285S.

*REPLACED BY FIELD MARSHAL FEDOR VON BOCK ON 17 JANUARY 1942
**REPLACED BY GENERAL GEORG VON KUECHLER ON 16 JANUARY 1942

During the withdrawal movements the following points were to be observed: POL supplies would have to be made available during the movement and upon arrival in the new line of resistance; no gun was to fall into Russian hands intact; no wounded were to be left behind; all railroad tracks, bridges, etc., were to be demolished; and all inhabited localities were to be burned down and the chimneys blown up.

A document that was very typical of the atmosphere then prevailing at the Army High Command headquarters was a memorandum General Halder addressed to all chiefs of staff in the Russian theater. The purpose of the memorandum was to counteract the "paralyzing effect that the tremendous number of enemy units identified opposite certain sectors had occasionally produced on certain field commanders." This kind of panic was contrary to the feeling of superiority typical for German soldiers. Halder pointed out that in many instances the immediate reaction of hopelessness caused by numerical inferiority was found to have been unjustified when the low combat efficiency of the Russian forces became manifest.

He continued by stating that field commanders ought not to succumb to a psychosis of numbers, "by reporting the tremendous number of enemy divisions and emphasizing the weakness of German units, which was only too well known to everyone from Hitler on down." In writing their estimates, intelligence specialists in the field would have to analyze all factors objectively. If that were properly done, ". . . the élan and morale of the German troops could [not] repeatedly give the lie to the figures submitted by worry-ridden statisticians."

The Crisis Reaches Its Climax (Beginning of February 1942)

Toward the end of January 1942 another critical situation developed in the Army Group South area, where the Russians attacked on a wide front on both sides of Izyum, broke through the German lines, and advanced practically unopposed. The gateway to Poltava and Dnepropetrovsk stood open, exposing the entire flank of Sixth Army and nearby bridges, across which ran the life lines of First Panzer and Seventeenth Armies. However, since the Russians did not exploit their advantage, Army Group South had time to strengthen the shoulders of the penetration in a makeshift manner. Army Group Center had succeeded in narrowing the gap near Sukhinichi by a series of local counterattacks, so that the danger at this point subsided. The cold weather hampered operations, since temperatures were still around -20° F.

In contrast to these fairly favorable developments, the situation of the German forces at the boundary of Army Group Center and North had deteriorated considerably. A gap of almost 120 miles yawned between Bely and Kholm, giving the *Kalinin Front* free access to the Vitebsk–Velikiye Luki area. Once in possession of the latter area, the *Kalinin Front* might pivot south toward Smolensk or north toward Pskov. Whether the Russian forces would be sufficiently strong for either maneuver was still a matter for conjecture at the end of January; by then Russian forces pouring through the gap veered sharply southeastward into the rear of Third Panzer and Ninth Armies. In conjunction with these ground operations the Russians began to airdrop supplies and reinforcements in the rear of Fourth Army. Despite the improvement near Sukhinichi, the overall position of Army Group Center became almost untenable. Thus began a life-and-death struggle.

Directly southeast of Lake Ilmen the situation also grew more and more critical. There, two corps, whose front formed a salient protruding to the east near Demyansk, could either stay in place at the risk of being encircled or they could withdraw to a shorter line at the base of the salient. Hitler decided to leave them in place, advancing for the first time the idea of tying down Russian forces by holding salients. In the specific case of Demyansk he was probably right because the Russian forces tied down by the two corps would otherwise have poured through the wide gap farther south. In general, however, only a salient that constituted a potential threat served a useful purpose. Whenever the Russians did not feel threatened by a salient, they merely kept it under observation and the Germans tied down their own forces without achieving what they had intended.

Farther to the north the Russians had also advanced across the Volkhov with the objective of gradually breaking the ring around Leningrad.

In this exceedingly tense situation the Germans sought consolidation in the hope that the Russians would overreach themselves in pursuing so many objectives at different points and would not be able to achieve any decisive success. This expectation, namely that the Soviets would dissipate their offensive strength, was not in vain. But before the German command was given respite, it was subjected to 10 more days of tension during which the situation grew even worse.

In the rear and on the exposed left flank of Army Group Center the situation had further deteriorated. The Russians landed some airborne reinforcements in the Vyazma area. Two Russian armies stood behind Ninth Army in the area west of Sychevka. Soviet spearheads had appeared in the vicinity of Velizh and Velikiye Luki. In the Army Group North area the encirclement of the German forces around Demyansk was imminent, and additional Russian units were crossing the Volkhov and advancing toward the northwest. On the positive side, Army Group South had been able to build a loosely knit front around the penetration in the Izyum sector and Army Group Center had eliminated the threat at Sukhinichi, thus warding off the danger of a double envelopment. German countermeasures were slow to get under way, mainly because low temperatures hampered essential movements. Thousands of tanks and motor vehicles were lost because of insufficient winterization.

The Russian Offensive Is Halted (20 February 1942)

By 20 February the crisis seemed to have passed its peak. Step by step the Germans stemmed the Russian offensive, bringing one danger area after another under control.

Army Group South had made the greatest progress. In the Izyum area, where Soviet aggressiveness seemed to have been exhausted, the Germans began to implement their plan to cut off the Russian salient and turn it into a pocket.

In the Army Group Center area the Russian penetration around Sukhinichi was under control and the situation in the rear of Fourth and Ninth Armies was sufficiently stabilized to present no immediate threat. The penetration into the Toropets region had not yet been checked, but since the Russians were not moving up reinforcements, the Germans hoped that this salient would eventually be contained.

In the Army Group North area the so-called Fortress Demyansk was encircled by the Russians. West of Demyansk, however, the Germans had formed a new front near Staraya Russa, from which relief of the encircled forces seemed possible. Along the Volkhov River the German forces had been able to prevent a widening of the Russian breach, and here too an operation to cut the salient at its base was under consideration. All Russian attempts to pierce the German front south of Lake Ladoga had failed.

In Finland the Russians started to seize the initiative at the beginning of 1942. They attacked along the Svir River in an attempt to clear the main line of the Murmansk railroad between Lakes Onega and Ladoga, and at the same time sought to drive back the German forces threatening the railroad from points in central and northern Finland. [See map 4.] Although these counterattacks remained fruitless, the problem of disrupting the Murmansk railroad traffic became a matter of increasing concern to both the Germans and the Finns. Large quantities of lend-lease material were reaching the Russians via this line. The Finns were unable to mount an operation against the railroad because the commitment of their forces on static fronts had left them without strategic reserves. They did, however, agree to carry out an operation against Belomorsk, the main junction of the Murmansk railroad on the White Sea, provided that the Germans first captured Leningrad. The Finns claimed that the forces needed to carry out and screen the Belomorsk operation would not be available until after Leningrad's fall. The strategic interdependence between the operations in southern Finland and those of Army Group North was greater than ever.

Critique

Generally speaking, the Russian counteroffensive had bogged down by the end of February 1942. In its course the Russians had seized the initiative on the entire front and had achieved major territorial gains, inflicting heavy casualties on the Germans whose combat effectiveness had been considerably reduced. Any immediate threat to the continued existence of the Soviet Government had been thwarted. But the Russians had failed to achieve a decisive reversal of the strategic situation. They had not annihilated entire German armies, let alone army groups. Though crumbling at many points and threatened at the rear and in the flanks, the German front had held. German losses had been heavy; the number of casualties had increased by 175,000 during January and February 1942 and had passed the million mark after eight months of fighting.

At the end of the winter the German position in the Russian theater might have been far stronger, if the Germans had been able to use an elastic, manpower-conserving defense system, instead of the rigid defense imposed by Hitler. As it happened, German effective strength dwindled and at the same time a number of divisions were forced to fight under conditions that contravened sound tactical doctrine. Piecemeal commitment of forces deprived the army group commanders of units which they urgently needed to cope with the critical situations that had developed at different points along the entire front.

Finally, Army Group Center stopped the Russian counteroffensive approximately along the line to which Field Marshal von Bock wanted to withdraw voluntarily in the first place. If he had been given the customary latitude within the framework of his mission, the withdrawal movement would have terminated along a line more favorable for stopping the Russian attacks, thus conserving manpower while still presenting a potential threat to Moscow. Instead, the center of the German front in Russia remained an open sore that did not heal for many months.

The fact that rigid defense methods did prove successful during the first winter, when the Russians committed a series of blunders, had a fatal influence on Hitler's conduct of operations during the following years. In any given situation the Fuehrer would justify his insistence on holding a position by referring to the fighting west of Moscow and to the so-called Fortress Demyansk, although prevailing conditions were in no way comparable to those of the winter of 1941-42.

VIII

PRELIMINARY PLANNING FOR A GERMAN OFFENSIVE IN THE CAUCASUS, 1942.

Exploratory Steps (July 1940–September 1941)

To Hitler, the oil of the Caucasus had always been one of the foremost attractions of Russia. He had mentioned the necessity of seizing the Baku oil fields as early as 31 July 1940, during one of the initial discussions of his plan to invade the Soviet Union. In the spring of 1941 the Armed Forces High Command activated the so-called Oil Detachment Caucasus for the purpose of taking over the oil fields. At that time the Germans expected that their advance into the Caucasus would be so rapid that the Russians would not be able to severely damage the oil wells, and the tables of organization and equipment of the oil detachment were established accordingly.

The next step in this direction was the preparation of Directive No. 32, circulated by the Armed Forces High Command among the three services on 11 June 1941—11 days before the start of Operation BARBAROSSA. This directive envisaged a drive from the Caucasus across Iran as a part of the plan for the continuation of operations against the British Empire following the defeat of the Soviets. At that time German expeditionary forces were to be activated in the Caucasus and sent across Turkey and Syria to Palestine and across Iraq to Basra. The same directive also visualized the use of the Arab liberation movement against the British in the Middle East, and Special Staff F was designated to initiate and coordinate the corresponding military and subversive activities.

A few days later, on 16 June 1941, German counterintelligence submitted to the Armed Forces High Command a plan for securing the Caucasus oil fields as soon as the internal disintegration of the Soviet Union would become manifest. A nucleus of 100 Georgians, trained by German counterintelligence agents in sabotage and revolt tactics, was in existence in Romania. These Georgians would have to be

brought to the oil fields by sea or air transport as soon as the German ground forces approached the Caucasus region. In a somewhat optimistic vein the plan foresaw the employment of the Georgians in two to three weeks after D Day.

On 24 July 1941 the Army Operations Division wrote a memorandum on the conduct of operations after the conclusion of Operation BARBAROSSA. With regard to the Caucasus it was anticipated that the British would seize and block this area as soon as the Germans approached the Sea of Azov. The first British troop concentrations were believed to be taking place along the northern and eastern border of Iraq. Because of terrain difficulties a German offensive from the southern slopes of the Caucasus across Iran into Iraq could not be executed before the spring of 1942. Meanwhile, data regarding the Caucasus were to be collected; a list of German tourists, who had climbed the Caucasus Mountains during recent years and knew the terrain and weather conditions, was drawn up, and books dealing with the same subjects were carefully scrutinized.

At the beginning of August the German Naval Operations Staff submitted an estimate of the probable reaction of the Soviet Black Sea fleet in the event of a German penetration into the Caucasus. It was believed that the fleet could seriously hamper operations by keeping the coastal road and railroad between Tuapse and Sukhumi under fire. Among the Soviet ships suitable for such operations were 1 battleship, 6 cruisers, and 15 modern plus 5 outdated destroyers. In the Black Sea area the German Navy had no units capable of stopping or disturbing the movements of the Soviet fleet. Coastal batteries would be of limited use; even if they did drive the Soviet ships farther off shore, the latter would still remain within reach of the coast. Air force protection was the only effective means of safeguarding coastal traffic.

In late September reports from agents and radio intercepts indicated that the Russians had from five to six divisions in the Caucasus and three in Iran. It was estimated that British troops entering the Soviet Union would take three weeks to get from Iran to the Caucasus and four weeks to the Crimea.

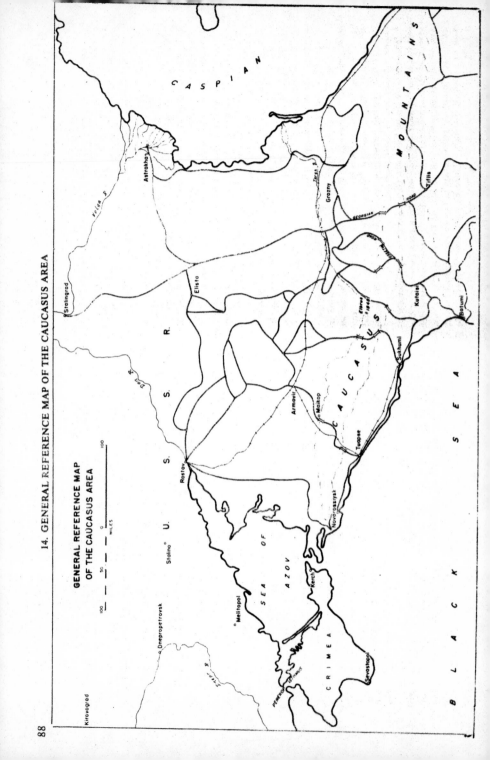

GENERAL REFERENCE MAP
OF THE CAUCASUS AREA

The *First Plan for a Caucasus Operation* (October 1941)

In October 1941 the Operations Division of the Army High Command drew up the first detailed plan for a Caucasus operation. The scope of the offensive was limited to seizing the oil resources of the Caucasus and to reaching the Iranian and Iraqi border passes for a possible farther advance toward Baghdad. [See *map 14*]. The operation was to be executed in six separate phases, extending from November 1941 to September 1942. These phases were outlined as follows:

1. Seizure of the approaches to the northern Caucasus, starting in November 1941;

2. A series of preliminary attacks leading to the seizure of favorable jumpoff areas by May 1942;

3. Launching the offensive across the Caucasus Mountains in two different stages in June 1942;

4. The advance across Transcaucasia toward the Turkish and Iranian borders;

5. Seizure of favorable jumpoff areas within Iran; and

6. Capture of the border passes leading into Iraq. The last three phases were to take place in the period July-early September 1942.

The feasibility of the entire offensive would depend on the course taken by current operations in the Russian theater. The second and third phases could be executed only if German troops reached the lower Volga during the winter of 1941-42. The scope of the preliminary attacks to be launched during the second phase would depend on the overall plan adopted for the offensive across the Caucasus. The latter could be launched via the two roads following the Black and Caspian Sea coasts respectively and over the mountain road leading to Tiflis. The interior roads crossed the mountains over passes more than 10,000 feet in altitude. These roads could be negotiated only by mountain divisions. The movement along the Caspian coastal road would be easier because only a few outdated Russian destroyers were liable to interfere.

During the first stage of the offensive proper, two motorized and two mountain corps were to be employed, driving toward Sukhumi and Kutaisi in the west, Tiflis in the center, and Baku in the east, respectively. As soon as any one of these forces had achieved a break-

through, one additional motorized corps that was being held in reserve was to move up and launch the pursuit. The commitment of this reserve force would determine where the point of main effort was to be placed during the second stage of the offensive.

The employment of two corps in the west during the first stage would be necessary because of the vulnerability of the lines of communications along the Black Sea. Moreover, in the west was the only opening for launching an enveloping drive, since unfavorable terrain conditions prevented any such maneuver elsewhere. During the second stage of the offensive the penetration into the mountains would have to be exploited by the reserve corps which could thrust either via the Black Sea coastal road to Batumi and from there via Tiflis to Baku; or across the mountains to Tiflis and from there either to Batumi or Baku; or along the Caspian shore to Baku and from there, if necessary to Tiflis.

While the offensive was in progress, German naval contingents would have to protect Novorossiysk and Tuapse by ta' ng over captured coastal batteries. In addition, some submarines would have to keep the Russian Black Sea fleet under control, and the Navy would also have to make available the shipping space needed for carrying supplies from Novorossiysk to Batumi once the Russian fleet had been eliminated.

The Luftwaffe would have to protect and support the ground forces; combat the Red Navy and its ports; commit airborne troops to capture the major cities; use dive bombers against the pass fortifications; and prepare transport planes to airdrop supplies.

This plan met with general approval at an exploratory conference held at Army High Command headquarters upon request of the Operations Division on 24 October 1941. An attack across the Caucasus was considered the quickest solution to Germany's Middle-Eastern problems. The effect of such an offensive would induce Turkey to join the Axis Powers. In addition, British forces that would otherwise oppose Rommel in North Africa would be tied down in Iran.

An offensive launched in the spring of 1942 would first lead to the seizure of the Caucasus oil fields, then open the passes from Iran to Iraq, and finally permit the capture of the Iraqi oil fields in the autumn of 1942, when the weather favored the commitment of large ground forces. The essential prerequisite for such far-reaching operations was the seizure of the west bank of the lower Volga from Stalingrad to Astrakhan. This realization implied that if, for instance, the Germans failed to capture Stalingrad, a complete reevaluation of the plans for an offensive against the Caucasus would become necessary.

Among the essential preparations for a Caucasus operation discussed at this conference were the production of military maps and tropical clothing as well as the activation and equipment of special mountain troops.

Caucasus Planning in November 1941

In a conversation with Field Marshal von Brauchitsch on 7 November Hitler mentioned that the seizure of the oil fields would have to be delayed until the following year. This delay had actually been anticipated by the Operations Division of the Army High Command. However, a new point was brought up by the Fuehrer when he added that he had no intention of going beyond the Russian border. The scope of the offensive was thus limited to the Caucasus; this change in plans was probably due to the slowdown in the 1941 advance caused by the muddy season.

According to all available intelligence the Red Army intended to put up stiff resistance in the Caucasus. By 9 November German intercept units had identified 5 army headquarters in that area. If exact, this information would imply the presence of at least 15 divisions, whereas prior to that time the presence of only 5 had been assumed. It seemed improbable that the Russians would move sizeable forces across their border into Iran. And it seemed even more unlikely that the British would send strong forces northward into the Caucasus. For the time being the situation in the Caucasus remained obscure.

In a conversation with General Halder on 19 November, Hitler stated that the first objective for 1942 would be the Caucasus. An offensive lauched for this purpose in March–April 1942 would bring the German forces to the Soviet border with Iran. Depending on the situation at the end of 1941, offensives in the center could subsequently be launched beyond Moscow toward Vologda or Gorki by the end of May 1942. Other objectives for 1942 could not yet be designated. Their scope would depend mainly on the capacity of the railroads. The question of whether a defensive wall separating Asiatic from European Russia was subsequently to be constructed remained open.

Hitler thus revealed a number of interesting facts. Even as late as 19 November he seemed convinced that the Germans would be able to capture Moscow before the end of 1941. Furthermore, he seemed to believe that the Caucasus offensive across difficult mountain terrain could be successfully executed within a few weeks in April and May, as a kind of southern interlude prior to another offensive farther north. Three days later, on 22 November 1911, Halder ordered a light infantry division organized for the Caucasus operation and mountain personnel withdrawn from combat. As late as 16 days before the turning of the tide in front of Moscow the atmosphere at Army High Command headquarters appeared definitely optimistic.

Effects of the Moscow Setback (January 1942)

An order dated 10 January 1942, originating from the Armed Forces Economics Office and the Organization Branch of the Armed Forces Operations Staff and signed by Hitler brought out the newly imposed material limitations—if not the change in scope—of the 1942 operations.

In the introductory paragraph Hitler stated that the long-range strategic plans remained unchanged; the Navy and the Luftwaffe were to be expanded for the showdown with the Anglo-Saxon powers. Until further notice, however, the operations scheduled for 1942 would not permit a reduction in armaments destined for the Army. On the contrary, the Army would have to be given even more than its ordinary share of manpower and armaments so that it could accomplish its mission for 1942.

In effect, the Army was to have top priority on armament production. Wherever shortages of raw materials developed, the Navy and Luftwaffe would have to take the cuts. Greater standardization, the introduction of more substitutes, and the increased use of captured munitions were recommended as means to overcoming production bottlenecks.

The ground forces were to be ready for offensive commitment by 1 May 1942; supplies for at least four months of continuous operations would have to be accumulated by that time. The units taking part in the offensive would have to be amply provided with supply and service troops as well as motor vehicles, while those committed along the Atlantic Coast would not need many trucks. Ammunition supplies for all weapons used in the Russian theater would have to be built up to one month's expenditure in addition to the basic load.

The Navy was to concentrate on submarine construction and maintenance. The Luftwaffe was to continue its current programs, except for a temporary curtailment of its ammunition and bomb production schedules.

Among the military-economic programs, oil had first priority. The railroad transportation, signal, and other programs were to be carried on along the same lines as before, whereas the motor vehicle output was to be increased. Military manpower requirements were to be coordinated with the industrial ones.

Perhaps the most striking note in this order was its pessimistic undertone. Written at a time when the Germans were desperately trying to stem the Russian tide west of Moscow, the order showed the many weaknesses in the German war machine which had become manifest after less than seven months of fighting in Russia. During the following weeks further planning for the summer offensive came to a standstill, probably because of the life-and-death struggle that raged along the Army Group Center front.

The First Preparatory Orders (February 1942)

With the acute danger past at the front, the military planners were able to pursue more actively the preparations for a summer offensive.

On 12 February 1942 the Operations Division of the Army High Command issued a directive for the conduct of operations after the end of the winter. An introductory statement anticipated that the Russian winter offensive would not succeed in destroying the German troops and their equipment. During the coming weeks the Germans would have to consolidate their lines, eliminate Russian forces that had penetrated into their rear areas, and generally attempt to seize the initiative. At the same time they would have to prepare themselves for the muddy period following the spring thaw.

The directive then went into great detail in describing the different aspects of the muddy season and the countermeasures to be taken. The Army High Command intended to use this probable lull in operations to rehabilitate and regroup its forces.

Army Group South was to hold its positions and make preparations for the planned offensive. First, the Russian penetration west of Izyum would have to be eliminated, then the Kerch Peninsula recaptured and Sevastopol seized, so that the forces stationed in the Crimea would become available for employment elsewhere.

Army Group Center was to seize Ostashkov and shorten its front line by eliminating various dents and penetrations.

Army Group North was to hold its lines near Kholm, Staraya Russa, and north of Lake Ilmen.

After the end of the muddy season all three army groups were to improve their front lines and establish continuous defensive positions, if possible. Because of the precarious supply situation, it seemed doubtful whether more than isolated strong points could be held along certain sectors of the front. Armored and motorized reserves would have to be assembled in accessible areas.

Units withdrawn from the frontline for rehabilitation would have to train their recently arrived replacements on the basis of past experience in combat. Because of a shortage of equipment, only a certain number of divisions could be fully rehabilitated. The ones selected for this purpose were the armored and motorized divisions as well as the army and corps troops of Army Group South, and three armored and three motorized infantry divisions as well as some of the army and corps troops of Army Groups Center and North. In the process of rehabilitation, each armored division was to have three tank battalions, and each motorized infantry division one. The armored divisions of Army Groups Center and North that were not to be rehabilitated would have to transfer some of their cadres to the south. Three armored and six infantry divisions of Army Group Center were to be moved to western Europe without their equipment. There they were to be completely rehabilitated and reequipped. The armored and motorized infantry divisions remaining with Army Group Center and North would have to be rehabilitated in the line without being issued any new equipment. The armored divisions in this category would probably have only one tank battalion. Approximately 500,000 replacements were supposed to arrive in the theater by the end of April 1942.

A special rehabilitation area for Army Group South was to be established near Dnepropetrovsk, while for Army Group Center similar areas could be set up near Orsha, Minsk, Gomel, and Bryansk. Those few units of Army Group North which were to be rehabilitated would probably be transferred to the Zone of Interior. Rehabilitation was to begin in mid-March at the latest. After the muddy season the fully rehabilitated units of Army Group Center were to be transferred to Army Group South.

The exigencies of the last few months had led to the commitment of a great number of technical specialists as infantrymen. The overall personnel situation and the shortage of technically trained men made it imperative either to return all specialists to their proper assignment or to use them as cadres for newly activated units. The future combat efficiency of the Army would depend upon the effective enforcement of this policy.

The high rate of materiel attrition and the limited capacity of the armament industry were compelling reasons for keeping weapons and equipment losses at a minimum.

In the implementing order to the army groups and armies, the Organization Division of the Army High Command directed on 18 February that those mobile divisions that were to be fully rehabilitated would be issued 50–60 percent of their prescribed motor vehicle allowance and infantry divisions up to 50 percent. Every infantry company was to be issued 4 automatic rifles and 4 carbines with telescopic sights; armor-piercing rifle grenades were to be introduced. Bimonthly reports on manpower and equipment shortages as well as on current training and rehabilitation of units were to be submitted by all headquarters concerned.

The element of surprise was essential to the success of the summer offensive. On 12 February Keitel therefore issued the first directive for deceiving the Russians about future German intentions. The following information was to be played into Soviet intelligence hands by German counterintelligence agents:

At the end of the muddy season the German military leaders intended to launch a new offensive against Moscow. For this purpose they wanted to concentrate strong forces by moving newly activated divisions to the Russian theater and exchanging battle-weary ones in the East for fresh ones from the West. After the capture of Moscow the Germans planned to advance to the middle Volga and seize the industrial installations in that region.

The assembly of forces was to take place in secret. For this purpose the capacity of the railroads was to be raised before the divisions were transferred from the West. German and allied forces would meanwhile launch a major deceptive attack in the direction of Rostov.

As to Leningrad, the prevailing opinion was that this city would perish by itself as soon as the ice on Lake Ladoga had melted. Then the Russians would have to dismount the railroad and the inhabitants would again be isolated. To attack in this area appeared unnecessary.

In addition, those German troops that were earmarked for the Russian theater and presently stationed in the West were to be deceived by the issuance of military maps and geographic data pertaining to the Moscow area. The units that were already in the theater were not to be given any deceptive information until the current defensive battles had been concluded. The same directive also requested the Army and Luftwaffe to submit suggestions for other deceptive measures. The maintenance of secrecy was strongly emphasized.

The Navy's Role (February 1942)

The German Navy's principal concern in the Black Sea area was the transportation of supplies for the Army. The difficulties were caused by the shortage of shipping space and the absence of escort and combat vessels. Measures taken to improve the German position in the Black Sea included transfer of PT boats, Italian antisubmarine vessels, small submarines, and landing craft; mine fields were also being laid. Orders had been issued to speed up these measures and support the Army by bringing up supplies. Russian naval forces in the Black Sea would have to be attacked and destroyed. The degree of success obtained would determine the outcome of the war in the Black Sea area. Attention was called to the fact that eventually it would become necessary to occupy all Russian Black Sea bases and ports.

On the other hand, the remainder of the Russian Baltic fleet stationed in and around Leningrad had neither strategic nor tactical value. Ammunition and fuel supplies were exceedingly low. About 12 of the high speed mine sweepers had been sunk so far, so that only 4 or 5 were left. About 65 out of 100 submarines had been sunk by the Germans.

Intelligence Estimate (20 February 1942)

In a summary dated 20 February 1942 the Eastern Intelligence Division of the Army High Command stated that the Russians were anticipating a German offensive directed against the Caucasus and the oil wells in that area. As a countermeasure the Red Army would have the choice between a spoiling offensive and a strategic withdrawal. Assuming the Russians would attack, it was estimated that their offensive would take place in the south. There they could interfere with German attack preparations, reoccupy economically valuable areas, and land far to the rear of the German lines along the Black Sea coast. If they were sufficiently strong, the Soviets would also attempt to tie down German forces by a series of local attacks in the Moscow and Leningrad sectors.

Numerous reports from German agents in Soviet-held territory indicated that the Red Army had been planning the recapture of the Ukraine for some time. At the earliest the Russian attack could take place immediately after the muddy season, i. e. at the beginning of May.

The Russian forces identified opposite Army Group South consisted of 83 infantry divisions and 12 infantry brigades as well as 20 cavalry divisions and 19 armored brigades; plus an unknown number of newly organized units.

Interference from British forces seemed unlikely. The latter would move into the Caucasus area only if their supply lines could be properly secured, a time-consuming process that had not even been initiated. On the other hand, lend-lease materiel was arriving in considerable quantities; the first U. S. fighter planes had been encountered along the German Sixth Army front.

Hitler's Preoccupations in Early March 1942

On 5 March an order signed by Keitel summarized the various instructions issued by Hitler to the services during recent weeks. In the general part of this order, the Army and Luftwaffe were reminded that premature attacks conducted without concentrating sufficient forces had failed on several occasions. Efforts to stop Russian penetrations all along the front had led to piecemeal commitment and dissipation of ground forces. The Russians would have to be stopped wherever they threatened vital communications. In the event of a Soviet breakthrough full-strength units were to be assembled along the shoulders of the salient and the gap was to be closed after the bulk of the Russian forces had passed through.

Minor rectifications of the defense lines were permissible so long as no important installations were thereby abandoned. No local attacks, the results of which were out of proportion with the losses, were to be launched. Luftwaffe support was to be requested only for essential operations, such as destroying concentrations of Soviet armor prior to an attack. Many a Russian attack could be delayed or altogether weakened beyond repair by disrupting Soviet lines of communications. To achieve greater effect, the heaviest bombs available were to be used for all-out air attacks. Since there was a shortage of artillery along many stretches of the front, effective air support for offensive operations was essential. Because of the current emergency, air transport was so scarce that no additional airlift operations could be carried out during the muddy period.

In the second part of the order the mission of each army group for the immediate future was set forth as follows:

a. Army Group South.

(1) If the Crimea was to be seized with a minimum of delay, the Kerch Peninsula would have to be captured before starting the siege of Sevastopol. The Russian ports and Black Sea fleet would have to be neutralized from the air before ground operations were started in the Crimea.

(2) The next step was to eliminate the Izyum salient by first letting the Soviets exhaust their offensive power in that area and then cutting off the salient by thrusts directed from the shoulders. The armored divisions of the First Panzer Army were to carry out these thrusts and were therefore given top priority on tank and motor vehicle deliveries.

b. Army Group Center. All forces available in the Army Group Center area were to be assembled for a Ninth Army thrust in the direction of Ostashkov. This drive was to take place before the spring muddy period. The lines of communications that had been frequently disrupted would have to be secured.

c. Army Group North. The airlift operations that had been initiated to bring the situation under control were to be stepped up. More reinforcements were to be moved up to permit the consolidation of the situation at Demyansk and prevent an encirclement along the Volkhov. Eventually, Sixteenth Army was to attack from the Staraya Russa area in a movement that was to be coordinated with the Ninth Army drive toward Ostashkov. The VIII Air Corps was to support this operation as well as the Volkhov maneuver.

Another directive, signed by Hitler on 14 March, dealt with the problem of Allied assistance to the Soviet Union. It stated that British and American efforts to bolster Russia's power of resistance during the decisive months of 1942 would have to be curbed. For this purpose the Germans would have to strengthen their coastal defenses in Norway to prevent Allied landings along the Arctic coast, particularly in the Petsamo nickel mine area in northern Finland. Moreover, the Navy would have to intensify submarine operations against convoys crossing the Arctic Ocean. The Luftwaffe was to strengthen its long-range reconnaissance and bomber units in the far north and transfer the bulk of its torpedo planes to that area. The flying units were to keep the Russian ports along the Murmansk coast under constant attack, increase their reconnaissance activities, and intercept convoys. Close interservice cooperation was essential.

The Situation at the End of March 1942

The overall situation remained static during the month of March. The Russians showed signs of exhaustion, while the Germans were incapable of launching any major counterattack. Like two groggy boxers, the opponents warily eyed each other, neither of them strong enough to land a knockout blow. The weakness of the Russians became manifest through a number of incidents. In the area around Velizh, for instance, the Germans captured rifles, the butts of which were unfinished, indicating that the weapons had been issued before they were ready. The shortage of infantry weapons, though nothing new, seemed more acute than ever. Russian prisoners stated that wooden rifles were being used for training recruits in the Zone of Interior. In another instance, the Russian cavalry divisions opposite Army Group South were so short of horses—their strength had dropped to approximately 60 horses per regiment—that the men had to be employed as infantry.

The true condition of the German forces could be gathered from a status report of 30 March 1942. Out of a total of 162 combat divisions in the Russian theater, only 8 were immediately available for any mission, 3 were capable of offensive missions after a rest period, 47 were available for limited offensive missions, 73 were fully suited for defensive missions, 29 were only capable of limited defensive missions, and 2 were not suited for immediate commitment. The 16 armored divisions in the theater had a total of 140 serviceable tanks, that is to say less than the normal complement of one division. Because of the shortage of motor vehicles and prime movers, few divisions were more than 20 percent mobile. The few available tanks and self-propelled guns were distributed among various armored and infantry divisions.

Under these conditions the arrival of the muddy season at the end of March, which practically enforced a truce in the fighting, was a relief for both protagonists. Although the mud was less severe than during the preceding autumn, it did not hamper operations for some time.

During March Army Group South was not engaged in any large-scale fighting, and Bock, who had assumed command of the army group after Reichenau's sudden death on 17 January 1942, used this lull to reinforce the wall around the Russian breach near Izyum.

GERMAN ASSAULT GUN advances ahead of infantry, 1942.

In the Army Group Center area the heavy fighting in the rear of Fourth and Ninth Armies continued. The Russians did everything in their power to supply their forces behind the German front, and they exerted constant pressure on Army Group Center's only supply line, the Smolensk–Vyazma–Rzhev railroad. German efforts to keep this route open were handicapped by a shortage of troops. Also, in the Vitebsk–Velikye Luki area there was a latent threat which the Germans were unable to eliminate. But they were fortunate that the Russians in this region had dispersed their forces over a wide area instead of concentrating them for a southward drive.

South of Lake Ilmen Army Group North had assembled a relief force to establish contact with the Demyansk pocket. The situation along the Volkhov front had deteriorated because a strong attack launched by the Russians northeast of Lyuban resulted in a deep breach, which—in conjunction with the Volkhov penetration—threatened to develop into a double envelopment of the German forces in that area.

IX

PREPARATIONS FOR THE GERMAN SUMMER OFFENSIVE

Directive No. 41 (5 April 1942)

There can be no doubt that Hitler himself conceived the plan for the German summer offensive. In addition to designating the principal objectives, he plotted most of the details and even went so far as to dictate the text. His self-confidence as military leader had greatly risen since he had overcome the winter crisis without abandoning a major part of Germany's territorial gains in Russia. In his recently acquired position of commander in chief of the Army he seemed less than ever disposed to listen to his advisers. Whereas the plans for Operation BARBAROSSA had been prepared according to German General Staff procedures, those for Operation SIEGFRIED—the summer offensive of 1942—were drafted by General Halder and his immediate assistants according to detailed instructions received from Hitler who dictated the final version. In so doing, the Fuehrer completely rewrote Directive No. 41, adding very important parts pertaining to the conduct of operations in particular. At the same time the code designation SIEGFRIED was changed to BLAU, and Hitler specified that the services be given separate instructions regarding the maintenance of secrecy and the scope of strategic propaganda directed at the Caucasus area.

Hitler's directive was issued on 5 April 1942. It read essentially as follows:

a. Introduction. The winter battles in Russia were approaching their end and the Germans had won a "defensive success of unequalled magnitude." The Russians had suffered extremely heavy losses and used up the reserves they had earmarked for subsequent operations.

As soon as weather and terrain conditions permitted, the Germans would regain the initiative so that they could eradicate the remaining Russian military potential and deprive the Soviets of the resources on which their economy was still based. All available forces of Germany and its allies were to be employed for this purpose, taking into account that the occupied territories in northern and western Europe, and especially their coast lines, had to be safeguarded.

b. Overall Plan for the Russian Theater. While Army Group North was to seize Leningrad and establish contact with the Finns, Army Group Center was to hold. In the south, German attack forces were to penetrate into the Caucasus. To attain the latter objective, the Army would have to proceed by phase lines. In planning the conduct of this offensive factors to be considered were the course of the front lines along which the winter fighting would be brought to a conclusion and the availability of manpower, equipment, and transportation.

All available forces would have to be concentrated for the principal operation in the south in order to first destroy the enemy forces in the Don bend, then seize the oil resources of the Caucasus, and finally cross the Caucasus mountain ranges. The Leningrad operation was to be made contingent upon developments in the overall situation.

c. Conduct of Operations. As a first step toward accomplishing these missions, the Army was to consolidate its position along the entire Russian front. That would require a number of limited-objective attacks which would have to be conducted with maximum power to assure local superiority and rapid success, and to strengthen the German troops' self-confidence.

Once this consolidation had been achieved, the Kerch Peninsula would have to be cleared and Sevastopol captured. During these preliminary operations the Luftwaffe and Navy were to disrupt Russian communications in the Black Sea. Moreover, the Russian forces that had dented the German lines at Izyum would have to be cut off along the Donets and destroyed.

After these preliminary operations the Army was to launch the Caucasus offensive proper. During the initial phases the Russian forces south of Voronezh and west and north of the Don would have to be destroyed. Since the divisions available for this operation could not detrain and assemble simultaneously, the offensive would have to be executed by consecutive phases that were to complement one another. The delivery of individual attacks in different parts of the theater would have to be so coordinated that maximum power could be developed at the right time at the decisive point.

Encirclements of Russian forces resulting from German break-throughs and envelopments would have to be tight; the enveloping forces would have to avoid any delay that would offer the Soviets an opportunity to escape. While movements were underway, the armored and motorized infantry units were to avoid losing contact with the infantry divisions; whenever the latter were unable to make headway, motorized elements were to lend them support.

The offensive was to start with a breakthrough from the area south of Orel in the direction of Voronezh. Two enveloping forces were to seize Voronezh. During the second phase, while some of the infantry divisions established a strong defensive line from Orel to Voronezh, armored and motorized divisions were to continue their southeastward drive along the Don, performing another double envelopment in conjunction with forces thrusting eastward from the Kharkov area.

During the third phase of the offensive the forces following the course of the Don were to link up near Stalingrad with those advancing eastward from the Taganrog area. Every attempt was to be made to seize Stalingrad or at least bring the city within reach of German artillery so that the Soviets would be deprived of its production and transportation facilities. Subsequent operations would be greatly facilitated if the bridges at Rostov could be seized intact and bridge-heads could be established south of the Don.

The German attack force on the right advancing eastward from Taganrog was to be reinforced with armored and motorized divisions in order to prevent major Russian elements from escaping across the Don. Defensive positions would have to be built along the Don while the advance was in progress. These positions would have to be amply provided with antitank guns and so constructed that, if necessary, they could be of service during the winter. Allied forces, supported by German troops, would have to man these positions, and German divisions would have to serve as strategic reserves behind the Don front.

Because of the advanced season the movements across the Don toward the south would have to be so timed that the Caucasus could be reached without major stoppage.

d. The Luftwaffe. Apart from giving direct support to the ground forces, the Luftwaffe was to protect the concentration of forces in the Army Group South area by strengthening the antiaircraft defense, particularly those of the Dnepr railway bridges. In the event that reconnaissance information should indicate the assembly of Russian attack forces, the Luftwaffe would have to disrupt Soviet lines of communications and above all destroy the railroad bridges across the Don

e. The Navy. In the Black Sea the Navy's main function was to carry out naval transports. Since the Russian Black Sea fleet had so far not been affected by military events, German naval vessels transferred to these waters would have to be prepared for combat without delay. The Russian Baltic fleet was to be neutralized in the Gulf of Finland.

Special security precautions were to be taken, which—together with strategic propaganda—were the subject of instructions issued simultaneously. The number of persons initiated in the plan for the summer offensive was to be held to a minimum; conversations about possible operations were strictly forbidden; no long-distance calls discussing preparations were to be made beyond army group, air force, and VIII Air Corps headquarters. All orders and messages were to be forwarded by courier in writing, and differences of opinion were to be cleared up in personal conferences or through an exchange of coded messages. Germany's allies were to be informed of only the most essential facts.

Strategic propaganda was to be directed at the Caucasian tribes to whom full independence was to be promised. Liaison officers were to be attached to allied propaganda agencies to guarantee adherence to German policies.

This directive leaves no doubt that Hitler's principal objective for the summer offensive of 1942 was the possession of the Caucasus and its oil resources. The shortage of combat troops and the precariousness of the transportation network made it necessary to place great emphasis on the preliminary operations, whereas the main drive toward the Caucasus was outlined only in its initial phase—the seizure of bridgeheads across the Don. More specific orders for a Caucasus operation were not issued until 23 July 1942, when the operation was in full swing and Hitler signed Directive No. 45. At the time Directive No. 41 was written, no basic conflict between the eastward thrust toward Stalingrad and the southward drive into the Caucasus was anticipated. Like Voronezh, for instance, Stalingrad was to be a stepping stone along the approach road toward the Caucasus. In the Fuehrer's mind, however, the desire to conquer the city on the Volga by house-to-house fighting gradually became a fixation. This was all the more difficult to understand because in 1941 he had rejected any direct attack on Leningrad and Moscow. The diversion of more and more forces toward Stalingrad was made to the detriment of the principal drive into the Caucasus, and eventually both efforts were to bog down for lack of strength.

Estimates, Delays, and Disappointments in April 1942

Intelligence Estimate

Despite the bitter experiences of the winter 1941–42, the Germans continued to underestimate their Russian opponent. According to an estimate submitted by the Eastern Intelligence Division on 10 April 1942, the Red Army had been greatly affected by the winter fighting. Newly activated units showed deficiencies in training, weapons, and equipment. Not only was there a shortage of manpower, but the limitations imposed by the loss of armament production capacity would hamper the further activation of armored units.

In 1942 the Russians would limit themselves to defensive operations, possibly interrupted by intermittent limited-objective offensives to harass the Germans. Being aware of the German plans for an offensive in the southeast, the Russians could be expected to use every means at their disposal to maintain their lines of communications with the Caucasus. As yet there was no indication that the Russians intended to launch a spoiling attack in the south. In the center they would try to consolidate the defense system around Moscow, whereas in the north the relief of Leningrad would probably be given top priority.

Few Russian units appeared to be at full combat efficiency. While the activation of new rifle divisions was feasible, that of armored divisions seemed no longer possible. Steel production was the bottleneck. No major Russian offensive was to be expected in the foreseeable future. The bulk of the Soviet forces would probably be massed in the south.

Making these ideas his own, Halder reported to Hitler that the great number of Russian divisions identified since November 1941 seemed to indicate that the Red Army had mobilized all its manpower resources and had used up a major part of them during the winter offensive.

Delay in the Preliminary Operations

On 16 April Generaloberst (Gen.) Fritz Erich von Manstein, commander of Eleventh Army in the Crimea, suggested to Hitler that the attack on the Kerch Peninsula be delayed until 5 May because he was still short some essential items of supply. Hitler approved Manstein's request, adding that the Luftwaffe would have to give strong support to the ground forces. As soon as Kerch was cleared, Army Group South was to pinch off and eliminate the Izyum salient, after which the siege of Sevastopol was to be begun. The timing of these three preliminary operations was to be made contingent upon the availability of essential air support. Because of the delay in the start of the first attack, the Sevastopol operation would not begin before mid-June at the earliest.

The Situation at Army Group Center

As a result of the shifting of forces to the West, to Army Group South, and to rehabilitation centers, Army Group Center was forced to abandon the attacks on Ostashkov and Toropez. Despite its reduction in strength, however, the army group was ordered to eliminate the partisan forces in its rear, consolidate its front line, reorganize its remaining units, and set aside reserves. After these missions had been accomplished, the army group was to undertake a series of limited-objective attacks.

Chain of Command

The first phase of the summer offensive was to be conducted by Army Group South, composed of Second and Sixth Armies, Fourth Panzer Army, and the Hungarian First Army. During the second phase First Panzer Army, the Italian Eighth Army, and probably also Eleventh Army were to intervene. The newly activated Army Group A was to assume control of the movements foreseen for the following phases, while Army Group South would become responsible for securing flank protection along the Don front.

Transportation

The divisions that were to participate in the German offensive were to be moved up in three echelons. The 41 divisions—21 of which were allied—that were to reinforce the units stationed in the south were none too many for an offensive of such dimensions. Since the Russians had the better railnet for their assembly, they might be able to jump off before the Germans. Much would depend upon the quantities of lend-lease equipment they would receive via Murmansk by June 1942.

The delays in the start of the preliminary attacks would necessarily affect the time of the offensive proper, all the more so because as late as April the Russians were still holding the initiative.

15. DIVISIONS TO BE MOVED UP FOR THE SUMMER OFFENSIVE

Echelon	Divisions				
	Total	German	Italian	Hungarian	Romanian
Totals	41	20	6	10	5
First	20	15		3	2
Second	12	5	3	4	
Third	9		3	3	3

Turkey Remains Neutral

Hitler, who believed that Turkey would sooner or later join the Axis Powers, ordered the German Ambassador in Ankara to offer the Turks 150 million marks worth of military equipment at a time when he could hardly spare a rifle. However, the deal was not consummated because Turkey refused the passage of German submarines and PT-boats through the Dardanelles into the Black Sea. In his search for another solution Hitler ordered the boats disassembled, transported cross country, and reassembled in Black Sea ports. This order was carried out, but it produced no significant results.

Logistical Preparations

Timing

During the first phase—the drive on Voronezh—the offensive forces were to be supplied from the supply depots of the Kursk district. After the seizure of Voronezh, the railroad connecting that city with Kursk would become the principal feeder line for the Don front. Nonorgrnic truck transportation columns were to carry the supplies for the spearhead divisions.

The Kharkov supply district was to support the attack forces participating in the second phase. An advance base was to be set up at Valuiki as soon as the Voronezh forces linked up with those coming from Kharkov.

During the third phase additional advance bases would have to be set up along the railroad leading from the Stalino supply district to Stalingrad and east of Valuiki along the Don. Supply points would also have to be established south of the lower Don as soon as German troops crossed the river for the drive into the Caucasus.

To carry out these different missions, a large number of truck transportation columns would have to be held in readiness. Special supply reconnaissance teams were to follow the spearheads during each movement.

Chain of Command

Until Army Group A assumed control in the southern part of the Army Group South area, the supply preparations for Operation BLAU were to be the responsibility of the newly formed Command Staff South.

Supplies

Aside from the initial issue carried by the troops, the following quantities of supplies were to be stored in depots:

16. SUPPLIES IN DEPOTS

	Short Tons		
	Ammunition	POL	Rations
Totals	68,000	39,600	55,000
Kharkov	18,000	11,000	15,400
Kursk	15,000	8,300	14,900
Stalino	35,000	20,300	24,700

Detailed preparations could be made only for the first two phases for which the necessary data were available. Depots in the Kharkov and Kursk districts were to break down supplies according to the estimated requirements of the forces that were to be assembled in these areas, whereas at Stalino supplies were to be stored in bulk.

Motor Vehicles

By the start of Operation BLAU it was hoped that most of the participating units would be adequately equipped with motor vehicles. Prime movers were still scarce. The preliminary operations as well as the long distances some of the motorized units would have to cover to reach the assembly areas might cause further attrition in organic motor vehicles before the start of the offensive proper. Despite intensive maintenance and repair efforts the spearhead divisions would probably have only 60 percent or less of their organic motor vehicles by the time the offensive was launched. Truck transportation columns with a total capacity of 11,000 short tons would be available by 20 June 1942 to compensate for the shortage of organic vehicles.

Rail Transportation

During the initial phases of the operation the attack forces could rely on three major rail lines with detraining points in the Kursk, Kharkov, and Donets Basin areas. During the third phase the left arm of the pincers directed at Stalingrad would lack rail support as it extended southeastward along the Don. The right arm would be dependent upon the single railroad connecting Stalino with Stalingrad. This was the only railroad by which the attack forces could be supplied once they were approaching the Volga.

Summary

The supply situation during the first phase appeared satisfactory with sufficient ammunition and rations apparently available for the second phase. But POL reserves would be consumed by 15 July, and the continuation of the offensive would have to be assured from current shipments.

Organizational Problems

Rehabilitation of Units

The predominant problem facing the Organization Division of the Army High Command was the rehabilitation of units. Altogether 3 armored and 5 infantry divisions committed in the Russian theater were selected to be exchanged for 1 armored and 9 infantry divisions stationed in the West. The troops to be withdrawn from the Russian theater were to be deloused twice: first before entraining and then again after detraining.

Some of the army and corps troops as well as the divisions that were to be rehabilitated within the theater could not even be pulled out of the front. They were to be rehabilitated in place, a very unsatisfactory procedure not propitious to raising the combat efficiency of the respective units. Leaves were to be granted to all those men who had served uninterruptedly in the theater since the start of the campaign. Two leave trains per week were scheduled for each army group.

Shortage of Technicians

The armored divisions complained about the continued shortage of technicians and the weakness of their cadres. Tank and truck drivers were at a premium. Several orders were issued requesting field commanders to return technicians and specialists to the assignments for which they were trained. To relieve the manpower shortage within the theater, native units were to be activated from the prisoners of Tatar, Caucasian, Georgian, Armenian, and Cossack nationality who would probably be captured during the summer offensive. These units were to assume some of the routine duties heretofore carried out by German troops, thus permitting a more judicious employment of the latter.

Construction of Fortifications

On 26 April General Halder issued an order calling for the establishment of a defense system. In view of the general weakness of the front lines, enemy breakthroughs could be prevented only by constructing fortifications, establishing switch positions, and building specific fortified areas.

The front lines were to be fortified in depth. Switch positions were to protect the Bryansk-Kharkov line. Since there was not sufficient manpower to construct continuous lines in the rear, it would be neces-

sary to establish fortified areas that could be held for prolonged periods by weak forces against superior enemy pressure. These fortified areas were to secure important supply and communications centers, such as Melitopol, Dnepropetrovsk, Poltava, Bryansk, Roslavl, Smolensk, Nevel, Luga, Gatchina and Pskov.

By securing the most important road and rail junctions, river crossings, etc., situated between the front line and the fortified areas in the rear, the Germans could create a defense system capable of successfully withstanding any Soviet armored elements that might break through the front.

Engineer staffs were to be responsible for the construction of the fortifications. Only indigenous labor was to be used because of the shortage of German manpower. The material needed for the construction program would also have to be procured from local resources.

Oil Brigade Caucasus

The Oil Detachment Caucasus, formed in the spring of 1941, was expanded because of recent experiences with the Russian scorched-earth policy. Since the oil fields would be more severely damaged than originally presumed, the detachment was brought to a strength of 10,794 men and redesignated Oil Brigade Caucasus. The brigade was issued 1,142 vehicles and 6 planes and ordered to stand by, ready to move into the Caucasus oil fields immediately behind the combat troops.

Casualties and Replacements

At the end of the winter fighting, on 30 April 1942, total German casualties, excluding sick, numbered 1,167,835 officers and men. A number of measures to save personnel had been introduced, such as lowering the T/O strength of the infantry divisions. Nevertheless, by 31 October 1942 the estimated shortage of replacements in the Russian theater would amount to 280,000 men, even if all operations proceeded according to plan. The Organization Division believed that it would be impossible to provide sufficient replacements for all three army groups. The three solutions therefore taken under consideration at the end of April were as follows:

1. To give Army Group south its full complement of replacements, in which case the situation at Army Groups Center and North would not be relieved until July 1942;

2. To fulfill only 80 per cent of the Army Group South requirements, as a result of which the position of the other two army groups would improve considerably by July 1942; or

3. To give Army Group South its full complement and accelerate the arrival of additional replacements by transferring during May and June to each of the two other army groups 100,000 men with only two months of training.

General Halder chose the third solution, fully cognizant of the disadvantage incurred by committing replacements with only two months of training. Actually, he had little choice in the matter. The monthly report on the rehabilitation of units in the Army Group Center area during April 1942 indicated that the unabated intensity of the defensive fighting as well as the withdrawal of divisions for transfer to the West had almost completely obstructed the reorganization and rehabilitation of the units that stayed in place. In general, the divisions which were to be rehabilitated in place would have only limited mobility and reduced combat efficiency, the shortage of motor vehicles and horses being their greatest handicap.

The Participation of Germany's Allies

During the summer of 1942 Germany's allies were to play a much more significant part in the Russian theater than heretofore. In an effort to intensify their participation in the struggle against the Soviet Union, Keitel had visited Hungary and Romania during the preceding winter and Hitler had made a personal appeal to Mussolini. The Armed Forces High Command was to provide all the weapons and equipment it could spare for the allied contingents. The political differences were to be partly overcome by interspersing Italian corps or armies between Hungarian and Romanian ones. In compliance

with requests received from Germany's allies, Hitler on 15 April ordered national units to fight under the command of their own army or at least corps headquarters. This decision was to cost the Germans dearly when their allies collapsed along the Don front under the blows of the Russian counteroffensive.

To ascertain smooth cooperation at different levels of command, the German Army organized a number of liaison staffs to be attached to allied division, corps, and army headquarters. Hitler showed his continued anxiety over the morale of the allied troops a few weeks later, when he stated that Italian and other allied military achievements should be given proper credit in German news releases. Fanatical loyalty on the part of the Germans would in turn inspire their allies with similar feelings.

The Germans counted on the assistance of the following allied forces:

17. GERMAN ALLIED DIVISIONS

Allied Divisions Available for the Russian Theater (Summer 1942)

Nationality	Total	Inf.	Mtz Inf.	Armored	Cavalry	Security
Totals	52	38	4	2	3	5
Romanian	27	22	---	1	3	1
Hungarian	13	9	---	1	---	---
Italian	9	6	3	---	---	3
Slovak	2	1	1	---	---	---
Spanish	1	1	---	---	---	---

On the other hand, Hitler was unable to satisfy the requests of Generaloberst (Gen.) Erwin Rommel after his meeting with Mussolini at the beginning of April 1942. No motorized army artillery and engineer units could be made available for the North African theater before the successful conclusion of the Caucasus offensive in the autumn of 1942. By June, however, Rommel's advance into

Aside from Germany's allies, a number of European states, even some of the recently vanquished ones, offered contingents of volunteers who desired to participate in the campaign against the Soviet Union—which for a time tended to assume the characteristics of a crusade against Bolshevism. But Hitler, distrusting his former enemies, reluctantly permitted only a limited number of Frenchmen to serve in national units up to regimental strength. Party political considerations induced him to transfer the responsibility for organizing foreign military volunteer units from Army to National Socialist Party (Waffen–SS) control.

Rear Area Security

Anxious to secure the lines of communications of the combat forces, General Halder decided that three German security divisions plus Hungarian and Romanian troops were to follow behind the advance. Each security division was to be composed of one infantry and one security regiment, one motorized military police, one artillery, and one signal battalion, as well as one Cossack troop. Military administrative headquarters and prisoner of war processing units were to be formed in addition.

Army Group South's Defense Line

One of the problems that constantly preoccupied Hitler during the preparatory period was the exposed flank that would extend from Voronezh to the area northeast of Kursk. The Fuehrer ordered this defense line amply provided with antitank guns. A total of 350-400 self-propelled 75-mm antitank guns—more than half of them captured French weapons—and some 150 captured Russian 76-mm guns were to be distributed along this front to repel Soviet medium and heavy tanks. Tractors and captured prime movers were to be employed to give a certain degree of mobility to those guns which were not self-propelled.

Egypt seemed so promising that Hitler suddenly decided to divert to North Africa a number of tanks, trucks, and weapons which had been reserved for the rehabilitation of two Russian-theater divisions.

The Role of Army Group A

The new Army Group A was to be formed under the command of Field Marshal Wilhelm List. To prevent premature discovery of the German intentions by the Russians, the arrival of all higher headquarters in the assembly areas was to be delayed to the last possible moment. The Army High Command was to control the movements of all Army Group A and Fourth Panzer Army units as well as those of the army and corps troops.

The cover names given to each of the Army Group A units were to convey the impression that they were engaged in fortification work. List himself was not to arrive in the theater until shortly before the start of operations. The forward echelon of his headquarters was transferred to Poltava on 12 May, the remaining elements were to arrive at Stalino later in May. By approximately 15 June, when the first phase of Operation BLAU was to be launched, Army Group A headquarters was to be ready to secretly assume command over the Eleventh and Seventeenth Armies, and possibly over the First Panzer Army. The overt assumption of command was to take place shortly afterward.

Feint and Counterfeint

At the beginning of May 1942 Molotov flew to Great Britain and the United States, where he was promised that a second front would be opened before the end of the year. On 2 May a news agency report from Moscow indicated that the Russians were expecting a German spring offensive launched from the Bryansk-Orel-Kursk area. The probable objective was Voronezh, after which the German troops would advance down the Don to seize Stalingrad, while other German forces thrusting from the Kharkov region would advance eastward.

This news report must have produced a certain effect, since only five days later the Chief of the Armed Forces Operations Staff issued a new directive concerning deception. Referring to the previous directive on the same subject dated 12 February 1942, Jodl divided the period before the start of Operation BLAU into two phases.

During the first phase, which was to last up to 25 May, the existing uncertainty with regard to the true German intentions was to be increased, and the preparations and movements for Operation BLAU were to be dissimulated by showing no point of main effort. Since some of the troops needed for the preliminary operations around the Izyum salient were to assemble behind Army Group Center, the Russians would have difficulty in recognizing the objective of the next major offensive. To German units the troop movements were to be explained as a series of simple exchanges of battle-weary divisions from the Russian theater for fresh divisions from the West. The rehabilitation of numerous divisions had long been overdue. As soon as the preliminary operations got under way, maps of the Moscow area up to the middle Volga were to be distributed to the Luftwaffe units.

The second phase was to start after 25 May. By that time the Russians would be at least partly aware of the German distribution of forces. If their attention was drawn away from Army Group South toward Army Group Center, it might be possible to deceive them with regard to the real German main effort and objective. This deception was to be achieved by replacing German units with allied ones at the front, thus simulating a weakening at a point where in reality strength was being built up. An attack on Moscow was to be simulated by assembling some of the attack forces at the boundary between Army Groups South and Center. By intensifying reconnaissance activities along sectors of the Army Groups Center and North fronts one might simulate offensive intentions. Other means suggested were deceptive radio traffic and supply activities; the formation of fictitious staffs; night march movements of rear elements of security divisions; the erection of dummy planes on airfields in the Army Group Center area; rumors spread by military attachés assigned to neutral countries; the planting of articles in military magazines published in neutral countries, in which special emphasis was placed on Moscow's significance as the center of Russian resistance, as the traffic hub, and the key to armament production, indicating that after the loss of Moscow the Red Army would be unable to offer active resistance west of the Volga.

To judge by the results, the net effect of these deceptive measures was disappointing, since on 16 June another news agency report from Moscow contained details concerning the German intentions and came very close to the real plans.

Warning Notes (May 1942)

Some hesitancy regarding the success of the German summer offensive was expressed by Jodl on 10 May when he stated to one of his associates that Operation BLAU was very risky because of the weakness of Army Groups Center and North. The Russians might try a stab at Smolensk even though it was doubtful that they could muster sufficient manpower and daring for such a venture. A little later Hitler agreed with Jodl that, once the Russian offensive in the south got under way, all available Russian forces would automatically be diverted to the south.

The Army felt much stronger on the same subject. In a report, submitted on 12 May in reply to a request for a survey of its potential strength in 1942, Halder struck some warning notes. The contents of this report are so revealing that it is presented here in an only slightly edited version.

The Armed Forces Potential in the Spring of 1942

1. Introduction

In the summer of 1942 the organization and potential of the German military establishment were to be geared to war against the Anglo-Saxon powers. This reorientation, based on a decision made in July 1941, gave the Luftwaffe and Navy priority over the Army.

By the late autumn of 1941 developments in the Russian theater made it obvious that, as a requisite for concentrating all efforts against the British, the USSR would first have to be decisively beaten in 1942. For this purpose the entire German war machine had to be reversed and redirected toward rehabilitating and strengthening the Army.

The effects of this reorientation in the armament effort would not, however, make themselves felt to the Army during 1942. Other factors that were also detrimental to the effectiveness of the ground forces were as follows:

a. The long duration of the winter battles with the resulting high attrition of materiel.

b. The unusual cold which affected production and communications.

c. The increasing shortage of raw materials and manpower.

The combined effects of these factors would have to be taken into account in assessing the true strength of the German forces in the spring of 1942.

2. Overall Numerical Strength

18. GERMAN DIVISIONS

Date	Total	Inf.*	Mtz. Inf.**	Armored	Security	Replacement***
1 Sep 41	210	148	15	21	26	31
1 May 42	225	158	16	25	26	31

*Including light, mountain, and fortress divisions.
**Including a transformed horse cavalry division and several 88 divisions.
***In the Zone of Interior and occupied territories.

The purely numerical increase in the number of divisions during the eight months from 1 September 1941 to 1 May 1942 was therefore 15 divisions plus an insignificant number of army and corps troops. A considerable part of these forces had been diverted to Norway and North Africa during the winter of 1941–42.

3. Manpower

Although 1,100,000 replacements—excluding hospitalized personnel returned to duty within the theater—were transferred to the Russian theater from 22 June 1941 to 1 May 1942, the infantry divisions of Army Group South were at approximately 50 percent of their prescribed strength, those of the other two army groups at 35 percent. By the beginning of the offensive the infantry divisions in the south were to be at full strength, while those of the other army groups were to be brought to 55 percent by August 1942.

Other factors to be considered were that experienced commissioned and noncommissioned officers who became casualties could not be adequately replaced for the time being; that the combat efficiency of the armored and motorized divisions was reduced because of the shortage of trained technicians and specialists; that differences in age, training, and experience both within and among units led to an overall reduction in combat efficiency compared to the preinvasion ground forces; and that the mental strain caused by the exertions of the past winter was bound to show its effect. On the other hand, there were also a few positive factors, such as the availability of a cadre of experienced officers and men for training replacements and the existence of a relatively efficient supply system. Everything would depend upon how much time the Russians allowed the German troops for rehabilitation and rest.

4. Firepower

a. Artillery. Because of the high rate of attrition in the Russian theater, the demands of all three army groups could not be fully satisfied in addition to fitting out newly formed units and rehabilitating wornout ones. The divisions of Army Group South would be brought up to their T/E allowances by the start of the offensive, but the other two army groups would have only three guns per artillery battery.

b. Tanks. In accordance with previous plans each armored division of Army Group South would have three tank battalions and each motorized infantry division one. The panzer divisions of the two other army groups, however, would have only one tank battalion each. At the start of the summer offensive the Germans would have 3,300 tanks in the Russian theater against 3,350 on 22 June 1941. The 1942 tanks were better armed than the ones with which Germany invaded the Soviet Union the previous year.

c. Antitank weapons. A considerable number of 37- and 50-mm antitank guns had been lost during the winter fighting, but these losses would be compensated for by the use of heavier caliber captured French and Russian guns. By introducing better guns, hollow-charge and antitank rifle grenades, etc., the defense against tanks would gradually be strengthened. Mines were available in sufficient quantities.

d. Antiaircraft Units. Only the spearhead divisions would have organic antiaircraft units. In general, however, the commitment of numerous corps and army flak battalions had improved overall antiaircraft protection. With operations extending over wide areas, the antiaircraft units would have to be spread very thinly.

e. Ammunition. The retrenchment on ammunition production imposed during the summer of 1941 and the high rate of expenditure of the following winter had led to a shortage of heavy-weapons, howitzer, and antitank ammunition, which was expected to continue through the autumn of 1942. By August 1942 shortages might affect operations. In this estimate the possibility of an increased expenditure before the outset of the offensive had not been taken into account. Expedients, such as imposing expenditure quotas and arranging for ammunition transfers from the West, had already been introduced.

5. Transportation

The heavy attrition of motor vehicles suffered during the winter battles—75,000 vehicles lost against the arrival of only 7,500 vehicle replacements for the period 1 November 1941–15 March 1942—complicated the effort of restoring full mobility to the ground forces by the start of the summer offensive. Current production was insufficient for both replacing past losses and equipping new units. Only the spearhead divisions would receive new vehicles. At the same time, most of the infantry divisions would be deprived of their motor vehicles and the motorized units in other sectors would be faced with a reduction in their organic vehicle allowance. Since spare parts production and repair installations would be incapable of fully satisfying the demands made by far-reaching offensive operations, whatever stocks and facilities were available would have to be diverted to the spearhead units.

To make matters even worse, there was an acute shortage of horses. During the winter 180,000 horses had died from hunger and exposure as well as enemy action, with only 20,000 replacements arriving in the theater. Although 109,000 horses had been shipped from the Zone of Interior by 1 May and another 118,000 had been requisitioned from occupied countries, the number of horses available by the start of the offensive would still be insufficient.

In summarizing the transportation picture, the Army estimated that the spearhead divisions in the south would have 85 per cent of their organic motor vehicle allowance by the time the offensive got under way. The infantry divisions would be restricted in their movements because of an almost complete lack of motor vehicles. Major operations in the other army group areas could be effected only along rail lines having adequate capacity. In any event, the logistical support that could be given to Army Groups Center and North during the summer would not be sufficient for conducting extensive operations.

6. Reserves

No further reserves would be available in the Zone of Interior. The unavailability of trained manpower and up-to-date equipment would prevent the activation of new divisions. Any replacements, weapons, and equipment that would become available during the course of the summer offensive would be needed to make up current losses. No further increase in the number of divisions was possible since the 18-year olds had already been inducted. Additional motorized and armored divisions could be activated only by disbanding existing infantry units.

7. Summary

A full rehabilitation of the German forces in the Russian theater before the start of the 1942 offensive would not be feasible. Personnel and materiel shortages hampered every effort to obtain greater mobility and raise combat efficiency. These shortages as well as the wear and tear on man, beast, and vehicle caused by the winter fighting seemed to have reduced the stamina of the German Army.

Halder's report revealed that the German ground forces that were to launch the summer offensive of 1942 could not compare with the troops that had invaded Russia a year earlier. The spearhead divisions would be almost up to strength, but the followup infantry was weak and slow, and no reserves were available. No wonder the Army High Command felt apprehensive about executing Hitler's overambitious plans. An equally somber note was struck by the Organization Division of the Army High Command in its memorandum to the Chief of the Armed Forces Operations Staff, dated 27 May 1942.

In reporting on the composition and condition of the Army Group South units by the beginning of the summer offensive, the Organization Division repeated that only part of the personnel and materiel losses suffered during the winter could be replaced. For this reason, all available replacements had been channeled to the spearhead divisions and the T/O & E's of numerous units had been modified to redistribute manpower and equipment. Two types of units had been created: highly effective attack forces and units having little punch or mobility.

Of the 65–67 German divisions that were to participate in the offensive in the south, only 21–23 were either being newly activated or fully rehabilitated behind the front, whereas the remaining 44 divisions were to be rehabilitated while committed at the front. Each of the fully rehabilitated infantry divisions would receive 1,000 replacements with only two months of training. The mobility of these divisions would be limited because they were short of horses and lacked most of their organic motor vehicles. The reconnaissance battalions were now equipped with bicycles. Contrary to previous reports, the spearhead divisions would have only about 80 percent of their organic motor vehicles.

In revising the distribution of forces greater consideration would have to be given to the unequal strength and mobility of the different divisions. Since no reserves of manpower or equipment were available, the rehabilitation of units would have to be accomplished with insufficiently trained men and untested equipment coming directly from the assembly lines. The possibility of forming strategic reserves before or during the course of the initial operations appeared unlikely.

The report further stated that German desertions had dropped sharply with the beginning of spring weather after having reached an alarming rate during the winter fighting.

Three preliminary operations were to take place before the launching of Operation BLAU. The first one, the seizure of the Kerch Peninsula, started on 8 May. Under Manstein's brilliant leadership, Eleventh Army forces soon began to clear the peninsula against strong resistance. The second operation, directed against the Izyum salient, was given the code designation FRIDERICUS. According to the German plan, the ground forces needed for the elimination of the Russian salient were to be assembled by 17 May. Five days earlier, however, the Red Army launched a strong spoiling attack south and east of Kharkov against the right of Sixth Army. This Russian drive threatened the entire logistical buildup for Operation BLAU because it was directed at the extensive depot and repair facilities in the Kharkov area, which were vital to the German supply system. The Russian maneuver also disrupted the rehabilitation of the spearhead units, since the threat to Kharkov led to a change in priorities and a diversion of tanks and self-propelled antitank guns to the danger area.

As soon as the fighting in the Izyum salient had taken a favorable course, Hitler withdrew some of the air support units from this area and committed them for the defense of Kharkov. By 13 May the situation around that city had grown so serious that the Fuehrer ordered the transfer of additional Luftwaffe contingents from the Crimea. He also decided to advance the date of the attack on the Izyum salient, originally scheduled for 18 May. In Hitler's opinion this counterthrust would be the most effective and fastest method of assisting Sixth Army in the defense of Kharkov. One of the most disquieting facts about the Russian attack was that, for the first time since the start of the campaign, the Red Army committed its armor in mass formation, thus copying the hitherto successful German tactics.

On 17 May—a day earlier than scheduled—two corps of Seventeenth Army forming the southern arm of the Izyum pincers jumped off, while the forces that were to compose the northern arm were still being assembled. During the first three days the German countermove did little to relieve the defenders of Kharkov. It was not until 20 May that the acute danger at Kharkov seemed to have passed. The effect of the Russian spoiling attack was to be felt throughout

107

the remaining weeks before the start of Operation BLAU, mainly because of the changes in schedule that became necessary.

Russian resistance on the Kerch Peninsula collapsed by 19 May. Five days later Hitler decided that the siege of Sevastopol, scheduled as the third and last preliminary operation, was to start on 7 June and the first phase of Operation BLAU eight days later. Under these circumstances the air support units would have to be withdrawn from the Izyum area by 6 June to assist the attack forces in the Crimea. After only three days in that part of the theater, the Luftwaffe contingents would have to be redeployed to the assembly area for Operation BLAU, where they had to arrive by 10 June at the latest. Considerations of wear and tear on planes and crews apparently did not enter the calculations on which this tight schedule was based.

On 28 May Halder suggested a change in the timing and execution of the preliminary attacks. He wanted to continue the successful German counterattack northeast of Kharkov in the Volchansk area first, leaving the Izyum salient to be eliminated next. By applying this procedure, the Russian forces would be systematically destroyed and the preliminary operations would be more directly related to the offensive proper. Hitler approved Halder's ideas in principle but decided to investigate the situation on the spot.

On 1 June the Fuehrer and a small staff flew to Army Group South headquarters at Poltava. Field Marshal von Bock and the field commanders whose troops had been directly involved in the battle for Kharkov reported on the situation, whereupon Hitler explained his ideas on the continuation of operations. Advantage would have to be taken of the extremely favorable developments around Kharkov by destroying the Russian forces near Volchansk and Izyum as quickly as possible. The principle to be applied was that "whatever forces could be annihilated now, would not be there to interfere with Operation BLAU," even if the practical application of this idea implied some change in plans.

On the basis of additional information provided by Bock, the Fuehrer decided that the preliminary operations would be executed according to a revised schedule, even if Operation BLAU had to be delayed. The new schedule was as follows:

a. The attack on the Volchansk area was to take place on 7 June.

b. The assault on Sevastopol was to begin on the same day.

c. The attack on the Izyum salient was to be launched on or after 12 June.

d. Operation BLAU on or before 20 June.

As it turned out the Volchansk operation had to be delayed because of bad weather. The assaults on Sevastopol started on time, but made little progress despite intensive preparatory fire and air force bombardments lasting five days. Because of the strong resistance encountered at Sevastopol, Hitler reversed his previous decision and did not withdraw the air support units after only three days. By 19 June some of the outer defenses of the fortress had been breached.

The Izyum operation had meanwhile taken a very favorable course, and by 25 June the First Panzer Army reached the Oskol River, thus cutting off the salient from Kupyansk to a point near Izyum, at the confluence of Oskol and Donets. The operation had been brought to a successful conclusion, and the pocket was being mopped up.

The Russians were meanwhile transporting reinforcements to Sevastopol by submarine. The fortress was still holding out, and its capture before the end of June seemed unlikely. As soon as Sevastopol did fall, a number of Eleventh Army divisions and all the heavy siege batteries would become available for another mission which Hitler considered as the second major objective of 1942: the seizure of Leningrad, permitting a link up with the Finns.

While these preliminary operations took place in the Army Group South area, Army Group Center units were engaged in a see-saw struggle in the rear areas of Fourth and Ninth Armies, which lasted throughout the spring. During the second half of June, Fourth Army finally got the upper hand and succeeded in wiping out a number of partisan and regular troop units in its rear. Around Velikiye Luki, however, the situation remained serious.

Army Group North had reduced and mopped up most of the Volkhov pocket, thus disposing of this threat near Leningrad. The German forces in the Demyansk pocket had been relieved by the end of

April, but the Ostashkov breach remained an open sore along the army group boundary.

During May 1942 Army Group Center had suffered fewer casualties than Army Group South in the Kerch and Kharkov fighting or Army Group North along the Volkhov and near Demyansk. The replacements transferred from the Zone of Interior during June were distributed as follows:

Total	130,000
Army Group North	25,000
Army Group Center	45,000
Army Group South	60,000

This left 7,000 replacements at the disposal of the Army High Command.

Last-Minute Incidents and Impressions (June 1942)

Approximately 10 days before the intended start of the summer offensive—19 June—the operations officer of the 23d Panzer Division, which was to participate in the crucial breakthrough west of Voronezh, flew to the front, taking with him a number of highly classified documents in violation of existing security regulations. He crash-landed in Russian-held territory, and the documents, which included a corps order outlining the entire attack plan for the first phase, had disappeared when a German patrol recovered his body three days later. Hitler relieved of command a number of officers whom he held responsible for this incident.

With this plan in Russian hands, the element of surprise was bound to have been lost during the crucial initial phase. Since a change in plans was no longer feasible because of the advanced season, the operation either had to be executed according to the plan or cancelled. Hitler decided to go ahead as planned.

This decision may have been partly motivated by his low opinion of the Red Army in 1942. During the daily situation conference on 25 June he stated that approximately 80 Soviet divisions had been destroyed during the preliminary operations. Russian resistance was much weaker than during the preceding year. The various phases of Operation BLAU would therefore be executed faster and easier than hitherto assumed by the Army planners. It might not even be necessary to commit all the armor earmarked for the second phase of the operation, and two of the armored divisions could perhaps be diverted to cut off the Sukhinichi salient in the Army Group Center area.

While the Fuehrer anticipated developments in Russia with so much optimism, he seemed worried about the possibility of Allied landing attempts in the West. The German defensive forces were too weak to interdict mass landings of parachute and glider troops. Hitler felt that some of the armored divisions, which were to return to the Russian theater after rehabilitation in the West, would have to stay on to reinforce the Atlantic defense system. He seemed to believe that he could defeat the Red Army without them.

The Army judged the situation more soberly: on 26 June Halder reported that the Russians were withdrawing troops along the entire front to form reserves. Moreover, they were suddenly launching massed air attacks against German troops moving into assembly areas near Kursk.

X

INITIAL OPERATIONS AND NEW PLANS (JULY 1942)

The First Phase (28 June–6 July 1942)

By 27 June those German forces that were to participate in the first phase of the summer offensive had moved into their assembly areas according to schedule. On the next day Fourth Panzer Army and Second Army jumped off with forces consisting of three armored, three motorized, and nine infantry divisions. Four Hungarian divisions covered the southern flank; in addition two German and six Hungarian divisions, constituting the reserves, were still enroute.

The mission of the spearhead divisions was to break through to Voronezh. [See map 16.] The infantry divisions were then to build up strong flank protection along a line extending from Livny to Voronezh, while the motorized forces were to thrust southeastward along the Don River. The forces available for this operation were none too strong. The protection of the Livny—Voronezh sector—about 100 miles wide—would divert most of the German infantry divisions, with the Hungarians taking over the defense of the Don south of Voronezh.

From the very first day of the offensive the Russians launched counterattacks, committing numerous armored brigades whose presence had not been discovered by German intelligence. Sizeable Russian forces were detraining in the Yelets area.

By 2 July the German spearheads were at the outskirts of Voronezh. The city fell after four days of furious fighting, during which the divisions of Fourth Panzer Army became more heavily engaged than Hitler had thought necessary. The first phase of the offensive was completed on that day, with flank protection being secured between Livny and Voronezh.

The Second Phase (30 June –7 July 1942)

During the second phase the Sixth Army forces, consisting of 2 armored, 1 motorized, and 16 infantry divisions, jumped off from the area northeast of Kharkov, crossed the Oskol River, and linked up with the armored spearheads of Fourth Panzer Army on the upper course of the Valuy River. The maneuver was completed by 7 July. To gain sufficient time for establishing defensive positions along the Don, the Russians had fought a series of delaying actions west of the river. In isolated instances, such as east of Kupyansk and opposite the first German bridgeheads across the Oskol, they seemed determined to make a temporary stand. Although some Soviet forces had been enveloped during the course of the German advance, few prisoners and little booty had fallen into German hands. In general, the offensive had thus far proceeded according to expectation.

The German personnel shortage induced Halder to send a memorandum to Army Group South on 2 July, requesting the latter to provide a new type of information. He first explained that current operations of Army Group South were conducted almost without reserves echeloned in depth. Because of the long distances to be covered to reach the objectives, this shortage of forces could have grave consequences unless the Army High Command knew at all times the strength, condition, and casualties of all units, particularly the armored ones. Only with this on hand could the Army High Command properly accomplish its functions.

Changes in the German Order of Battle (July 1942)

The first two phases of the offensive had been directed by Field Marshal von Bock, whose command, Army Group South, was redesignated Army Group B on 9 July. [See chart 4.] Four days later Bock was replaced by Generaloberst (Gen.) Maximilian von Weichs, the former commander of Second Army, ostensibly because of Hitler's dissatisfaction with Bock's conduct of the Voronezh operation. In reality Hitler wanted to tighten his control over the conduct of the German summer offensive.

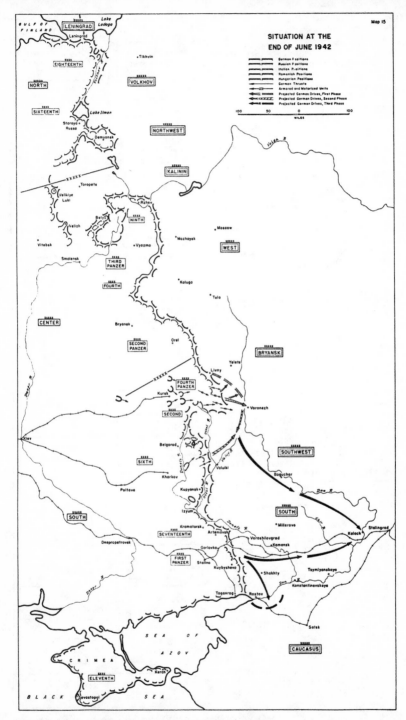

Map 15. SITUATION, End of June 1942   111

19. GERMAN ORDER OF BATTLE, Beginning of July 1942

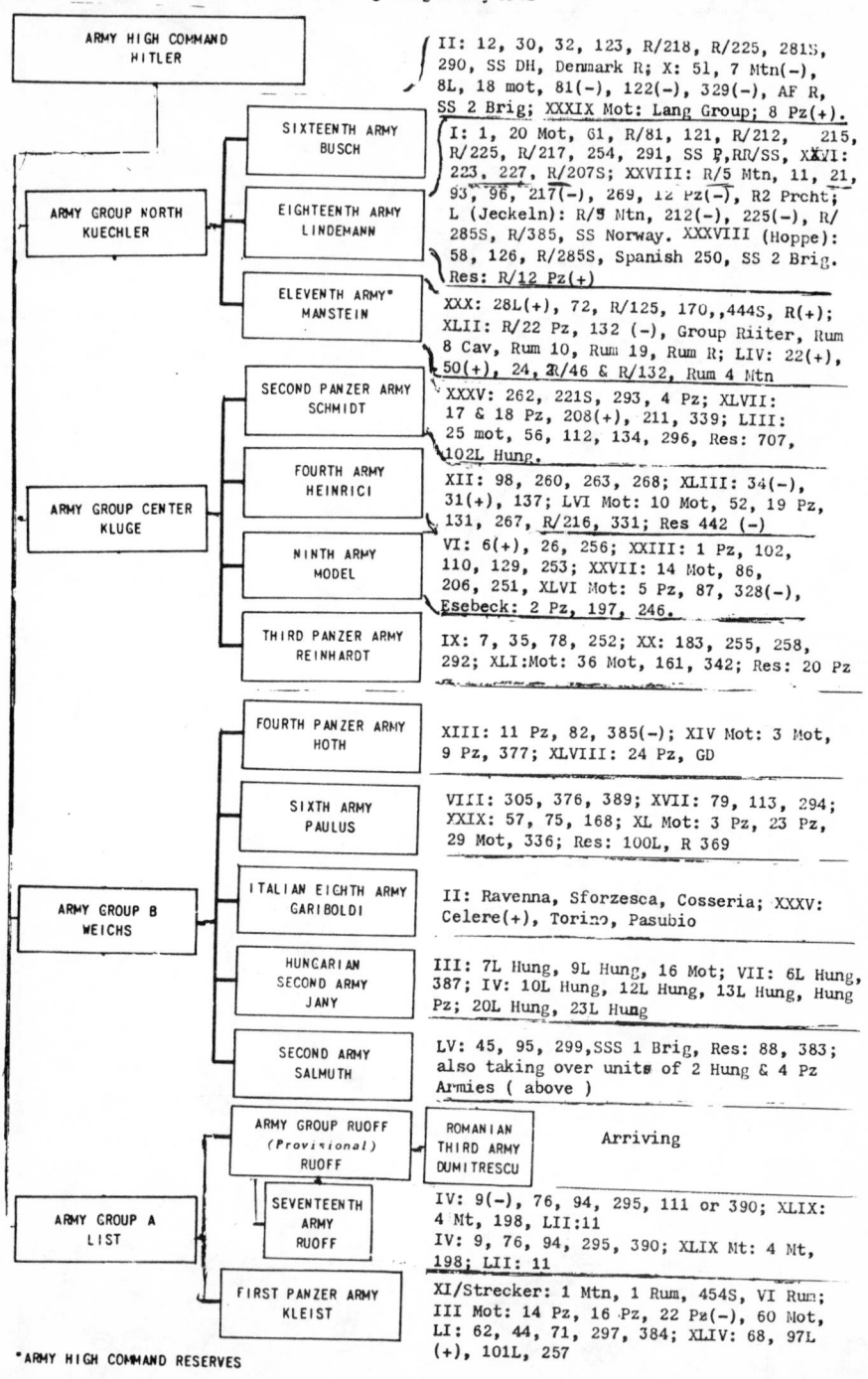

ARMY HIGH COMMAND HITLER

II: 12, 30, 32, 123, R/218, R/225, 281S, 290, SS DH, Denmark R; X: 51, 7 Mtn(-), 8L, 18 mot, 81(-), 122(-), 329(-), AF R, SS 2 Brig; XXXIX Mot: Lang Group; 8 Pz(+).

ARMY GROUP NORTH KUECHLER

SIXTEENTH ARMY BUSCH

I: 1, 20 Mot, 61, R/81, 121, R/212, 215, R/225, R/217, 254, 291, SS P,RR/SS, XXVI: 223, 227, R/207S; XXVIII: R/5 Mtn, 11, 21, 93, 96, 217(-), 269, 12 Pz(-), R2 Prcht; L (Jeckeln): R/5 Mtn, 212(-), 225(-), R/285S, R/385, SS Norway. XXXVIII (Hoppe): 58, 126, R/285S, Spanish 250, SS 2 Brig. Res: R/12 Pz(+)

EIGHTEENTH ARMY LINDEMANN

ELEVENTH ARMY* MANSTEIN

XXX: 28L(+), 72, R/125, 170,,444S, R(+); XLII: R/22 Pz, 132 (-), Group Riiter, Rum 8 Cav, Rum 10, Rum 19, Rum R; LIV: 22(+), 50(+), 24, R/46 & R/132, Rum 4 Mtn

ARMY GROUP CENTER KLUGE

SECOND PANZER ARMY SCHMIDT

XXXV: 262, 221S, 293, 4 Pz; XLVII: 17 & 18 Pz, 208(+), 211, 339; LIII: 25 mot, 56, 112, 134, 296, Res: 707, 102L Hung.

FOURTH ARMY HEINRICI

XII: 98, 260, 263, 268; XLIII: 34(-), 31(+), 137; LVI Mot: 10 Mot, 52, 19 Pz, 131, 267, R/216, 331; Res 442 (-)

NINTH ARMY MODEL

VI: 6(+), 26, 256; XXIII: 1 Pz, 102, 110, 129, 253; XXVII: 14 Mot, 86, 206, 251, XLVI Mot: 5 Pz, 87, 328(-), Esebeck: 2 Pz, 197, 246.

THIRD PANZER ARMY REINHARDT

IX: 7, 35, 78, 252; XX: 183, 255, 258, 292; XLI:Mot: 36 Mot, 161, 342; Res: 20 Pz

FOURTH PANZER ARMY HOTH

XIII: 11 Pz, 82, 385(-); XIV Mot: 3 Mot, 9 Pz, 377; XLVIII: 24 Pz, GD

SIXTH ARMY PAULUS

VIII: 305, 376, 389; XVII: 79, 113, 294; XXIX: 57, 75, 168; XL Mot: 3 Pz, 23 Pz, 29 Mot, 336; Res: 100L, R 369

ARMY GROUP B WEICHS

ITALIAN EIGHTH ARMY GARIBOLDI

II: Ravenna, Sforzesca, Cosseria; XXXV: Celere(+), Torino, Pasubio

HUNGARIAN SECOND ARMY JANY

III: 7L Hung, 9L Hung, 16 Mot; VII: 6L Hung, 387; IV: 10L Hung, 12L Hung, 13L Hung, Hung Pz; 20L Hung, 23L Hung

SECOND ARMY SALMUTH

LV: 45, 95, 299,SSS 1 Brig, Res: 88, 383; also taking over units of 2 Hung & 4 Pz Armies (above)

ARMY GROUP RUOFF (Provisional) RUOFF

ROMANIAN THIRD ARMY DUMITRESCU

Arriving

ARMY GROUP A LIST

SEVENTEENTH ARMY RUOFF

IV: 9(-), 76, 94, 295, 111 or 390; XLIX: 4 Mt, 198, LII:11
IV: 9, 76, 94, 295, 390; XLIX Mt: 4 Mt, 198; LII: 11

FIRST PANZER ARMY KLEIST

XI/Strecker: 1 Mtn, 1 Rum, 454S, VI Rum; III Mot: 14 Pz, 16 Pz, 22 Pz(-), 60 Mot, LI: 62, 44, 71, 297, 384; XLIV: 68, 97L (+), 101L, 257

*ARMY HIGH COMMAND RESERVES

The first group of officers appointed to the staff of Army Group A arrived in Poltava at the end of May. When the new headquarters assumed control at the beginning of July, a forward echelon moved to Stalino, where the future headquarters of the army group was to be established. From the outset the command net broke down repeatedly because the signal troops were insufficiently trained.

The Army Group A Offensive

The Operation Plan

Army Group A was to intervene during the third phase. Its forces were to jump off from the Taganrog-Artemovsk area, break through the Russian lines, and drive eastward across the Donets River as far as the Don bend, where they were to link up with the Sixth Army and Fourth Panzer Army spearheads driving down the Don. By this maneuver the Russians were to be trapped in the Don bend. Some allied forces were to provide flank protection—the Italians on both sides of Boguchar, the Romanians along the sector adjacent to the east. Other army group elements were to thrust southward, envelop Rostov, and establish bridgeheads south of the Don.

The Russian *Southwest*, *South* and *Caucasus Fronts* were commanded by Marshal Timoshenko, whose headquarters was in Stalingrad. Intelligence reports indicated that the defeats and losses suffered during the spring of 1942 seemed to have had little effect on the performance of the Russians. To explain the Russian soldier's attitude one had to understand his way of thinking in terms of tangible evidence. Since he ate better rations, saw more and more comrades joining him in combat, and noticed the relative stability of his sector, he probably felt that a definite change for the better had taken place since the last year's disastrous defeats.

Total German casualties for June had been slightly lower than those suffered in May, but higher by 10,000 than expected by the Army High Command. Approximately 157,000 reinforcements had arrived in the Russian theater, exceeding the number of losses by about 31,000 men.

In calculating future manpower distribution quotas for August, it was estimated that 70,000 replacements would be available in August 1942. Of this total 4,000 men would be needed in northern Finland, 10,000 for activating a special desert unit and as replacements for Rommel's casualties in North Africa, and 9,000 to make up for the July deficits of First Panzer and Seventeenth Armies. Of the remaining 47,000 men, 15,000 would go to Army Group A, 10,000 to Army Group B, 14,000 to Army Group Center, and 8,000 to Army Group North. In view of the scope of the summer offensive the Army Groups A and B quotas were not too reassuring.

On 1 July 1942 the total strength of the German Army field forces, including civilians with assimilated ranks, was 3,948,200; the number of officers included in this figure was 150,100.

The Army Group A Attack

On 7 July Field Marshal List assumed command of Army Group A, composed of the First Panzer, Eleventh, and Seventeenth Armies. Two days later his newly formed army group launched its attack with First Panzer Army thrusting toward Voroshilovgrad. The advance proceeded according to schedule. On 11 July an order signed by Timoshenko was captured. In it Timoshenko instructed his unit commanders to halt the German offensive by using delaying tactics. Since the Germans considered the Russian lower command echelon incapable of executing such a complicated mission, Army Group A issued orders to hit the Russians wherever they bogged down during the retreat and to seize as much of their materiel as possible.

By 13 July Army Group A had made such good progress that Hitler wanted to initiate the southward thrust toward the Caucasus. He therefore instructed List to advance southward in the direction of Konstantinovskaya, seize the Don-crossing facilities in that city and at Tsymlyanskaya, envelop the Russian forces west of the Donets and south of the Don by thrusting westward to Rostov, and cut off the Salsk-Stalingrad rail line. To carry out these missions Fourth Panzer Army and one infantry corps were transferred from Army Group B to Army Group A. The infantry divisions of Army Group A were to move up in forced marches so that they could assist the armored spearheads in preventing a Russian withdrawal.

Army Group B was to provide flank and rear protection for this maneuver by moving the Italian Eighth Army via Millerovo to the middle Don and covering the Chir River. On 15 July air reconnaissance information indicated that the Russians were speeding up the evacuation of the Donets Basin and were withdrawing south and southeastward.

German and Russian Weaknesses

Even before mid-July a shortage of POL began to hamper the movements of the spearhead divisions of Army Group B. Airlift operations were under consideration when, on 15 July, Fourth Panzer Army reported that its further progress would be assured by the capture of sizeable quantities of gasoline. Soon afterward, however, the Germans discovered that the dump they had seized intact contained only about 200 tons of fuel, not even enough to fill the tanks of one weak armored division.

By contrast, the First Panzer Army still had sufficient gasoline to continue its advance as scheduled. The Russian units opposing this army were disorganized; recently captured prisoners originated from as many as 30 different divisions and brigades. A tendency toward mass desertion became manifest at various points, such as at Millerovo, where 1 officer deserted with 500 enlisted men. Prisoner interrogation reports conveyed the impression that the Russian command had lost control in certain areas and that the confusion in the enemy ranks was spreading.

The Russian retreat was directed southward behind the Don with men and equipment crossing the river by ferries and across emergency bridges. At the same time trains out of Stalingrad were moving fresh troops westward. To counteract this maneuver Fourth Panzer Army was ordered to drive straight toward Konstantinovskaya. The army was to protect its flank in the Millerovo area and east of the lower Donets.

Directive No. 43

On 11 July Hitler issued Directive No. 43 which dealt with the German flank attack from the Crimea across the Kerch Strait into the Caucasus. After mopping up the Kerch Peninsula and Sevastopol—the latter had fallen on 1 July after a surprise landing of German assault detachments north of the fortress—Eleventh Army was to make preparations for crossing the Kerch Strait by early August.

Strong units were to land in the rear of the enemy's coastal fortifications and capture the ports of Anapa and Novorossiysk, thus depriving the Russians of these two naval bases. Most of the Eleventh Army forces were then to advance along the northern slopes of the Caucasus and seize the Maikop oil fields. A secondary thrust along the coastal highway via Tuapse was to be envisaged.

The Navy was to prepare crossing facilities, support the landing forces, and—together with the Luftwaffe—protect the operations from interference by the Russian Black Sea fleet. As part of the preparatory measures the Luftwaffe was to neutralize the Russian harbor installations and naval forces in the Black Sea. During the operation the Air Force was to give direct support to the landing forces. The possibility of employing airborne troops was to be taken into consideration.

An attempt to deceive the Russians was to be made by pretending that strong Eleventh Army forces were being shifted into the area north of the Sea of Azov. Counterintelligence agents were to parachute into the Maikop area to protect the oil fields, execute sabotage missions against the railroad lines leading to the Taman Peninsula, and destroy harbor and coastal installations.

Five days after issuing this directive Hitler moved to his newly established headquarters in the Ukraine, situated in a small triangular woods 10 miles northeast of Vinnitsa along the highway to Zhitomir. Hitler, his intimates, and his military staff—the field echelon of the Armed Forces Operations Staff—were billeted in log cabins and prefabricated barracks. The Army High Command set up its field headquarters in Vinnitsa proper.

The Continuation of Operations

On 16 July a conference of Army Group A commanders, their chiefs of staff, and the chief of staff of Fourth Air Force took place at Gorlovka. In his introductory remarks List stated that the advance had proceeded much faster than anticipated, since the army group forces had already reached the Don.

He also revealed that First Panzer Army, which had jumped off with 40 percent of its prescribed strength, now had only approximately 30 percent. There was no overall reduction in tank strength, because current losses were being replaced from new production. Each division of First Panzer Army had one tank battalion. Whereas the German divisions of Seventeenth Army were considered good, the Italian ones—with the exception of one classified as "quite good"—had not yet been involved in any fighting. This army had no non-organic artillery units and was particularly anxious to receive some self-propelled assault guns. Four of the Fourth Panzer Army divisions were considered good, two very good. Their automotive equipment was very poor, and it was solely by expedients that the army kept rolling.

List then outlined his plan for future operations: the spearhead divisions of First Panzer Army were to cross the Donets near Kamensk and turn southward to Shakhty; some of the infantry units were to follow the course of the Donets and advance in a southeastward direction to protect the flank of the Fourth Panzer Army. The latter was to cross the Don near Konstantinovskaya and pivot west or southwestward according to the situation prevailing at that time. Infantry divisions were to follow with a minimum of delay to protect the army flank north of the Don, their deployment depending on developments in the Stalingrad area. On 18 July the Seventeenth Army was to launch an eastward or southeastward attack from the Kuybyshevo area. The double purpose of this attack was to tie down the Russians and close in on Rostov as soon as possible.

By 19 July the Russians were withdrawing the bulk of their forces toward Rostov. They covered their retreat by leaving strong rear guards, particularly opposite the right of Seventeenth Army. List intended to throw an ever-tightening ring around Rostov while

Fourth Panzer Army forces were to send two armored corps across the Don and form bridgeheads as soon as possible. Their task was complicated by the fact that, when they finally reached the Don at the confluence of the Donets, the bridges had been blown and the Russians were entrenched on the south bank of the river. According to an intelligence estimate dated 18 July the Russians had been able to withdraw two-thirds of their infantry strength across the Don. No figures regarding the armored brigades were available. By that date the total number of prisoners taken by Army Group A was 54,000. Because of the disorganization and loss of material caused by the withdrawal, the combat strength of the Russian units had dropped considerably.

The Situation of the Other Army Groups by 20 July 1942

By 20 July only the infantry divisions of Sixth Army and the units of one panzer corps of Army Group B continued to advance in the direction of Stalingrad. The bulk of the German forces in the south were engaged in the Rostov operation under the control of Army Group A. [See *map 16.*] Flank protection along the Don up to the area east of Boguchar had been established. The Hungarian Second Army had taken over *its* designated sector south of Voronezh, while the Italian Eighth Army was marching northeastward from the Voroshilovgrad area in order to relieve the German forces in the Boguchar sector. The German Second Army front between Voronezh and Livny had defied a series of savage armored assaults in the vicinity of Voronezh.

Army Group Center had cleared the rear area of Fourth Army of partisan forces. The immediate threat deep in the flank of Ninth Army had also been eliminated. In the Toropets area the front had been strengthened, but here the grave potential danger persisted. Moreover, the Russians maintained continuous pressure along the entire front, particularly in the Second Panzer Army sector. Their local attacks seemed to be intended to relieve the Soviet forces in the south. However, by 20 July no critical situation had developed.

On the other hand the scope of the partisan operations behind the German front had changed noticeably. Whereas in the past the Rus-

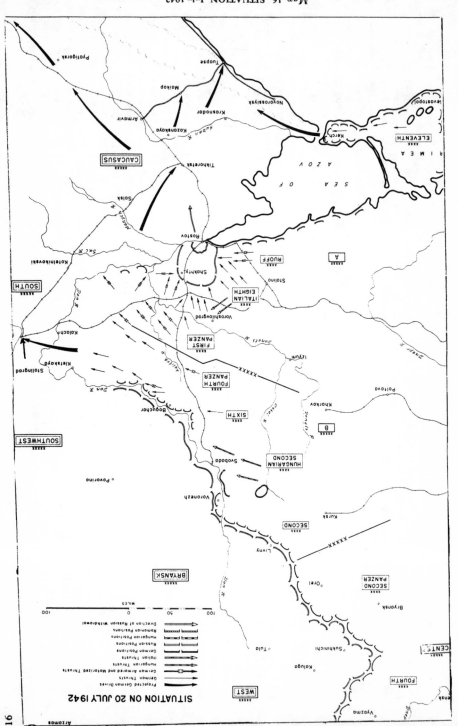

Map 16. SITUATION, July 1942

116   Arzamas

sian command had used partisan units to soften up sectors that were subsequently to be attacked by regular troops from the front, guerrilla operations were now extending far into the German rear areas. Instead of employing large partisan units as in the past, the Russians committed more and more small raiding detachments and sabotage teams to cut off the German lines of communications and inflict losses on reinforcements moving to the front.

In addition three air forces had been formed out of flying units previously attached to individual armies. It was estimated that approximately 800 serviceable planes supported the Russian ground operations against Army Group Center.

Army Group North had to contend with local attacks, mainly at Staraya Russa and along the Volkhov, which had been repelled without too much difficulty. German preparations for an all-out assault on Leningrad progressed very slowly.

A mid-July report on the rehabilitation of the Army Groups Center and North units indicated that their personnel and materiel situation had improved considerably. Most of the infantry divisions had been reduced to six infantry battalions each and the artillery batteries to three guns each. Their mobility had improved with the arrival of horses and the introduction of more effective automotive repair procedures. The motor vehicle situation nevertheless remained very serious. Motorized elements averaged only half their authorized allowances; the majority of the divisions were capable only of limited objective attacks.

Developments along the fronts of Army Group Center and North had no adverse effect on the German offensive in the south, and Hitler was able to concentrate on his attack plans without fear of diversion.

Directive No. 44 (21 July 1942)

Directive No. 44 pertained to warfare in northern Finland. The rapid progress of the operations in the south gave rise to the hope that the Soviet Union would soon be cut off from the Caucasus. As a result, the Soviets would lose their oil resources, and the vital supply route for lend-lease shipments via Iran would be blocked. This blow,

together with the loss of the entire Donets Basin, would be fatal to the Soviet military position.

In Hitler's opinion the next step would be to cut off the northern supply route by which the Allies kept the Soviet Union in the war. This had to be achieved by cutting the Murmansk railroad, which carried the bulk of lend-lease supplies during the winter months. [See *map 4*.] The importance of this route would increase when unfavorable weather prevented effective interception of the convoys in the Arctic Ocean.

The Twentieth Mountain Army, together with the Fifth Air Force, was therefore to seize the Murmansk railroad near Kandalaksha during the autumn of 1942. To facilitate this drive, Leningrad was to be captured in September at the latest, thus releasing Finnish forces, and one German mountain division was to be transferred to Finland.

A Finnish attack against Belomorsk was to be coordinated with the Twentieth Mountain Army offensive. In general, the most important task of the German forces in Finland remained the protection of the Petsamo mines, since Germany would probably have to cease the production of high-alloy steel for airplane and submarine engines without nickel shipments from Finland.

Oddly enough, the Finnish theater was the only one in which the Russians did not enjoy numerical superiority, since about 500,000 Finns and Germans faced approximately 300,000 Russians. However, contrary to the hopes expressed in Directive No. 44, this superiority could not be brought to bear because the prerequisite to any major operation—the capture of Leningrad—had not materialized; Army Group North had not proved sufficiently strong to seize the city. The German forces stationed in Finland did not influence the struggle for victory in the south, since no decisive action took place in the Finnish theater during 1942.

Directive No. 45 (23 July 1942)

On 21 July a recently captured Russian General Staff officer stated during his interrogation that the Russians intended to defend Rostov to the bitter end. At Army Group A headquarters, however, the impression prevailed that Russian resistance in the city would soon collapse because the garrison had lost much of its equipment and morale seemed to be low. This opinion was soon justified: Rostov fell on 23 July except for a few isolated nests of resistance in the western part of the city.

At this decisive moment Hitler began to show increasing interest in Stalingrad, the Volga city that was still approximately 100 miles from the German spearheads. The old Russian dictum that the motherland could not be defeated unless the invader got across the Volga seemed to have gained new significance in Hitler's mind. Several of his requests to divert two panzer divisions from the Rostov operation had previously been ignored in the heat of battle. Now he issued a direct order transferring one panzer corps composed of two armored divisions from Fourth Panzer to Sixth Army and thus from the Caucasus to the Stalingrad operation. The concept of an orderly advance by consecutive phase lines, which had been followed since the beginning of the summer offensive, gave way to two simultaneous drives in divergent directions, one toward the oil lands, the other toward Stalingrad.

Directive No. 45, dealing with the continuation of the summer offensive, was issued on 23 July. In the preamble Hitler stated that during an offensive of little more than three weeks' duration, the long-range objectives set for the southern attack forces had been attained for all intents and purposes. Only a few small contingents of Timoshenko's armies had been able to escape and reach the other bank of the Don, where they would probably be reinforced from the Caucasus area. Another Russian force was being assembled in the Stalingrad area, where the Soviet command apparently intended to offer strong resistance.

As its next objective Army Group A was to encircle and annihilate those enemy forces south and southeast of Rostov which had escaped across the Don. Strong motorized units were to advance southwestward and cut the rail line connecting Tikhoretsk with Stalingrad.

In addition to losing the panzer corps transferred to Army Group B for the continuation of the drive toward Stalingrad, Army Group A

was to release the Motorized Infantry Division Grossdeutschland which was to stop its advance as soon as it reached the Manych River and prepare its units for transfer to the West.

After accomplishing the mission of destroying the Russians south of the Don, Army Group A was to seize the Black Sea coast and thus paralyze the Russian Black Sea fleet. As soon as the movement of the main army group forces had progressed sufficiently, elements of Eleventh Army were to cross the Kerch Strait and advance along the Black Sea coastal road.

Another force, consisting of mountain and light divisions, was to cross the Kuban River and seize the elevated ground near Maikop and Armavir. The mountain divisions were to cross the western Caucasus passes and operate in conjunction with the forces advancing along the Black Sea coast. At the same time an attack force consisting of motorized elements was to move into the Grozny area, block the passes of the Ossetin and Georgian military roads leading across the central Caucasus, and then thrust along the Caspian toward Baku.

In addition to building up a defense line along the Don, Army Group B was to advance toward Stalingrad, destroy the Russian forces assembling in that area, and block the corridor between the Don and the Volga. Motorized units were then to drive down the lower Volga toward Astrakhan and there block the principal branch of the river.

The Luftwaffe was to support the ground forces crossing the Don and advancing toward Tikhoretsk, and concentrate on destroying Timoshenko's forces and the city of Stalingrad. Occasional raids were to be conducted on Astrakhan, and shipping on the lower Volga was to be disrupted by the sowing of mines. During the further course of the operation the Air Force was to operate in conjunction with the ground forces advancing toward the Black Sea ports and protect them from Russian naval interference. Other Luftwaffe units were to support the thrust via Grozny to Baku.

Because of the crucial importance of Caucasus oil to the future German war effort, air attacks against oil wells or oil tanks were to be made only in case of absolute necessity. The Russians, however, were to be deprived of Caucasus oil deliveries by German air attacks that were to disrupt the rail and pipe lines and destroy the port installations.

The Navy was to lend its support during the crossing of the Kerch Strait and prevent the Russian Black Sea fleet from interfering. Moreover, the Navy was to organize light forces for disrupting Russian communications across the Caspian Sea.

The local operations previously planned for Army Groups Center and North were to be executed with a minimum of delay in order to produce the greatest possible effect on the opposing forces. Army Group North was to seize Leningrad by the beginning of September. For this purpose five divisions as well as the nonorganic medium and heavy artillery units of Eleventh Army were to be transferred from the Crimea to the north. Two German and two Romanian divisions were to be left in the Crimea temporarily.

Special attention was called to maintaining the secrecy of this directive.

Directive No. 45 resulted in the diversion of one motorized infantry division of Army Group A and five divisions of Eleventh Army from the Caucasus operation. Hitler's absolute confidence in victory induced him to leave in the Caucasus only sufficient forces to carry out a pursuit. The breach in the Russian front seemed so enormous that the shifting of a few divisions from Army Group A to Army Group B could not possibly affect the Caucasus drive. At the same time Hitler felt that such a move would guarantee a speedy advance to the lower Volga. The Russian forces assembling in the Stalingrad area would be overrun by the German spearhead divisions. After reaching the city the latter would immediately turn southeastward and continue their drive toward Astrakhan and the Caspian Sea.

Thus in a way Hitler reverted to the original concept on which the Operations Division of the Army High Command in October 1941 had based its plan for the Caucasus operation. According to this plan an offensive across the Caucasus Mountains could be envisaged only after the German flank along the lower Volga had been secured. The instructions issued in Directive No. 45 constituted a belated attempt to secure the flank along the Volga while relatively weak forces simultaneously advanced into the Caucasus.

Tanks

On 25 July the number of tanks in serviceable condition in the Army Group A area totaled 435 for 8 spearhead divisions or an average of 54 tanks per division. The best equipped panzer division had 109 tanks, the poorest 24.

Gasoline

The First Panzer Army's shortage of gasoline was so great that all motorized elements of the XLIV Infantry Corps were immobilized and the infantry units were unable to move because of the breakdown of the supply system.

By 25 July the gasoline situation had grown more critical than ever. When General Halder inquired at Army Group A headquarters why gasoline supplies were so unsatisfactory, he was told that the shortage was caused by bad weather, the long distances covered during the offensive, and the priority given to the Sixth Army for its assault on Stalingrad. Airlifted supplies had temporarily alleviated shortages, but the bulk of the essential POL requirements could not be moved by this mode of transportation. Since the available truck transportation had proved insufficient, an improvement could be expected only after the Stalino-Shakhty railroad had been repaired. Both panzer armies were temporarily immobilized by lack of gasoline.

Stalingrad Takes Priority Over the Caucasus (End of July 1942)

On 29 July the last rail line connecting the Caucasus with central Russia was blown up at several points by German armored elements. The Caucasus was isolated and Hitler seemed to believe that it was his for the taking. On the next day Army Group A was warned that the heavy fighting near Stalingrad would force the Army High Command to transfer one additional German corps and two Romanian ones with a number of divisions to Army Group B in order to assist Sixth Army in its struggle. The Fourth Panzer Army headquarters might also be pulled out to take charge of this support thrust, in which case only one of its corps would continue to participate in the drive toward Maikop under First Panzer Army control. The definite decision would depend on developments in the Stalingrad situation.

That same evening List told Halder that the transfer of three corps, which apparently was under consideration, would endanger the eastern flank of the southward thrust into the Caucasus. Halder replied that the transfer would take place after the corps had reached the south bank of the Don and that their diversion in the direction of Stalingrad would actually constitute an alternative flank protection. List thereupon insisted that at least the Grossdeutschland Division remain with Army Group A to protect its flank against a Russian surprise thrust. Halder reassured him that the division would not be transferred to the West before mid-August. On the other hand, he had little hope of any further delay since Hitler had recently asked him: "What is the use of victories in Russia, if I lose western Europe?"

Halder continued by saying that Hitler did not believe the Army Group A flank would be in danger. List did not share this opinion. He wanted at least the Grossdeutschland Division in reserve. The army group commander then reminded Halder that the success of the Caucasus operation would depend primarily on the ready availability of POL. Hitler's plan struck him as a great gamble, since driving into the Caucasus with relatively weak forces, whose flank was not sufficiently protected, meant taking extraordinary risks.

While these conversations were taking place Russian troops were retreating into the Caucasus, with no sign of a new front being built up farther to the south. Stalin's order, that every officer and enlisted man would have to fight to the end without giving way, showed that the Russian command was aware of the seriousness of the situation.

On 31 July Halder sent an order to Army Groups A and B in which he confirmed the transfer of Fourth Panzer Army. In the introductory remarks he stated that with the severing of the rail communications between the Caucasus and Stalingrad the Russian front south of the Don was split wide open. The Russians in front of Army Group A would attempt to stop the German advance into the Caucasus,

but it seemed doubtful whether they would have the necessary forces to do so. At Stalingrad they would throw all their resources into the battle to maintain control over their life line, the Volga.

Army Group A's immediate mission was to seize the Black Sea coast and thus paralyze the Russian fleet, which in turn would guarantee the security of the German lines of communications across that body of water.

On 1 August the Fourth Panzer Army with two German and one Romanian corps, a total of eight divisions plus corps and army troops, would be transferred from the Caucasus to the Stalingrad operation. Army Group A was to assemble its remaining motorized units under First Panzer Army for a drive in the direction of Maikop. From there some army elements were to cut off the withdrawing Russian forces, while others were to drive via Tuapse toward Batum. Some motorized units would have to protect the eastern flank of the army. Mountain divisions were to be employed for the thrusts across the passes in the Caucasus. The much contested Grossdeutschland Division would be available for eight days more, after which it was to prepare to entrain on 12 August at Stalino.

The mission of Army Group B was to remain unchanged.

XI

THE PERIOD OF STAGNATION (AUGUST - OCTOBER 1942)

Developments to Mid-August 1942

German hopes that Army Group A would be able to encircle the enemy forces in the region immediately south of the lower Don were unfulfilled. The Russians evaded destruction by withdrawing to the Caucasus, whereupon the Germans seized Krasnodar and Maikop against light resistance. Their divisions followed the retreating Russians closely and penetrated into the western Caucasus up to the mountain passes. Fully realizing the danger which threatened them the Russians successfully blocked the only road leading over the mountains to Tuapse.

In the Crimea elements of Eleventh Army prepared the crossing of the Kerch Strait, while the bulk of the army forces entrained for Leningrad. In the central Caucasus area First Panzer Army moved in the direction of the Grozny oil fields, but very slowly being greatly handicapped by a shortage of gasoline at the very time when Russian resistance was stiffening.

The operations of Army Group A thus gave the impression of a dispersed effort with 20 divisions advancing along a front of more than 500 miles. The army group's two points of main effort—northeast of Tuapse and at Pyatigorsk—were 200 miles apart. Most of the air support units had been shifted to the Stalingrad area after the army group had crossed the Don. The supply situation was very unsatisfactory. Because of the shortage of rolling stock, the only rail line leading from the Rostov area into the Caucasus could not satisfy more than the most elementary requirements, and insignificant shipments across the Sea of Azov failed to alleviate the shortages.

The situation of Army Group B was equally disappointing. The Russians in the Don Bend took advantage of the slowness of the

Sixth Army advance—caused by the 10-day lack of gasoline and a momentary shortage of ammunition—and suddenly offered strong resistance. Although this maneuver led to the encirclement of some Russian forces, it also helped the Soviet command to gain time for the strengthening of the defenses of Stalingrad. In any event, by

18 August the Germans had cleared the Don bend and prepared for the final reduction of the city. After some confusion, caused by an almost 180° turn of its forces, Fourth Panzer Army had moved into the area north of Kotelnikovski and was ready to push toward Stalingrad from the south. Flank protection along the Don was provided by the Italian Eighth and Hungarian Second Armies, which—supported by a few German divisions—occupied wide sectors. [See *chart 5.*] The Romanian Third Army, scheduled to take over the sector on both sides of Kletskaya, was unable to take its place because of rail transportation difficulties. For the time being Sixth Army had to assign German divisions to this sector which in turn reduced the striking power of the assault forces at Stalingrad. During the preparatory attacks the Luftwaffe gave close support and simultaneously carried out some strategic bombing missions against the lines of communications connecting Stalingrad with Moscow.

The German supply situation was alarmingly bad. The assault forces were dependent on a single, low-capacity railroad which ran eastward from the Donets Basin. Available truck transportation was insufficient to bridge the long distances between the supply bases and the spearhead units.

Hitler had ordered Army Group Center to launch a pincers attack against the Russian salient around Sukhinichi. The two armored divisions of Fourth Panzer Army that had been transferred from Army Group B during the second half of July because of the shortage of POL in the south were to participate in this attack. Field Marshal von Kluge strongly protested against this mission, indicating that the consolidation of the Rzhev front was far more urgent. On 7 August a conference at Hitler's headquarters near Vinnitsa ended with Kluge's

20. GERMAN ORDER OF BATTLE, 12 August 1942.......*ugust 1942)*

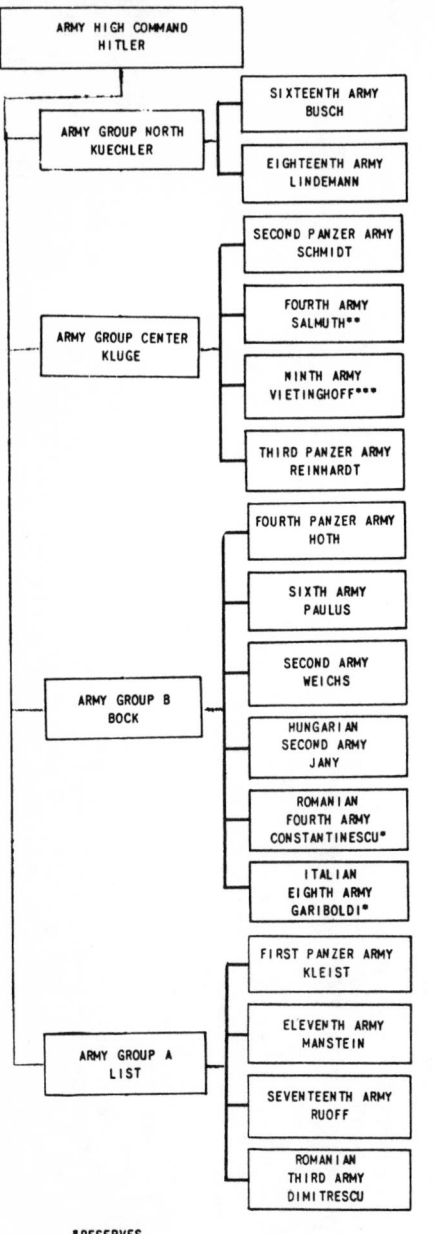

*RESERVES
**TEMPORARILY REPLACING GENERAL
HEINRICI
***TEMPORARILY REPLACING GENERAL
MODEL

exclaiming that he would not disobey a direct order to launch the Sukhinichi attack, but that the responsibility would be Hitler's.

The attack failed despite all German efforts. Soon afterward Army Group Center became engaged in such heavy fighting that air and ground reinforcements had to be diverted from other parts of the theater. Finally, strong Russian attacks against Ninth Army at Rzhev were repelled in sharp local actions. Meanwhile Army Group North was continuing its preparations for the attack on Leningrad.

The distribution of Luftwaffe units corresponded to that of the ground forces. Of some 1,230 operational aircraft available in the Russian theater in mid-August 1942, approximately 720 supported Army Groups A and B.

The Eastern Intelligence Division estimated overall Russian strength on 15 August as follows:

21. RUSSIAN STRENGTH

	Total*	Russian western front*	Reserves*	Other fronts*
Infantry Divisions	287	134	73	80
Infantry Brigades	142	47	66	29
Cavalry Divisions	33	7	20	6
Armored Brigades	131	34	86	11

*Equivalent of full-strength units.

Personnel and Other Problems (16–18 August 1942)

In a letter to Marshal Keitel, General Halder again drew the attention of the Armed Forces High Command to the seriousness of the Russian Army's personnel situation. According to recent estimates the Russian theater would be short of at least 720,000 replacements by 1 November 1942. The 400,000 men who would be inducted and trained in the interim period might compensate for current losses, but would not reduce this deficit, and the requirements of other theaters had not been taken into account. In any event, the estimated shortage of more than 700,000 replacements would involve serious risks.

In addition to the vexing personnel shortages at the front, the partisan problem had assumed such importance that Hitler issued Directive No. 46 on 18 August in order to standardize German operating procedures against the enemy in the rear areas. In this directive the Fuehrer ordered every German in partisan-infested areas to participate in the antiguerrilla struggle. However, though the new policy was well intended, its enforcement suffered from a chronic shortage of personnel and equipment which permitted great numbers of partisans to escape from one well-set trap after another.

This same personnel shortage created another problem. Germany's allies, who had had to bear such heavy burdens during the summer offensive in order to supplement the Wehrmacht's strength, now stood along greatly exposed sectors of the Don front. In this connection Hitler was apprehensive lest Stalin repeat his classic maneuver of 1920: an attack across the Don near Serafimovich in the direction of Rostov, similar to the one the Bolsheviks had launched against Wrangel's White Russian Army with such devastating results. The Fuehrer felt that the Italian Eighth Army which was responsible for the security of this Don sector would be incapable of stopping such an attack. He therefore urged repeated[ly] that the 22d Panzer Division be withdrawn from Stalingrad and reassibilitated behind the Italian Eighth Army sector.

The Romanians who were providing the largest contingent among Germany's allies were the subject of a memorandum Halder sent to Army Groups A and B on 18 August. Those Romanian units assigned to Army Group A—with the exception of the four mountain divisions committed in the Crimea and Caucasus—were to secure the area west and southwest of Astrakhan after the Russian Black Sea coast had been cleared and the fleet eliminated. The plans, however, would be subject to approval by Marshal Antonescu who was to assume command of a newly activated Romanian army group composed of the

Romanian Third and Fourth and German Sixth Armies. The army group would secure the German flank along the lower Volga after the fall of Stalingrad.

The Dieppe raid, 18–19 August 1942, came as a complete surprise and somewhat of a shock to the Germans. Hitler's immediate reaction was to strengthen his defenses in the West, an objective that could be attained only at the expense of the Russian theater. The personnel and equipment diverted to North Africa, which was more than justified by Rommel's brilliant exploits, also constituted a drain on Germany's limited resources. A few weeks later Hitler directed the diversion of more troops to reinforce the Crete garrison. He believed that a large-scale Allied invasion of the Mediterranean island fortress was imminent and ordered the crack 22d Infantry Division transferred from the Crimea to Crete.

The Situation in the Caucasus (Second Half of August 1942)

On 19 August Army Group A headquarters estimated the situation in the Caucasus as follows: Russian resistance in the northwestern parts of the Caucasus Mountains was extremely stubborn. Approximately 20 Russian reserve divisions known to be in the Caucasus had not yet been committed for the defense of this area, perhaps because they were insufficiently trained and equipped. The fact that the Red Army considered Caucasian replacements as unreliable might have delayed their employment.

There was no indication of any assembly of Russian forces in the Astrakhan area. The Russians apparently did not intend to threaten the flank and rear of Army Groups A and B from that side. On the contrary, repeated air attacks on Elista—the German-held town in the gap between Army Groups A and B—seemed to indicate that the Russians were worried about a German thrust toward Astrakhan.

In its conclusions the report stated that the Russians seemed to employ delaying tactics in the Caucasus. They were continuing the evacuation of industrial machinery and military forces. Because of the advanced season, however, it was not to be expected that they would completely evacuate the Transcaucasus. In carrying out their mission, the Army group forces would have to face a hard and time-consuming struggle along the entire Caucasus front even though sizeable Russian forces had been destroyed during the past weeks.

The steadily growing lines of communications, the vast territory to be kept under control, the scarcity of motor fuel, and the increasing terrain obstacles were the principal factors that would slow down the advance.

Two days later a German propaganda release proudly announced that at 1100 on 21 August a detachment of mountain troops had raised the German flag on Mount Elbrus. But the conquest of the 18,481-foot peak of the Caucasus Mountains did not alleviate the oil shortage.

The acute shortage of gasoline was at this point the primary cause for the delay in the advance, because it prevented the heavy truck columns from moving up supplies from distant railheads. Instead, the Germans had to use short, undamaged or repaired sections of rail lines and establish truck shuttle services between detraining and entraining points. The delays incurred by transshipping bulky supplies were reflected in the unsatisfactory progress of the army group forces.

By 28 August the Russian forces opposite Army Group A had set up their defenses. The Red Army had regained control over its units, reorganized its forces, and moved up reinforcements from Transcaucasia, Iran, and also—via the Caspian—from central Russia. By the end of August strong Russian ground forces, having the advantage of local air superiority, blocked the access to Novorossiysk along well-built, deeply echeloned defense lines and launched occasional counterattacks. The Russians also were on the offensive along the Tuapse road, where German motorized units were restricted to the few existing mountain roads.

The advance of the German mountain corps was delayed by smaller, but equally well-entrenched forces. The Italian Alpine Corps that was to participate in the thrust across the Caucasus failed to arrive, apparently because the Italian Eighth Army refused to transfer the corps to the respective German army command. Along the Terek

River bend the Russians had concentrated strong ground forces that had the advantage of local air superiority.

At the end of August the Russians were employing 10-12 divisions along the Black Sea coast, 1 or 2 in the mountains, and 8 divisions along the Terek front for a total of 19-22 divisions. Additional forces and replacements were arriving. The Soviets seemed to be determined to hold their Caucasus positions until the outbreak of winter. Nevertheless, they were continuing to evacuate industrial and agricultural supplies and machinery from the Caucasus area.

On 31 August Hitler, who was very dissatisfied with the situation at Army Group A, received Marshal List, its commander, at his headquarters. List explained that he intended to continue his thrusts into the western Caucasus at three points:

1. Near Anapa and Novorossiysk and, after the seizure of these two cities, along the coastal road;

2. On both sides of the mountain road to Tuapse; and

3. Along the Sukhumi road, where the mountain troops were to make their main effort.

In the central Caucasus, List suggested, the First Panzer Army should destroy the Russian forces in the Terek bend and seize the Grozny oil fields beyond that river. Hitler approved these plans.

General Warlimont visited Army Group A and a number of its subordinate headquarters during the last days of August and reported that morale was high. The responsible commanders apparently felt confident that they would be capable of accomplishing their missions.

The Opening of the Battle for Stalingrad (End of August 1942)

Early on 23 August one corps of General Paulus' Sixth Army crossed the Don in force and reached the Volga north of Stalingrad that same evening. On the following day heavy Russian counterattacks endangered the German toehold which, however, was strengthened by the arrival of additional units on the west bank of the Volga.

Fourth Panzer Army and Sixth Army had the mission of seizing Stalingrad and securing the lower Volga. The two armies totaled

25 divisions, some of which were greatly understrength. The Russian *Sixty-Second Army*, composed of some 8 divisions under General Chuikov, was responsible for the defense of Stalingrad. The Germans had local air superiority, being supported by some 1,000 aircraft of all types. During the last days of August, the Germans advanced with relative ease through the outer suburbs of Stalingrad.

While this advance was proceeding in a satisfactory manner, Hitler continued to be preoccupied with protecting both flanks of the forces driving across the Don toward Stalingrad. He ordered one of the few remaining motorized infantry divisions of Army Group A detached from the drive into the Caucasus and shifted to the Elista area west of Astrakhan to secure the growing gap between Army Groups A and B.

On the other flank the Russians attempted to gain another bridgehead against the Italian Eighth Army deployed along the Don. Although the Russians attacked cautiously and with only relatively small forces, the Italian right withdrew apparently without offering resistance. The Russians thereupon moved a guard cavalry corps into the area of penetration and two days of heavy counterattacks were required before the situation was restored on 27 August. Two additional Russian bridgeheads existed opposite the Hungarian Second Army which held the Don sector adjacent to the Italian left. Farther to the north the Germans observed that the Russians were gradually transferring attack forces from the Voronezh to the Stalingrad area.

On 28 August Generaloberst (Gen.) Wolfram von Richthofen, Commander, VIII Air Corps, made a personal reconnaissance of the region, during which he consulted with the commanders of Fourth Panzer and Sixth Armies. The consensus was that no interference from strong enemy forces was to be expected in the Stalingrad area. Luftwaffe reconnaissance aircraft flying northward were unable to discover any Russian forces in a terrain that offered little cover or concealment. Richthofen's general impression was that the Russian command was disorganized in this area.

Halder, however, contested the accuracy of this information and Hitler thereupon decided to move the forward echelon of Army Group

B headquarters far to the front and airlift infantry replacements to Sixth Army in order to speed up the conquest of Stalingrad.

The German Leadership Crisis (September 1942)

Throughout the summer of 1942 General Halder [Chief, Army General Staff] had noted in his diary that he was experiencing increasing difficulties in working with Hitler. The latter's chronic tendency of underrating Russian capabilities had gradually assumed grotesque proportions, finally developing into a positive danger. In fact, the situation had become more and more intolerable for the military. According to Halder, it was almost impossible to accomplish anything useful. Hitler's exercise of command was characterized by pathological reactions to impressions of the moment and by his complete lack of understanding of command procedures.

Under such circumstances the military men in top-level positions were bound to be the first victims of any unfavorable turn of events. As early as 30 August, for instance, while German progress was still quite satisfactory, Halder noted that the Army leaders had once again been the target of the Fuehrer's abuse. According to Hitler, they suffered from intellectual conceit, mental inflexibility, and a complete incapacity of grasping essentials.

During the first days of September the military events continued to be favorable for the Germans. On the first day of the month German troops succeeded in crossing the Kerch Strait and landing on the Taman Peninsula. After seizing Anapa, they joined in the drive along the Black Sea coast toward Novorossiysk. A few days later Marshal List [Commander, Army Group A] suggested that the bulk of II. Mountain Corps engaged in the central Caucasus be pulled out after leaving some blocking units near the passes. This mountain corps could be more advantageously employed in the Maikop area to achieve a breakthrough toward the coast. Since he did not share List's opinion, Hitler sent General Jodl [Chief, Armed Forces Operations Staff] to investigate on the spot and discuss the matter with List.

Upon his return Jodl reported that List's plan seemed sound and he advocated its implementation. In the subsequent argument Hitler accused List of not having followed orders and of having dispersed his forces over much too wide an area. In his reply Jodl tried to prove that List had followed to the letter all orders he had been given. The Fuehrer thereupon became extremely irritated and asked that his orders to List, including notes of verbal instructions, be submitted to him. In addition, he instructed that court stenographers be brought from Berlin to Vinnitsa to take down the minutes of all future military conversations and conferences.

On 9 September Hitler was informed by Halder that List intended to let the Russians attack the German bridgeheads across the Terek until their strength had been exhausted, and that he would then resume the offensive. Hitler considered this idea as fundamentally wrong since its execution would imperil the very existence of the German bridgeheads against which the Russians were moving a constant stream of reinforcements.

This last misunderstanding, coming after so many similar conflicts, led Hitler to consider a number of changes in top-level positions. List was asked to hand in his resignation, which he did on the evening of 9 September. For the time being Hitler decided to assume command of Army Group A in person, so that in addition to his civilian functions he now held the position of an army group commander in Russia, commander in chief of the German Army, and commander in chief of the German armed forces. Three top echelons of military command has thus been unified in a singular manner.

The chief of staff of Army Group A, General von Greiffenberg, remained at army group headquarters at Stalino as "head of the message center and transmitting agent for orders." Halder was notified on the same day that Hitler intended to relieve him because he "was no longer equal to the psychic demands of his position." (General der Infanterie (Lt. Gen.) Kurt Zeitzler replaced Halder on 24 September.

The conflict between Hitler and Jodl—brought to the surface by Jodl taking List's side—was so deep that Hitler considered the dismissal of his closest military adviser. He was to be replaced by Paulus who a few months later was to play such a tragic role when he surrendered the remnants of the Sixth Army at Stalingrad. Keitel's position as Chief of Staff, Armed Forces High Command, was also jeopardized with Goering trying to replace him with one of his own protégés. General Warlimont, Jodl's immediate assistant, fell in disfavor and was sent on extended leave from which he did not return to duty until his superior—who had survived the turmoil—recalled him after the Allied landings in North Africa in November 1942.

In the opinion of an eyewitness who was at Hitler's headquarters at Vinnitsa during the period under review, the crisis which developed in September 1942 was far more than a conflict over the misinterpretation of orders and was by no means settled with the relief or temporary absence of a few military men. Hitler himself showed signs of such deep and lasting depression that the causes must have been less superficial than was generally assumed. For the first time the Fuehrer seemed to have realized that Germany could not win the Russian campaign and would therefore lose the entire war. It took him many weeks before he was able to restore his outward composure, and then he achieved it only by immersing himself in the innumerable military and political details of his daily work.

Faulty Intelligence and Its Interpretation

On 9 September the Eastern Intelligence Division submitted an estimate according to which the Russians seemed to have no sizeable reserves along the entire front. On the contrary, in order to form points of main effort, they had to shift units over long distances. Because of insufficient training and a shortage of equipment the troops still available and the units presently in the process of activation would probably not be ready for commitment for some time. Halder accepted this estimate and concluded that the Russians lacked strategic reserves.

Such favorable information was always well received by Hitler who, on 13 September, ordered Army Group B to launch a pursuit in the event Russian resistance north of Stalingrad should collapse. At the same time the existing plans for a thrust toward Astrakhan were to be reexamined and data regarding their execution submitted. Hitler then instructed the army group commander to launch local attacks at the boundary of Sixth Army and the Italian Eighth Army, correct some dents in the German lines in the Don bend, and construct a switch position behind the German front west of Voronezh. Obviously, the Fuehrer took great interest in every tactical detail concerning the army group adjacent to his own.

The German Offensive Grinds to a Halt (26 September 1942)

None of the objectives of the summer offensive were attained by the Germans. Although Army Group A made local gains in the direction of Tuapse and Grozny, these minor successes were not decisive. The army group had exhausted its strength. The only major oil fields that had fallen into German hands—those at Maikop—were almost completely destroyed. In 1941 their output had amounted to 2.5 million tons or 8 per cent of the total USSR production. The oil wells and refineries were demolished. Only two storage tanks and a few stretches of pipeline were found intact.

Army Group B's assault on Stalingrad met with unexpected resistance. Beginning 14 September the Russian garrison received a steady flow of reinforcements, and on 16 September Sixth Army under General Paulus was given control of all German units that had entered the city, including some Fourth Panzer Army elements. As early as 20 September Halder noted that the attack forces were gradually succumbing to exhaustion. But for the next two months the battle raged within the city, marked by feats of magnificent heroism on both sides. The Russian toehold west of the Volga was split into four separate bridgeheads with a total frontage of some 15 miles running through the built-up downtown area. The main 5-mile bridgehead held by the Russians had a depth varying from 600-3,000 feet on the west bank of the river.

During these weeks of house-to-house fighting Stalingrad lost its initial significance as a flank protection anchor for the Caucasus offensive. Instead of a means to an end, Stalingrad had become an end in itself. More and more troops poured into the city from both sides. After the Romanian Third Army had finally arrived and taken up its positions along the Don between the Italian Eighth and the German Sixth Armies, Paulus was able to shift into the city those German divisions that had hitherto protected his flank.

The Romanians felt none too happy about the new assignment they had received. In an inquiry addressed to the Operations Division of the Army High Command on 24 September, they pointed out that the Romanian Third Army would have to defend a 105-mile sector with 69 battalions, or an average of 1.5 miles per battalion. Considering that the Romanians had no mobile forces for counterattacks and no self-propelled antitank guns, the Romanian line was very weak. If present plans were implemented, the situation of the Romanian Fourth Army would be even worse, since only 33 battalions would have to hold a frontage of 250 miles, an average of almost 8 miles per battalion. This army would be scarcely strong enough to keep its sector under observation.

The Germans did not attach too much importance to these alarming weaknesses; in their reply they pointed out to the Romanians that everything would depend on the outcome of the battle of Stalingrad. They also answered evasively the other Romanian inquiries regarding German armored support, the availability of motor transportation, etc.

The fighting in the sectors of Army Groups Center and North had resumed with new intensity. Strong Russian attacks against Second and Third Panzer Armies and Ninth and Eighteenth Armies were repelled only with considerable effort. The Russians were by no means at the end of their strength. On the contrary, despite the life-and-death struggle raging in the south, they were attempting to gradually regain the initiative in these parts of the theater. The German Eleventh Army forces earmarked for the attack on Leningrad had to be committed to ward off these Russian assaults, so that the all-out offensive on the city of Leningrad—the second major objective of the summer of 1942—had to be abandoned.

The German offensive had bogged down everywhere and the imminence of the muddy period, quite apart from all other factors, made its resumption impractical. The personnel situation in the Russian theater, which had slightly improved until the end of July, had deteriorated considerably since then.

22. GERMAN PERSONNEL STRENGTH VARIATIONS, Summer 1942

Month of 1942	Losses*	Reinforcements**	Strength	
			Increase	Decrease
May	134,230	158,900	24,670	------
June	126,050	157,500	31,450	------
July	156,600	177,800	21,200	------
August	256,100	89,750	------	166,350
September	185,000	83,750	------	101,250
October	130,100	97,200	------	32,900

* Including personnel transferred out of the theater.
** Including convalescents returned to duty.

German Estimates in October and Early November 1942

General Zeitzler, the new Army Chief of Staff, indicated at the daily situation conference on 9 October that the complete calm along wide stretches of the front could not yet be interpreted with complete certainty. Either the Russians had withdrawn a number of units to rehabilitate them or they were transferring them to some other points for a winter offensive. Under these circumstances it would be particularly important that the German army groups form reserves for such a contingency.

Army Group A

Intelligence agents informed their contacts in the Army Group A area that American and British materiel and technicians were arriving at Baku, Batum, and in the Transcaucasus. The disposition of the Russian forces in the Caucasus, as plotted from radio intercepts, was as follows:

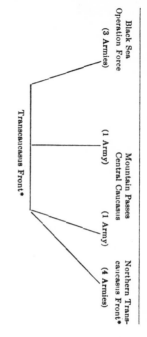

Black Sea Operation Force	Mountain Passes Central Caucasus	Northern Trans-caucasus Front*
(3 Armies)	(1 Army)	(4 Armies)

Transcaucasus Front*

(1 Army)

*Equivalent to an army group.

During the first half of November there was a notable increase in reinforcements arriving in the eastern Caucasus area. According to various reports 3 divisions had arrived in Baku, 4 were transferred from Baku to Tiflis, 1 to Makhachkala on the Caspian, and 18 additional troop transports were on the way to the latter.

Army Group B

By mid-October Army Group B received many reports of troop concentrations in the Saratov area, which seemed to confirm that the Russians were making initial preparations for an offensive near Stalingrad. Air reconnaissance had so far failed to confirm these reports, but this was by no means a proof of their inaccuracy, since Russian concentrations had often gone unnoticed from the air until practically completed. In any event, the Germans were then too deeply committed in Stalingrad to turn back from an operation which had become an obsession with Hitler.

Reports from the front indicated that traffic in the Serafimovich area increased nightly, but Army Group B interpreted these movements simply as supply traffic serving to replenish stocks consumed during recent combat actions. It was precisely from this point that the Russian counteroffensive was launched on 19 November.

On 26 October Sixth Army reported confidently that, even though strong Russian resistance might prevent the army from completing the seizure of Stalingrad before 10 November, the city would be completely in German hands by that date.

In his conversations with the men in his immediate entourage Hitler often revealed his concern over a major Russian offensive, perhaps a winter offensive, across one of the allied sectors along the Don in the direction of Rostov. Russian troop movements and the construction of bridges in the Italian and Romanian sectors were indications of the Soviet command's offensive intentions. Hitler ordered some newly organized Luftwaffe ground divisions moved up to strengthen the allied sectors. With these reinforcements on the line, a few German Army divisions could be transferred behind the allied positions, where they could be held in reserve during their rehabilitation. Meanwhile, he ordered the air force to bomb intensively Russian bridge sites and presumed staging areas in the forests along the northern bank of the Don.

The intelligence summary for the second half of October reported the arrival of Russian reinforcements in the Kletskaya–Serafimovich area. The cross-river traffic near Kletskaya had increased, and rail-road traffic northwest of Stalingrad had grown heavier. So far none of these reinforcements had been committed in battle. Radio silence in the Saratov area was complete. Similar indications of troop concentrations were observed opposite the Italian Eighth and the Hungarian Second Armies along the Don, where several bridges had been constructed to consolidate Russian-held bridgeheads. The Germans did not yet know whether the forces arriving in the Saratov area were combat-ready units or new ones in the stage of activation or training. The mere presence of these units however, was significant if considered in connection with potential Russian offensive intentions.

By 3 November intelligence sources reported that the Russians were preparing an attack against the Romanian Third Army. Whether this offensive would be a diversion or an operation with a far-reaching objective was not known. During the following days the Russians seemed to carry out large-scale movements opposite the Romanian Third Army. On the night of 8-9 November some 2,000-2,500 vehicles had been observed in the area north of Klets-kaya. The establishment of the headquarters of the *Southwest Front* northwest of nearby Serafimovich was considered as definite proof of offensive preparations in this area.

The Estimate of 6 November

This convincing evidence of an impending Russian attack in the Army Group B area was apparently not properly interpreted by the Eastern Intelligence Division. In an estimate dated 6 November this agency expressed the opinion that the Russians were concentrating their forces opposite Army Group Center. Whether they would be capable of conducting another major operation in the south seemed doubtful; in any event, indications for the launching of such an offensive in the south in the near future were lacking. That the Russians had altogether abandoned their previous intentions of thrusting across the Don could not be verified.

The following reasons were given for a major Russian offensive on the Army Group Center front:

1. There was a definite need for a rapid success that could be achieved more easily in the center than in the south. Moreover, such an offensive would definitely dispel the German threat to Moscow;

2. The favorable course of the Russian front opposite Army Group Center offered advantageous jump off positions for a Red Army offensive against Smolensk;

3. In the event of success the offensive could be pursued to the Baltic, thus cutting off the German forces in the Leningrad area; and

4. Any operation across the Don, directed against German-held Rostov, would present greater logistical and technical problems than the one in the center. Even if such an offensive in the south succeeded,

it would destroy only the southern wing of the German forces without offering the strategic possibilities of the thrust in the center. This did not imply that the Russians would not launch a secondary offensive across the Don.

According to available information the Russian preparation for the offensive in the center had not sufficiently advanced to permit its start before the muddy season. The arrival of German reinforcements and German radio deception were given as reasons for having delayed the attack. Although the Russian forces so far identified in assembly areas would appear relatively small for an operation against Smolensk, this factor had little significance since motorized units could be moved up within a short time. Moreover, some of the assembled forces might not have been identified. Also, the Russians had often shown a tendency of overextending themselves by reaching for objectives that were not properly related to their available strength.

During recent offensive operations the Russians had first launched infantry attacks to open gaps in the minefields and had then committed their tanks for penetrations in depth. They had shown remarkable skill in dissimulating their offensive plans by excellent deception which made it difficult to estimate the extent of their preparations. Whether the Russian offensive would be launched on 7 November, as stated by Russian prisoners, was doubtful. Actually, its start would depend both on Russian preparedness and weather conditions. Taking into account all known factors, the launching of the offensive on the ——ny Group Center front could be expected with the start of freezing temperatures.

This estimate, made only 13 days before the Russian counter-offensive was launched in the south, showed that the Russians had succeeded in deceiving the Germans as to their true intentions. The reasoning used to prove the theory of an offensive in the center rather than in the south was an interesting example of intelligence rationalization.

On 12 November—seven days before the Russians jumped off—the Eastern Intelligence Division correctly estimated the threat to the Romanian Third Army, but arrived at the conclusion that the scope of the offensive would be limited to cutting the railroad line that connected Stalingrad with the west. The purpose of such a Russian operation would be to force a German withdrawal from Stalingrad and to resume the Volga boat traffic.

The Oil of the Caucasus

German Efforts at Production

Late in September German counterintelligence personnel were still planning a *coup de main* in order to spare certain important installations in the Baku area from complete Soviet destruction. German agents were to infiltrate behind the Russian lines, contact reliable persons employed at the respective installations, and prepare so-called fake demolitions. The latter would be easily repaired once the Germans had seized the respective area.

By early November the unfavorable course of events forced German counterintelligence to switch from fake-demolition attempts to real acts of sabotage. The most successful sabotage act was perpetrated at Grozny, where parachute agents blew up a large Russian ammunition dump, causing great damage and heavy casualties.

The Oil Brigade Caucasus was meanwhile continuing its efforts against heavy odds. In a memorandum dated 29 October Oil Brigade Headquarters complained about the situation at Ilskaya, a town southwest of Krasnodar. There, the German outpost line went straight through the oil fields. Inspecting officers from Oil Brigade Headquarters had requested the responsible tactical commander to advance his defensive positions by 900 yards. This request had gone to the chief of staff of Seventeenth Army, who expressed his concern over any such action since German forces faced greatly superior Russian units in that sector. From the German point of view this refusal was all the more regrettable because the Russians had apparently left their drills intact and production could have started sooner there than elsewhere.

The Ilskaya wells produced no oil while under German control. Neither did most of the other wells at Maikop or elsewhere in the Caucasus. Reviewing the German effort to exploit the Caucasus oil resources in his economic survey of 1942, General Thomas stated that the staff of Oil Brigade Caucasus had taken the continuance of the German advance into the Caucasus for granted. Expecting that they would be able to exploit the rich Grozny oil fields, the Oil Brigade personnel had failed to concentrate their efforts on the Maikop and other fields, which had been in German hands for several months. The technical difficulties encountered by the Germans because of Russian demolition of oil wells and transportation facilities were far greater than anticipated. After inspecting the Maikop area the technical experts reported that it would be more effective to use the drilling equipment and personnel of the Oil Brigade in Romania or near Vienna than in the Caucasus.

This suggestion was not accepted. Instead, the Oil Brigade operated at Maikop and elsewhere under precarious circumstances, and the Armavir-Maikop railroad was not reconditioned until too late. When the brigade finally struck oil, its commander was ordered to evacuate and blow up the laboriously reconstructed installations; the small quantities of oil produced could not be taken along due to the lack of transport facilities.

Russian Supplies

In reviewing the Russian oil supply, General Thomas expressed the opinion that blocking the Volga at Stalingrad would not by itself suffice to reduce the Soviet Union's POL supplies to such a degree that it would impair the Russian conduct of operations in 1943. This could be achieved only if all supplies from Baku were cut off completely by the spring of 1943. In this case Russian stocks would be exhausted by the summer of 1943. The Soviet armed forces and civilian economy would be severely handicapped without oil from the Caucasus. Since approximately 70 percent of the total high-octane gasoline consumed in the Soviet Union was produced from Baku oil, the seizure of the Baku wells and not the occupation of the lower Volga from Stalingrad to Astrakhan would lead to extensive paralysis of the Russian Air Force.

This report, like so many others by which General Thomas tried to warn the men who were responsible for Germany's military planning, served only one practical purpose: to make its author even more unpopular in National Socialist circles.

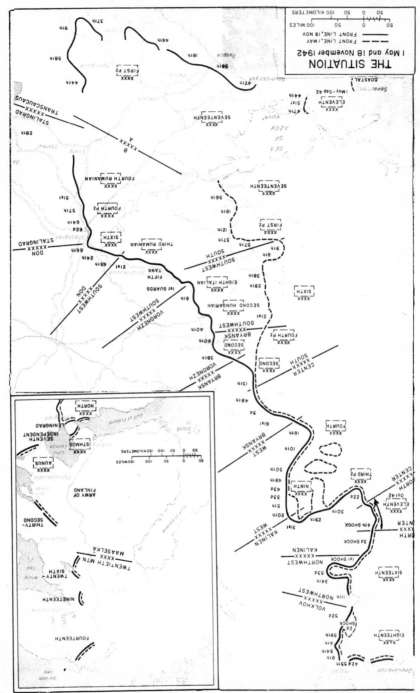

THE SITUATION
1 May and 18 November 1942

————— FRONT LINE, 1 MAY
– – – – – FRONT LINE, 18 NOV

132

Local Engagements (October–Mid-November 1942)

During October and early November the strength of Army Groups A and B was further dissipated in local engagements on the road to Tuapse, in the Pyatigorsk area, and particularly within Stalingrad. [See *map 17.*] During heavy fighting the Germans achieved some local gains and improved their positions, but in many instances they had to ward off Russian counterattacks. These local engagements, however, had no effect on the overall situation. The autumn muddy season, which started in mid-October, brought no relief to the weary troops.

The Romanian and Italian sectors were still far from strong. No German divisions were available to support the allied sectors in case of emergency, because the motorized divisions originally earmarked for this purpose were fully engaged in the battle for Stalingrad and could not be released by the Sixth Army. On the contrary, on 2 November the Fuehrer approved Zeitzler's suggestion to pull organic engineer battalions out of certain divisions in the south and commit them at Stalingrad. A request to stop the offensive for eight days to give the German troops a much-needed rest was disapproved by Hitler. The supply situation, particularly in ammunition and gasoline, remained extremely critical, railroad transportation being unequal to the task of moving basic requirements to the front.

The situation of Army Group Center had improved with the gradual consolidation of the front line; a continuous line had been established even around the Russian-held Toropets salient. The Russians launched attacks in different sectors, but with little practical effect. On 22 October Hitler discussed the new shock tactics used by the Russians in the Army Group Center area, which consisted of massing forces along a narrow stretch of the front in deeply echeloned formation. To counteract these tactics, the Fuehrer advocated the use of the same defensive methods which the French had employed during the major German attack at Reims in 1918. They had kept their artillery at great distance from their MLR, firing large quantities of ammunition to meet the onslaught. Hitler did not realize, however,

that the Germans in 1942 could not expend as much ammunition as the French in 1918.

In the Army Group North sector, intermittent fighting around the German-held Demyansk salient did not lead to any major change in the front line. South of Lake Ladoga the situation became tense for the Germans who checked a Russian breakthrough toward Leningrad at the cost of heavy casualties. The strong artillery forces shifted from the Crimea—about 800 guns—were to be used to tighten the ring around Leningrad.

On 31 October and 1 November Hitler, his entourage, and the Armed Forces Operations Staff returned from Vinnitsa to their former headquarters in East Prussia.

XII

CRITICAL ANALYSIS OF THE GERMAN SUMMER OFFENSIVE IN 1942

Different Concepts of Strategy

According to the postwar conclusions of Generals Halder, Heinrici, etc., the German summer offensive should never have been launched. The German Army had emerged greatly weakened from the ordeal of the winter 1941–42. It had no strategic reserves. To concentrate the essential forces for a large-scale offensive, wide sectors of the Russian front had to be stripped of all their local reserves. Even though the Russians were equally weak by spring 1942, they had manpower reserves and natural resources that were not available to the Axis Powers.

In Halder's opinion the appropriate German strategy for the summer of 1942 would have been to stabilize the front, eliminate the numerous Russian salients and dents in the German lines, and shorten the front line to save personnel. While using active defense tactics at the front, the German Army could have reorganized and refitted for an offensive to be launched at the first favorable opportunity.

Hitler, however, was adverse to any such delay in the continuation of the offensive. In his opinion the Russians had been hard hit during their winter onslaught, and if given time, would get back on their feet. He doubted whether the German Army would be in a more favorable position in 1943 than in 1942. Also, Germany would have to seek a decision in Russia that year, because the Allies might attempt an invasion of western Europe in 1943. While direct and indirect United States aid to Britain and Soviet Russia was steadily increasing, Italy's military and economic power was gradually deteriorating. The crushing blows suffered by the Italian armed forces in the African and Mediterranean theaters had affected the staying power of Germany's principal ally in Europe. Moreover, by adopting a defensive strategy, Germany would lose face with Japan and the neutral powers. Finally, Hitler believed that a dictatorship, to maintain itself, had to produce an incessant stream of successes. An offensive in 1942 would be all the more necessary because, with the military-economic situation steadily growing worse since the start of the Russian campaign, time was working against Germany.

Differences over the Choice of Objective

The original objective of the campaign against the Soviet Union was "to eradicate the remaining Russian military potential and deprive the Soviets of the resources on which their economy was still based." The experience of 1941 indicated that this objective could not be attained unless the Russians were prevented from withdrawing. Halder at the time asserted that this would be extremely difficult in the south, where the Russians could afford to trade space for time without suffering a decisive defeat.

The situation could have been different in the center, where the Russian capital was still within German reach. A deep enveloping sweep launched from the Voronezh-Orel region to points east and northeast of Moscow would have had a telling effect. There was little doubt that the Russians would again have summoned all their strength to defend their capital as they had done during the preceding winter. An offensive in this area would therefore have given the Germans a far better chance to deal the Soviets a knockout blow than an operation in the south.

The German offensive in 1942 was, however, launched in the south because Hitler felt that a decisive victory could be won in southern Russia. Germany's growing shortage of strategic materials influenced the Fuehrer's thinking so much that he became convinced the Soviets were suffering from similar handicaps after having lost so many rich provinces to the Germans. He argued that if their vital oil supply from the Caucasus was threatened, they would use all their remaining manpower and materiel for its defense. Another factor was that possession of this oil would be of greater importance to the German war effort than anything Moscow had to offer.

According to the postwar writings of General Halder and his associates, Hitler's decision to launch an offensive in the summer of 1942 in the southern part of the Russian theater was at best a doubtful gamble. His objective could have been obtained only if the Russians had committed the bulk of the Red Army in the Don bend and if the Germans had succeeded in cutting off and destroying these Soviet forces.

Mistakes in the Execution of the German Offensive

In addition to being handicapped by Hitler's basic mistake of choosing the wrong time and place for his second attempt to defeat the Soviet Union, the German summer offensive was affected by the following factors:

a. *Strength vs. Objectives.* The relationship between the objectives of the summer offensive and the forces available for attaining them was not sound. The objectives—conquest of the Caucasus and linkup with the Finns via Leningrad—were too distant and difficult to attain with the forces that could be mustered. The solution to proceed by phases in southern Russia was a useful expedient, so long as the objective in each case was reached before the next phase was tackled. The first two phases were executed according to plan, but by the end of the third phase—23 July 1942—the objective of cutting off and destroying the Russian forces in the Don bend as a preliminary step to the invasion of the Caucasus had not been achieved. The proper action would have been to stop and consider every facet of the existing situation. Instead, Hitler issued Directive No. 45 which committed his exhausted forces to two simultaneous drives into the Caucasus and toward the Volga.

b. *Faulty Intelligence Estimates.* Even though the Germans had built up an efficient system of collecting information, their evaluation and interpretation often was colored by wishful thinking. The desire to avoid unpleasant incidents with the realities of the situation. Hitler had underestimated the Russians from the beginning of the campaign. Ever since June 1941 he had been convinced that the Red Army was on the verge of defeat and the Soviet regime ready to collapse. He repeatedly asserted that if the German Army could deliver only a few more blows in the summer of 1942, the entire house of cards would tumble. If anyone objected to his arguments, Hitler would ask him, "Are you insinuating that the Russians could outperform us?"

c. *Logistical Difficulties.* The various supply reports and statistics distributed before the start of the summer offensive reflected a certain overconfidence and self-assurance that were not fully justified. Even though stocks in depots and dumps seemed ample, transportation of supplies to the rapidly advancing troops was bound to create numerous problems unless the few existing rail lines could be complemented by a tremendous truck and airlift effort. But it was no secret that the German armed forces had neither the necessary trucks and cargo planes nor the gasoline, not to mention the persistent inadequacy of maintenance and repair facilities, and the shortage of qualified technicians, spare parts, etc. From the outset there was actually not the slightest hope that the supply services would be capable of keeping up with an advance to the Volga and beyond the Caucasus.

d. *Mistakes in Occupation Policy.* Hitler's attitude toward the Russians found its expression in the occupation policies applied by the National Socialist Party functionaries. Overriding the repeated protests of the commanders in the field, Hitler's henchmen perpetrated such ruthless acts of suppression that they destroyed all chances for gaining the support of the population of the occupied territories.

e. *Inflexible Luftwaffe Tactics.* Throughout the summer offensive of 1942 the Luftwaffe had continued its rigid adherence to the tactics that had proved so successful in earlier campaigns but had failed in Russia in late 1941. The method of concentrating practically its entire strength on close support of the armored spearheads was ineffective because of the depth and width of the theater. The striking forces of the Luftwaffe, drawn far away from their bases and beset by maintenance difficulties, were exposed to Russian attacks on their lines of communications.

136

In the autumn of 1942 these developments led to a revision of policy by which Luftwaffe tactics and organization were adapted to the needs of the Russian theater. Balanced air forces, better equipped with defensive aircraft, were to assist the ground forces in repelling any possible Russian counteroffensive, but they were "too little and too late."

f. Hitler's Intuition. It is remarkable how early Hitler realized at which point the major Russian counteroffensive would hit the German and allied lines. But he was incapable of drawing the proper conclusions from his realization. When the Russians launched their attack and succeeded in trapping the Sixth Army within a few days, Hitler was unable to make the right decision. For this reason the German summer offensive of 1942 ended in a heavy defeat that could not be recouped, especially since it was soon to be followed by a second catastrophe, the capitulation of the German and Italian armies in Tunisia. The battle of Stalingrad—the climax and aftermaths of which will be described in a later volume dealing with the period 1943–45—initiated the series of defeats that brought about Germany's collapse and ruined Hitler's recently acquired reputation as a *Feldherr* (Great Captain).

GERMAN TANK rumbles through Kiev.

NORTHERN RUSSIA

Half of the German free in the Soviet Union operated within the areas of Army Group Center and North. These forces did not participate in major offensives in 1942. As the southern offensive progressed, the northern armies watched the campaign as did the Finnish "cobelligerents" (The Finns were not, technically, German Allies). Until the offensive actually struck on 19th November German Army Intelligence continued to predict that the Russians would launch their major offensive against Army Group Center and not towards Stalingrad. Even after the offensive began, German planners continued to delude themselves that Russia was committing its last reserves to exploit an "unexpected" victory in the South.

This impression quickly changed after a week, when the Russians launched six armies against the Rzheu salient and a Shock Army (with a 5 to 1 advantage) toward Velikiye Luki. (See Map 18). Both offensives against Army Group Center began on 25 November. The larger attack hit the Germans where expected and met prepared resistance. The troops were proven veterans of past campaigns and mobile reserves had been readied. Within two weeks the Germans had thrown back the Rzheu offensive to its original line. On 11 December the Russians attacked with increased intensity, losing 300 tanks in two days. The offensive ended by 16 December without significant Russian success except for a small salient that held out several more weeks.

The offensive by the Third Shock Army was more successful. Within two days most of a German division (83rd) at "Velikiye Luki was encircled and a garrison 15 miles to the west risked a similar fate. A relief operation near Christmas failed. A second effort was launched on 4 January 1943, and finally succeeded in extricating a few hundred survivors by 16 January. About 5000 Germans perished in the town, while another 12,000 were lost in the rescue attempts.

THE RUSSIANS ENCIRCLE STALINGRAD

The German attack in Stalingrad had lost momentum by 6 October, when Paulus temporarily halted his forces to regroup. His infantry and engineer troops had become badly depleted with strength typically near 50% in these units. By that date losses totaled almost 40,000, including nearly 8,000 killed, in the 6th Army. The attack burst forward again when fresh units arrived on 14 October, until the end of the month. (See Inset, Map 18)

By early November freezing weather and shortages had badly slowed the German advance. Meanwhile, German intelligence predicted that a Soviet counter offensive could be expected at any time (after the fall rains) and last several weeks. The intelligence branch noted a large build up opposite the Third Rumanian Army (See Map 16). Hitler feared that the Russians would attempt a single large thrust towards Rostov. When bridge construction was observed in the area, in early November, he ordered a fresh corps to move from France in order to bolster the northern wing of Stalingrad.

It is significant that through the first week of November, the intelligence branch mistakenly believed the Russians would attack north toward Army Group Center. Only in the second week of November, was more attention given to a build up on the Don, South of Stalingrad (See Map 20). By 12 November the intelligence branch began looking at an attack to the rear of Stalingrad, but along the lines suggested by Hitler, from the north only, towards Rostov. Weichs, commanding Army Group B, realized by 9 November that there was a dangerous build up in front of the 4th Rumanian Army south of Stalingrad and, therefore elected not to shift a reserve division (29th) from south to north of Stalingrad. On 16 November, Weichs decided to shift the weak 22nd Panzer division further south to back the Third Rumanian Army, and combine with the untested Rumanian Armored Division to form the XLVIII Panzer Corps.

The Soviets had meanwhile assembled a local numerical advantage of at least 2 to 1 through October and mid November. They allowed their front line in Stalingrad to bleed white as critical reserves massed. There were five Soviet armies ready to begin the attack. The numerical

18. SOVIET OFFENSIVE AGAINST ARMY GROUP CENTER AND NORTH

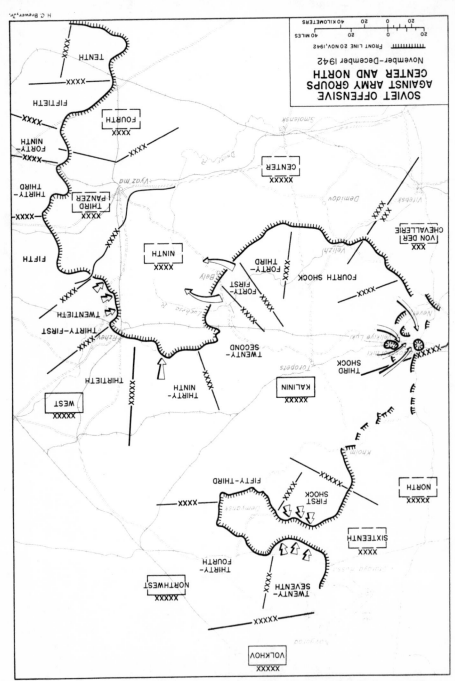

SOVIET OFFENSIVE
AGAINST ARMY GROUPS
CENTER AND NORTH
November–December 1942

FRONT LINE 20 NOV. 1942

20   0   20   40 MILES
20   0   20   40 KILOMETERS

H. C. Brewer, Jr.

odds were further enhanced by the fact that the blows would fall on the poorly led and ill-equipped Rumanian Armies. Meanwhile the German 6th Army in Stalingrad resumed its attacks, oblivious to the threat of a Soviet *Blitzkrieg* attack.

On the snowy, sub-freezing morning of 19 November 1942, the Russian attacked north of Stalingrad (See Map 21). The Rumanian Third Army rapidly disintegrated. On the next day the blow fell on the VI Rumanian Corps of the Fourth Rumanian Army, south of Stalingrad; with similar results. In two days, most of the Rumanian frontline units had been broken.

The German XIV panzer corps attacked northwards from Stalingrad on the 20th, too weak to seal the penetration and too late to avoid entrapment. In the South, the German Fourth panzer army was split. Its 29th Motorized Division and IV Corps were pushed toward Stalingrad; the 16th Motorized Division and shaken VII Rumanian Corps remained outside. They were unable to prevent the Russians from pouring past; just as the 48th Panzer Corps was too weak, north of the pocket. By 23 November with the fall of the German garrison at Kalach (about seventy miles from the initial attack) Stalingrad was surrounded.

In terms of numbers, about one quarter million men, the equivalent of two armies, were cut off from Germany. This included five corps (IV, VIII, XI, LI, and XIV Panzer); with twenty-three divisions (1st Rumanian Cavalry; 20th Rumanian, 44, 71, 76, 79, 94, 100 Light, 113, 295, 297, 305, 371, 376, 384, and 389th Infantry; 3rd, 29th, and 60th Motorized; 14th, 16th, and 24th Panzer; and the 9th Anti-aircraft Divisions) with various construction and service troops, including Eastern auxiliaries. In fact, by 1944 standards these forces would have constituted an "army group" of three or four armies. The loss of such a military force would cripple Germany.

A rational military leader would have evaluated the critical situation and attempted to extricate the divisions. Hitler was already beginning to lose touch with reality and took another of the many decisions that proved his lack of military ability. Rather than authorizing a breakout from the city, he declared Stalingrad to be a "fortress" and attempted to conduct a relief operation. He created a new army group "Don" around the 6th Army and what was actually an understrength Panzer

Army (4th) and placed it under the command of Field Marshall Von Manstein. Air Marshall Goering promised to ship 600 tons of supplies daily into the city to maintain combat readiness of the encircled forces (and never managed more than 300).

Military leaders in the pocket, of the relief forces, and of the air units involved) protested that the capability to defend and relieve Stalingrad simply did not exist. On 5 December, 6th Army reported about one day of artillery ammunition (one-third of a "primary issue") remaining. The air commander Col. General Von Richtofen pointed out that he had only 60% of the required transport aircraft. Manstein ended his order on the relief operation with doubts about adequate strength, as needed to maintain a corridor to Stalingrad. Never-the-less, on 12 December, during the daily conference, Hitler pointed to Stalingrad on a map and stated that the city could not be given up under any circumstance.

On that same day Manstein finally launched the rescue operation, code-named "Winter Storm". Meanwhile, the Russians again struck north of Stalingrad on 16 December, overrunning the remnants of the Rumanian Third Army and an Italian Corps (See Map 22). By the 19th, Manstein's relief forces, spearheaded by the LVII Panzer Corps, penetrated to thirty-five miles outside the pocket and he ordered his subordinate army to prepare for a breakout. Hitler refused to approve withdrawal citing the lack of fuel within the pocket, which would cause abandonment of equipment.

When in two days further progress proved impossible, and as the Italian Army broke apart, Manstein again urged steps be taken for a breakout. The Sixth Army Chief of Staff indicated that fuel availability dropped to twelve miles, and another three days would be needed for a breakout attempt. He also pointed out the likelihood that such an attempt could force evacuation unless added supplies and replacements could be provided. On that basis Hitler refused to sanction a breakout. Thus, Winter Storm had failed.

Two days later Manstein provided Hitler three options. He stated that an added panzer corps would be needed to continue the relief operation. Otherwise, the Sixth Army should (1) be ordered to breakout

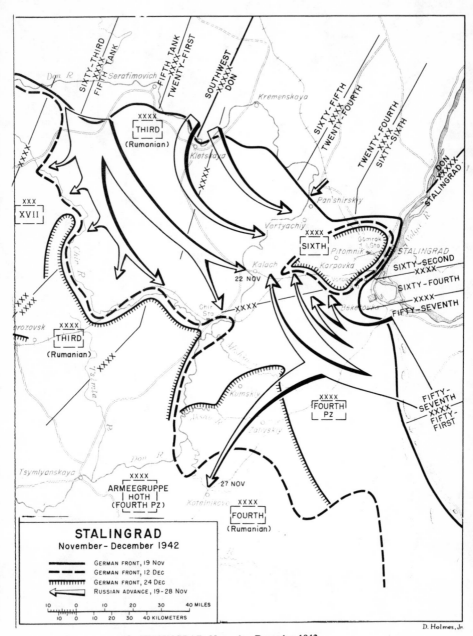

19. STALINGRAD, November–December 1942

with no guarantee of success or, (2) the army should defend in place with adequate airlifted supplies. Hitler wasted another day with counter questions and, by default, the 6th Army was condemned to a static defense with inadequate air supply. On the next day, the 24th, Manstein's LVII Panzer Corps was beaten back by the Russians. The day after Christmas, Paulus reported that his army was too weak for a breakout and could only be saved by outside forces.

The relief forces had by now become badly outnumbered and in danger of encirclement. Army Group A in the south had still not begun to retreat and Manstein pointed out how essential these units would be in the Army Group Don area. On the 26th, the Rumanian VII Corps disintegrated on the flank of the relief forces. On the 28th, only a rapid retreat saved the LVII Panzer Corps from encirclement and Manstein reported that his forces were not adequate to defend the existing front. By the end of the month, both a rescue and adequate re-supply of Stalingrad had failed as the Russians consolidated the objectives of the offensive.

It was the Sixth Army that was to save Army Group South by engaging Russian forces. Hitler continued to refuse necessary withdrawals and Manstein's frustration grew. Fourth Panzer Army continued to struggle against encirclement attempts and vainly sought needed reinforcement from Army Group A in the Caucasus. Army Detachment Hollidt carried out a precarious 100-mile retreat during the first week of the 1943, sometimes losing contact with Army Detachment Fretter-Pico on its left. Hitler attempted to stop this retreat when a vital airbase, needed for Stalingrad, had to be abandoned. He soon realized that any defense east of the Don's was not tenable.

A continuous front did not actually reform until the second week of January, although even then, the First Panzer Army had not linked with the right flank of the Fourth Panzer Army. Kleist, commanding Army Group A, asked Hitler for specific directions on 13 January, and recommended a retreat toward Rostov. Colonel General Zietzler, Chief of Staff of OKH, urged Kleist to fall back toward Crimea. Manstein struggled to maintain his front. In the north, Weich's Army Group B had been a helpless spectator to the Stalingrad tragedy, but now joined it. On the 13th the Russian Fortieth Army struck the Second Hungarian Army on the Army Group South flank.

In the third week of January, Army Group B began to collapse as the remainder of the Italian Eight Army and the Hungarian Army fell apart, thus leaving a 180-mile gap south of Voronezh. The left flank of the Army Group - the German Second Army - recoiled to avoid encirclement. Manstein with pressure along his entire front, kept advising the High Command about the urgency of the situation. Hitler continued indecision discouraging withdrawal while promising seemingly inadequate reinforcement.

The last week of January 1943, was likely one of the most tragic in German military history. On 25-26 January, the German Second Army was temporarily encircled by a Russian *Blitzkrieg* attack. This destroyed more units and Voronezh fell with 50,000 prisoners. The renewed Soviet Winter offensive struck all three southern Army Groups. Hitler finally ordered most of the 1st Panzer Army north toward Rostov (See Map 23). It was too little, too late. The 6th Army perished in Stalingrad. Added to losses of four allied armies, dead and missing-half a million men. Meanwhile, desperately needed armies, with over four hundred thousand men, retreated toward Crimea from the Caucasus. Meanwhile at Casablanca, at Roosevelt's behest, the Allies announced a policy of unconditional surrender.

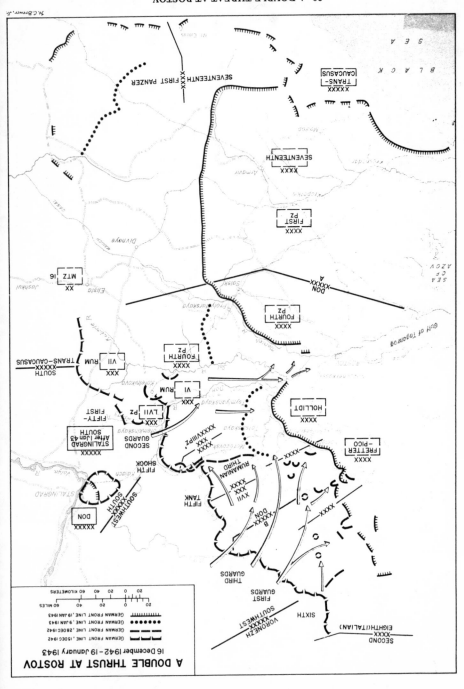

A DOUBLE THRUST AT ROSTOV
16 December 1942 – 19 January 1943

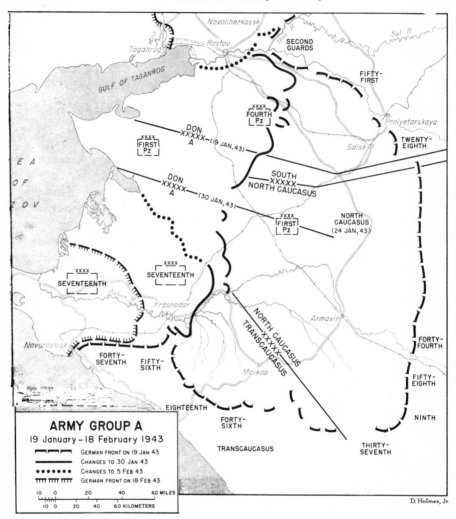

ARMY GROUP A
19 January – 18 February 1943

━━━━━ GERMAN FRONT ON 19 JAN 43
━━━━━ CHANGES TO 30 JAN 43
•••••••• CHANGES TO 5 FEB 43
┳┳┳┳ GERMAN FRONT ON 18 FEB 43

10 0   20   40   60 MILES
10 0   20   40   60 KILOMETERS

D. Holmes, Jr.

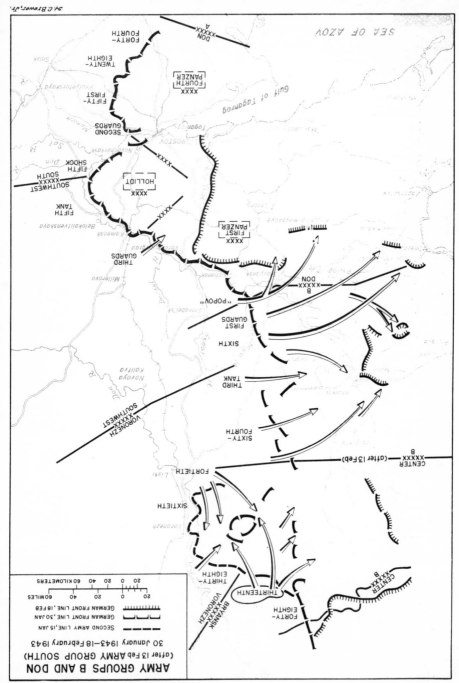

144

22. ARMY GROUP B AND DON

ARMY GROUPS B AND DON
(after 13 Feb) ARMY GROUP SOUTH)
30 January 1943–18 February 1943

ARMY GROUPS NORTH AND CENTER

On the northern fronts, the two army groups took steps to shorten their line (See Map 24). Army Group North, after careful preparation, eliminated their Demyansk pocket between 20 February and 18 March. Army Group Center took similar action in the Rzhev Salient, code name Operation Buffalo, and conducted an evacuation from 1 to 23 March. The two withdrawals reduced the front by over three hundred miles. With the exception of right flank of Army Group Center, both fronts were relatively quiet, and front line units could even be deployed against the ever growing partisan threat.

On the front of the Second Panzer and Second Army, the Russian winter offensive had made major inroads thus exposing a long flank north of Kursk, around Orel. Here Kluge and Zietzler could not get permission to withdraw. This was where Hitler schemed to initiate his 1943 offensive to sweep southwards and meet a pincer advancing north from Belgorod. With the newly available units from the reduced front and with arriving replacements, Army Group Center began massing a large part of what could have been Germany's strategic reserve.

THE SOUTHERN ARMY GROUPS

After the fall of Stalingrad, the situation continued to be fluid as the Russian offensives continued. The Soviets pressed their advantage and continued their Winter Offensive (See Map 25). In the first week of February, Russian spearheads began pushing west along the boundary between Army Groups B and Don. Manstein's forces faced a serious threat of becoming cut off. He called for "drastic" actions on 5 February, to reinforce his flank. Hitler flew Manstein to his headquarters on the 6th for a conference. In the four-hour confrontation, Hitler accepted full blame for Stalingrad, but refused to relinquish supreme military control. He finally agreed to permit withdrawal behind the Mius river.

In the next two weeks Army Group Don retreated and consolidated its new positions. Masses of troops and civilians evacuated the Caucasus and units were shifted northwards (including 50,000 troops by air). In front of the Soviet offensive, Army Detachment Lanz with three of the best German motorized divisions (Grossdeutschland, SS Das Reich and SS L.A. Hitler) and other assorted units, defended Kharkov. They would not succeed in holding off from Soviet armies.

The newly created SS Panzer Corps demonstrated arrogance and the typical incompetence of political command. The SS units were pushed out of the city causing army commander Lanz to be replaced by Kempf on 20 February. Army Group Don was redesignated as Army Group South and Hitler arrived to exert some control (in reaction, perhaps to Manstein's comments of 6 February) on 17 February. Meanwhile, the Russian onslaught continued and a 100 mile breach developed between Army Group B and South. The Russians also had broken across the Mius river line in several places.

GERMAN COUNTERATTACKS

The next month would see the impact of command emphasis. The air and land units planned to rescue Stalingrad had begun arriving in force. The Fourth Air Force, for example, controlled over 50% of the Eastern front aircraft and would average 1000 sorties per day until spring. This was three times the January average. New formations finally arrived from the west and moved northward from the Caucasus. The SS Death's Head division moved east from Kiev and the Fourth Panzer Army reformed south of Army Detachment Kempf which was still retreating (See Map 26).

On 23 February the First Panzer Army struck against Tank Group Popov (with six tank "corps") and decimated it in a series of encirclement battles. The Fourth Panzer army struck toward Kharkov and retook the city after rapid advances averaging 100 miles per day. The SS Corps entered the city on 11 March, in disregard of direct orders, and retook it in three days of street fighting. A final push toward Belgorod captured the city on 18 March. Army Detachment Kempf regrouped and also advanced eastward. This ended the Soviet Winter Offensive in the South.

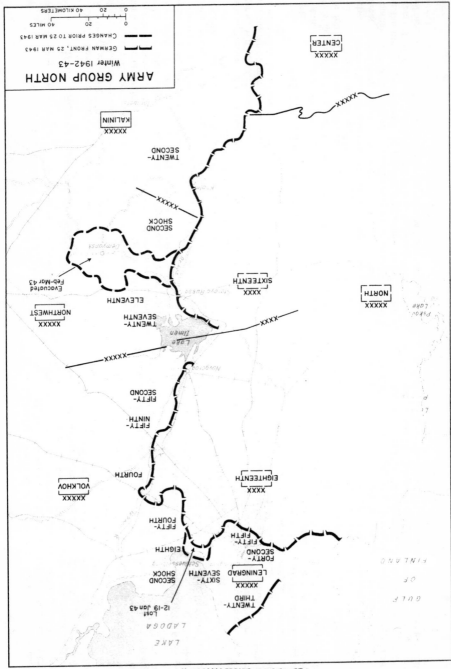

23. ARMY GROUP NORTH

ARMY GROUP NORTH
Winter 1942-43

GERMAN FRONT, 25 MAR 1943
CHANGES PRIOR TO 25 MAR 1943

0   20   40 MILES
0   20   40 KILOMETERS

CENTER
XXXXX

KALININ
XXXXX

TWENTY-SECOND

SECOND SHOCK
XXXXX

Evacuated Feb-Mar 43

ELEVENTH

TWENTY-SEVENTH

SIXTEENTH
XXXX

NORTH
XXXXX

NORTHWEST
XXXXX

Lake Ilmen

Pskov Lake

FIFTY-SECOND

FIFTY-NINTH

FOURTH

VOLKHOV
XXXXX

EIGHTEENTH
XXXX

FIFTY-FOURTH

EIGHTH

FIFTY-FIFTH

FORTY-SECOND

LENINGRAD
XXXXX

SECOND SHOCK

SIXTY-SEVENTH

TWENTY-THIRD

Lost 12-19 Jan 43

LAKE LADOGA

GULF OF FINLAND

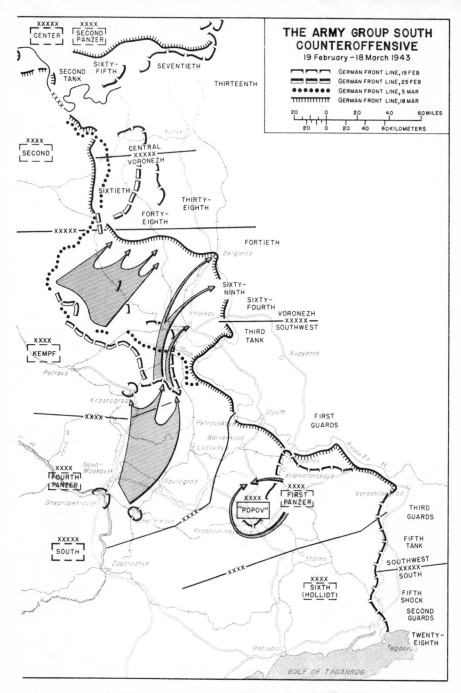

24. THE ARMY GROUP SOUTH COUNTER OFFENSIVE

CALM IN THE EAST

As the winter snows melted; swollen rivers and mud made warfare difficult. On the southernmost, flank Army Group A was ordered to eliminate a beachead south of Novorossisk to preclude use of the town as a naval staging area for the Black Sea fleet. By 23 April the five-day attack was discontinued as a complete failure.

Along the entire Russian front it was a time to lick wounds. New weapons arrived; replacements, hurriedly thrown into combat, had to be trained, needed machinery was added and repaired. Somehow the veteran divisions had to be honed to their old edge. Even if that could be done there also needed to be some preparation to fill the holes left by the five armies destroyed in the past four months.

DISASTER IN THE WEST

On 13 May, the African Fifth Panzer Army collapsed along with its Italian Allies. In the last weeks of fighting almost 300,000 Axis troops were lost, including almost 90,000 Germans, adding to 65,000 German captured earlier or evacuated because of wounds. Total German losses on both fronts from February through May 1943, included 100,000 killed and 90,000 missing, plus tens of thousands of wounded that would not fight again. Added to the more severe earlier losses it became clear that Germany's fortunes had irrevocably changed.

The situation of the Axis allies was particularly dismal for the Germans. Its major partner was broken. Italy would, in fact, formally capitulate in four months. The Japanese fleet had been severely damaged in 1942 and, with the evacuation of Guadacanal in February 1943, Japan began a series of almost unbroken reheats. The pretense of a neutral Vichy France ended. Finland was sending feelers to the United States and Britain to intercede in its behalf with Russia. Hungary would nurture its remaining strength with its borders, sending only token forces to the front.

Rumania urged Hitler to make peace with the west and end the two-front war. It also sent peace feelers to the west through the Argentinna ambassador. Bulgaria became less aggressive. Potential allies, such as Turkey and Spain became adamantly neutral. The puppet rulers of Slovakia and Croatia also expressed their concerns about further commitments. Germany would increasingly have to depend on its own human and economic resources.

GERMAN REACTION

Hitler surveyed the results of winter and spring. Already steps were being taken to close all non-essential German industries. Mobilization was intensified. Increasing use was made of *Volksdeutsche* in occupied states. Forced induction of Soviet defectors and volunteers increased. For the first time even ethnic Russians became acceptable for German service. The essential war industries often had to replace able bodied Germans and accept foreign slave labor. This was to be the start of total war.

Many German military leaders realized that the days of grand offensives had ended. There was discussion of possibly building a fortified line in the east and simply holding off Russian onslaughts with mobile reserves. Hitler was against this and felt that a decisive victory was needed to reduce the Russian threat and to restore the confidence of his allies in German ability. He announced Order 6 for Operation Citadel in mid April, to be launched on a six day notice in early May. This was to be a major encirclement battle, on the scale of 1941, and expected to net half a million prisoners. It was to be followed by another encirclement, Operation Panther, to the south.

On 3-4 May, Hitler held a conference with Manstein, Kluge, Model, Guderian, Speer and the chiefs of OKH and OKL. Model, as commander of the northern breakthrough army, convinced Hitler to delay the offensive until June because of inadequacy of his armor. This was done despite the objection of the other army and air force leaders. Arguments by Guderian and Speer to cancel the offensive, however, probably proved decisive. They felt that the expected tank losses would not permit armored forces to be rebuilt. Hitler became convinced that more and better tanks had to be built, but ignored the admonition to not squander armored forces and German reserves.

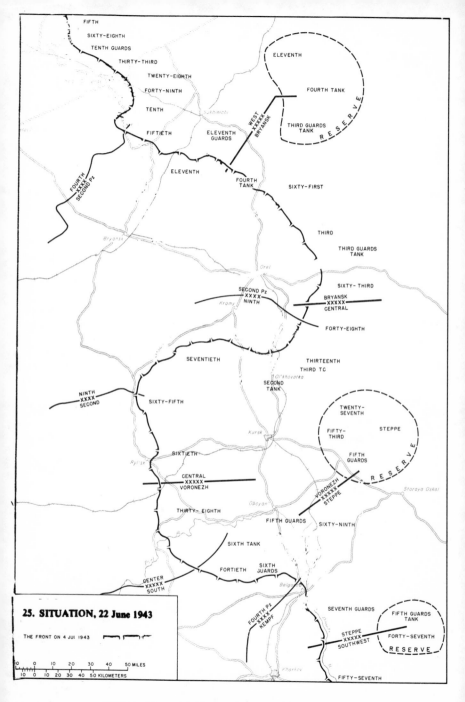

25. SITUATION, 22 June 1943

THE FRONT ON 4 JUL 1943

The map above should replace the one on page 149.

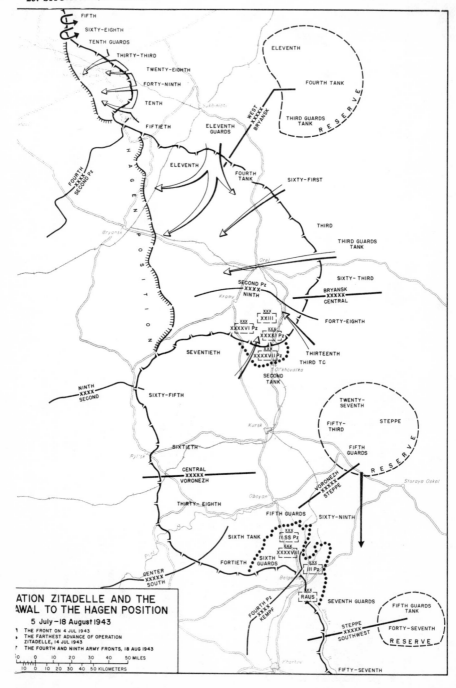

FIFTH
SIXTY-EIGHTH
TENTH GUARDS
THIRTY-THIRD
TWENTY-EIGHTH
FORTY-NINTH
TENTH
FIFTIETH
ELEVENTH GUARDS
ELEVENTH
FOURTH TANK
SIXTY-FIRST
THIRD
THIRD GUARDS TANK
SIXTY-THIRD
FORTY-EIGHTH
THIRTEENTH
THIRD TC
SEVENTIETH
SIXTY-FIFTH
SIXTIETH
THIRTY-EIGHTH
FIFTH GUARDS
SIXTY-NINTH
SIXTH TANK
FORTIETH
SIXTH GUARDS
SEVENTH GUARDS

WEST
XXXXX
BRYANSK

FOURTH
XXXX
SECOND Pz

SECOND Pz
XXXX
NINTH

BRYANSK
XXXXX
CENTRAL

NINTH
XXXX
SECOND

SECOND TANK

CENTRAL
XXXXX
VORONEZH

VORONEZH
XXXXX
STEPPE

CENTER
XXXXX
SOUTH

FOURTH Pz
XXXX
KEMPF

STEPPE
XXXXX
SOUTHWEST

ELEVENTH
FOURTH TANK
THIRD GUARDS TANK
RESERVE

TWENTY-SEVENTH
FIFTY-THIRD
STEPPE
FIFTH GUARDS
RESERVE

FIFTH GUARDS TANK
FORTY-SEVENTH
RESERVE

XXX
XXXXVI Pz
XXX
XXIII
XXX
XXXXI Pz
XXX
XXXXVII Pz

XXX
II SS Pz
XXX
XXXXVIII
XXX
III Pz
XXX
RAUS

FIFTY-SEVENTH

H A G E N   P O S I T I O N

Sukhinichi
Bryansk
Orel
Kromy
Ol'khovatka
Kursk
Ryl'sk
Oboyan
Belgorod
Kharkov
Staraya Oskol

OPERATION ZITADELLE AND THE
WITHDRAWAL TO THE HAGEN POSITION
5 July – 18 August 1943

THE FRONT ON 4 JUL 1943
THE FARTHEST ADVANCE OF OPERATION
ZITADELLE, 14 JUL 1943
THE FOURTH AND NINTH ARMY FRONTS, 18 AUG 1943

10   0   10   20   30   40   50 MILES
10   0   10   20   30   40   50 KILOMETERS

advantage over the Russians. He understood the implications of un-conditional surrender on Nazi leaders (and murderers) and forced Germany into the storm that would follow.

To the dismay of the front line leaders a postponement to 12 June was announced. Perhaps Hitler hoped that the Russians would attack first and relieve him of making a decision; more likely he actually believed that the new heavy tanks would be decisive when available.

On June 10, as the deadline approached, OKH called a conference to propose a delay until the Russians initiated combat. This put off a possible decision until 18 June when the Operations Staff of OKW then also came out in favor of cancelling Citadel. In light of the disaster in Tunisia and an expected Mediterranean invasion, OKW proposed forming the two offensive armies for Citadel into strategic reserves to be deployed near railroads. The two-front war was to begin in earnest.

Hitler refused the advice and announced, on the same day, that Citadel would go forward. This decision was disseminated on 20 June. In the next few days Hitler decided to launch the offensive on 5 July. The armies moved into position (see map 27).

After two years in Russia, half way into the Russo-German War, the tide had turned. Hitler took an irrevocable decision that would break the arm of his eastern armies and expend much of Germany's hoarded reserve. Hitler had no way of knowing that Russia learned of Citadel and prepared, not only to receive it in force, but to strike back. Their counter offensive would eliminate the entire Orel salient. Nine Russian armies in reserve waited to strike the German offensive.

OUTLOOK

The Axis could foresee resources stretching against ever increasing Allied numbers and weapons production. Time did not favor a strategy of caution. Losses in June 1943 were 13,400 killed and 1300 missing but this was to be the least costly month of the eastern war. Future losses would never be less than thrice as great. It is doubtful that even the fanatic Nazi leadership actually expected to prevail.

The time for prudent and flexible defensive warfare had come, with the possible hope of eventually wresting a favorable peace. Hitler instead chose a bold but rigid strategy that deprived his armies of their inherent

XV

CRITICAL ANALYSIS OF THE WINTER CAMPAIGN OF 1942/43

MISDIRECTION

The fundamental error in the Stalingrad Offensive is clear in retrospect. There should never have been a "Stalingrad" campaign. Such a street-by-street battle of attrition was completely uncharacteristic of German *Blitzkrieg* warfare. The basis of German offensive warfare was to bypass centers of resistance and reduce them as time and resources permitted. (Consider the siege of Leningrad in the north.) Instead Hitler committed his strongest army to the city and was even encouraging attack at the time the Russians sprang their trap.

The failure of Stalingrad is similar to the ancient Roman failure at Cannae against Hannibal. There are few better camparisons. Just as the Romans pushed into the center of the Carthiginian line raising shouts of victory, so also the Teutonic Centurions arrogantly plunged toward the Stalingrad bridgeheads. Just as the Carthiginians fell upon the Roman rear, so also the Russians swept upon the supply lines of the attacking army. Just as the Romans could not deploy their archers and phalanx, so also was German artillery and armor within the pocket rendered useless. Just as the entire Roman army was destroyed, so also the German legions perished.

The reasons for the engagement in the city can likely be found in Hitler's personality. Perhaps he was obsessed by the name of the Stalingrad, which translates to "Stalin's city." After the failure to capture the city in a swift offensive Hitler decided to reinforce the attack. It is characteristic of fanatics to intensify their efforts after they lose sight of the cause.

The cause of the Stalingrad offensive was the need to seize the resources of south Russia, especially oil, and secure the right flank of the German front. The army plans were adequate to accomplish this. If the Germans could breach the Volga and hold its mouth then they would have essentially split the Russian front and been able to mop up the Caucasus armies at will. The Don and Volga rivers could have provided a natural northern shield while this was accomplished.

Once the southern Russian units had been neutralized. The mobile units of Army Group A could join with the northern armies for an attack through Stalingrad and northwest toward Moscow and Leningrad. Even if such an offensive had not been possible in 1942, the seizure of the Astrakhan region would have provided a much shorter front than one stretching in a large bulge through the steppes west of the Caspian.

Instead, Hitler decided to attempt both goals simultaneously and he split his forces. The *"schwerpunkt"* principle of Blitzkrieg was violated. The main effort was toward a city of political rather than military significance. The cart had been put before the horse. The structural foundation for such a conquest simply did not exist.

Hitler also deluded himself about the ability of his Allies and planted the offensive between their insecure flanks. Their poor equipment, inadequate training, and inept leadership was ignored. Perhaps the generals must share the blame in allowing soldiers from mountainous Hungary and Rumania to be deployed on the Russian plains. Even the Italian Alpine units were sent to the steppes. These were the units that logically belonged in the Caucasus.

If German formations had held the flanks of Stalingrad, the Russian breakthrough would not have succeeded (as was demonstrated at Rzhev). The fundamental problem, was that the Germans lacked the units to accomplish the two strategic offensives at the same time. There were not enough units, Allied and German combined, to successfully accomplish both objectives.

EXPECTATIONS

Intelligence reports also misled the command. Until the very start of the Russian offensive the chief of Foreign Armies East, Gehlen, predicted a Russian offensive toward Army Group Center. As brilliant as his past (and future) tactical information may have been, it failed to anticipate Russian strategic capabilities except in the vaguest terms.

Of course, Gehlen was correct. The Russians did launch a major offensive against Army Group Center. They even managed a respectable offensive against Army Group North. The failure was that the German intelligence organs did not foresee a major offensive on all three fronts. The Germans had deluded themselves into underestimating Soviet capability.

The weather was another factor that acted against the Axis. The temperatures in Stalingrad in November, December, and January average 36°F, 27°F, and 19°F, respectively. In 1942-43 the winter started earlier and a deep freeze had set in during early November. On the day the Soviet offensive began it was well below freezing and snowing. Reduced visibility favored the attacker.

In December the weather became more mild and thawing interfered with German counterattacks. Daily variations were extreme and commonly produced fog, clouds, rain, snow and hampered German aerial resupply. After Christmas the temperature dropped well below zero for several days. The weather became more severe in January 1943. As in the previous winter the Russians knew what to expect from their weather and prepared for it. Meanwhile the German armed forces had not been adequately reequipped for winter warfare.

HITLER'S JUDGEMENT

Stalingrad was one of the many catastrophies caused by Hitler's "intuitive" perceptions. Past blunders had been far outbalanced by his successful gambles. After Stalingrad he would more than make up for his political successes earlier in the war. Uncharacteristically, even Hitler assumed full blame for the disaster of Stalingrad.

His political blunder was compounded by Nazi treatment of the Soviet minority groups, especially the nearly thirty million Ukrainian and six million White Russians. His brutality allowed the Great Russians, with barely one hundred million people (and less than 60% of the population), to convince the non-Russian (Soviet) peoples that they actually were fighting a great patriotic war for the nation, rather than for the communist party. Nazism (and Allied indifference) converted many anti-communists to Russian service. Aside from the obvious loss to

military manpower, this also drove many of the occupied peoples to band into partisan formations, some fighting both nazis and communists.

Economic errors compounded Hitler's political blunders. He failed to appreciate the supply difficulties of the endless country with its dirt roads and few rail lines. The front line troops in 1942 had started with equipment and manpower shortages partly because wartime industrial mobilization had only started in early 1942. Total war was not declared until after Stalingrad. There was a lack of essential materials and manpower and what was available could not be deployed properly because an adequate transport system did not exist.

Psychological Warfare

Skill, Efficiency, and Motivation are essential to success of any enterprise. Most histories adequately discuss the first two factors but only mention the third. But it was probably the motivation of the Soviet armies and people was the most decisive factor in the German defeat. The often fanatical if uneven, quality of Soviet resistance can not be explained by such factors as NKVD and party brutality, or commissar discipline as has often been suggested. Patriotism was the actual source of motivation.

Stalin was silent until 3 July, nearly two weeks after the invasion. Then in a well prepared speech he appealed to the people to rally to the defense of "Mother Russia". It is significant that Stalin's appeal was not worded in terms of party doctrine using the "communism as a world struggle theme". Such an approach to a people that lived under brutal tyranny for over a decade; and on an army officer corps torn by a viscious purge; would likely have failed. Thus the Soviet dictatorship stimulated its nation with the same adrenalin that flowed naturally in the American people after Pearl Harbor.

It is worthwhile to say a few words about propaganda and psychological operations at this point. Man's effort to gain his ends by threat or persuasion is as old as history but a systematic and scientific study of how this is to be done is relatively new - starting mainly in WWI and being developed prior to World War II.

Propaganda can be defined as "any form of information, ideas, doctrines, or special appeals in support of national objectives designed to influence the opinions, emotions, attitudes, or behavior of any specified group in order to benefit the sponsor". (U.S. Army doctrine). Propaganda or other action having the same purpose directed at hostile foreign groups is termed to be Psychological Warfare. Psychological Warfare by itself has produced few victories, but by playing on the emotions generated by the stress of war, and by heightening fears or dissatisfactions, it has often sparked men into taking a desired action. Through providing false yet believable information, it can also impair enemy decision making.

To be effective propaganda must: 1) gain attention, 2) be understood, 3) arouse a need, and 4) suggest a solution. To succeed a propagandist must have an extensive knowledge of man's nature and what influences it; particularly cultural factors. The last is crucial. The target group's reaction will largely depend on its "set" or "expectancy". The message must "make sense" to its audience. The propagandist may seek to relate a proposed behavior to the resolution of a conflict and the reduction of frustration that occurs when a behavior pattern is blocked, and will avoid motivation towards goals which cause emotional frustration. Generally a propagandist seeks to change certain attitudes in order to induce specified types of behavior. In general the successful propagandist will clearly specify his audience and target attitude in order to avoid rejection of his message. He will attempt to make the behavior he is seeking "meaningful" to the target group.

The tremendous number (about 90 million) of minority nationalities in the Soviet Union made it a fertile field for what had been the classic Nazi foreign policy of "set against each other and conquer" as illustrated in France. Prior to the Russian invasion, Rosenberg who Hitler charged with exploiting the Eastern territories, had already formed several (non-Great Russian) committees of Ukranians, Georgians, Armenians, Azerbaid-jainians, Turkestanias, and Cossacks, and trained representatives at their propaganda school. The saner political minds of Germany advocated a propaganda theme suggesting that Germany woudl free the soviet peoples of Russian communist domination.

On the other hand Hitler, rejecting the counsel of his Russian ambassadors Schulenberg and Koestring (whom he called "the two worst informed men on Russia"), was carried away by optimism of an easy Russian conquest and his hatred for communism. He decided on outright annexation of the Baltic states, the Ukraine, and other parts of Russia (31 July 1941). The population was to be slave labor! Rosenberg was slightly more moderate in that he favored preferential treatment be given to the national minority gorups, but his *Ostministerium* was already projecting that 40 million "Great Russians" would have to be "eliminated" (even though Rosenberg later protested about German brutality of prisoners and civilians).

Instead of entering Russia as saviours of the people from communism, German policy became enmeshed with racial opinions of men like Hitler and Himmler, so that all Slavs, especially the Great Russians, were viewed as "sub-human". The crusade against communism came to be directed against the Russian people, while it called on the rest of Europe to help fight the scourge of Bolshevism. This type of approach created obvious attitudes in the minds of the conquered and it did not take long for the Slavic Soviet citizens to realize that the Germans were after them and not their government. Certain generals advocated this racist policy of exploitation as evidenced by the "commissar order" and instructions (from OKW) that Russian war prisoners were not entitled treatment according to the Geneva convention.

Other generals strongly objected. In November 1941, the chief of OKW Field Marshall von Brauchitsch, submitted to Hitler, a recommendation that anti-communist Russians be incorporated into German military units (this was only officially approved after February 1942). He stated "Russia can only be beaten by Russians."

The 3 million prisoners captured by the Germans in the first three months of war offered a potent and militarily trained force with which to attack the Soviet Union. Stalin was well aware of this potential and even declared (Order 260) "that all Soviet prisoners of war will be considered traitors to their country". He even bombed several prisoner of war camps, followed by leaflets with "So will it be with all those who betray the cause of Lenin and Stalin." The NKVD issued an order for reprisals against the prisoner's families.

In the final analysis it was the wide gulf between German action and promises which drew the Russian people to support their government. While Nazi propaganda promised "liberation", abolishment of the collective farms, and fair treatment to defectors and prisoners, the people could see the brutal behavior of the conquerors. The strong separatist tendencies of the conquered lands were poorly exploited and most nationalist groups often formed large splinter partisan units that fought both Russians and Germans.

By late-summer 1941, Stalin's "Rally to defend the Motherland" message was becoming increasingly meaningful to the Russian people. German deeds spoke louder than their words. By 1945, about 1 million Soviet citizens had served in German uniform. The outcome of the war would almost certainly have been different if Germany had made a genuine effort to motivate and mobilize the non-Russian half of Soviet population.

Lend Lease Supplies

Some post war writers have claimed that Russian victory would not have been possible without Western Lend-Lease supplies. Total British, Canadian and U.S. Lend-Lease shipments from 22 June 1941 to 12 May 1945 amounted to sixteen million long tons; including 8.4 million tons of food, metals, and petroleum. Seventy percent of this (11.3 million tons) was shipped after June 1943, and ten percent (1.6 million tons) had been sent prior to July 1942. About 1/3 (1 million tons) of the July 1942 to June 1943 shipments would have arrived in time to make a difference for the decisive Stalingrad campaign. During the first half of the Russo-German war, perhaps about one-tenth to one-sixth of total lend-lease could have been deployed.

In terms the larger proportion this includes (among many other categories) the delivery of about 2100 aircraft, 6500 jeeps, 61,600 trucks, 740 medium tanks, 4,800 motorcycles, 1200 tractors, 300 locomotives, 1600 railway cars, 16000 submachine guns (45 cal) and 5400 radio stations. In the face of Russian denial, it would be difficult to prove that most of this aid made a major difference. The Russians justifiably claim that our tanks and aircraft were often not up to their standards.

What does stand out, however, is the amount of mobility we provided to the Russians. If we assume that the 2600 motor vehicles are required to motorize a Russian Corps, then the total number of vehicles shipped to Russia before Stalingrad (about 365 thousand) was adequate to motorize 140 Russian Corps. In other terms, the west gave the Russians enough vehicles to motorize all of their combat divisions, twice. (assuming the June 1941 level of mobilization). And for each motor vehicle that was sent, so also was one ton of petroleum products!

The food provided was quite substantial. About 640 thousand tons of lend-lease food were distributed to the Russians in their first 600 days of war. This was enough to give each Russian 1.4 lbs. of nutrition per day.

Could the Russians have beaten the Germans without Western aid? The answers must be qualified: in front of Moscow in 1941, definitely; in Stalingrad during the winter of 1942-43, probably. Given the major blunders made by the Germans in both the 1941 and 1942 campaigns it is likely that Russians courage and tenacity would have prevailed, despite inadequate food and mobility.

It is unlikely that the Russians would have created a blitzkrieg capability in late 1942 if they lacked motorization. A panzer attack on Stalingrad would have been a close situation. The Russians could have held their southern flank but the German crises situation would probably have been less serious than it actually became. The possibility of concurrent offensives on the central and northern fronts in 1942 would have been unlikely and fewer Russian lives may have been squandered in wasted offensives. Leningrad might have remained in jeopardy. Without Western lend-lease a German army probably not have been lost at Stalingrad and the decisive battles would likely have been fought in 1944, rather than before July 1943.

LOSSES

The Russian victory at Stalingrad marked the turning point in the European Theater of War. The obvious reason for such a conclusion is based on German casualty figures. Less obvious but more important are the casualties of the German Allies and the loss of Soviet oil capacity. In addition it became clear that the Russians had learned the rudiments of Blitzkrieg tactics, as demonstrated by two strategic pincer attacks.

German casualties in the period 18 November 1942 to 1 February 1943 totalled more than 100,000 dead and almost 180,000 captured. In addition to the units destroyed in Stalingrad, another seven divisions had been decimated in the Don bend (62,298,304,385,387 Infantry and 22,27 Panzer Divisions). To put these losses in perspective we should recall that in all the German combat prior to June 1941 the total German losses (killed and captured) were less than 100,000 men. During the entire previous Russo-German war (from 22 June 1941 to 18 November 1942) total German losses had amounted to three-quarter million men. In other words, in less than three months, the Germans had lost one-third the manpower of the previous thirty-nine months. This does not even include wounded, of whom about one-third would also not return to the front.

The specific losses of the German Allies are not clear but they were at least as great as German losses in numbers. Both the Rumanian Third and Fourth Armies collapsed. The Italian Eighth Army lost over 100,000 captured. The Hungarian Second Army disintegrated with about 80,000 captured.

Italy could no longer provide an effective force in Russia and this defeat played a major role in the forthcoming Italian capitulation in September 1943. (As of January 1943 the Italians had lost about 450,000 men, of which about one-third had been lost in Russia). The Rumanian Armies did not return to the front until 1944 (although several corps continued to operate in south Russia) and they went over to the Russians that August. For the rest of 1943 the Hungarians could be used for little more than rear security duty. In proportion to their population the three Axis allies suffered at least as much as the Germans.

Finland was also shaken by the German collapse. On 3 February the Finnish president met with his cabinet to discuss extricating Finland from the war because he felt that the fortunes of war had turned decisively against the Germans. A few days later the matter was secretly presented to Parliament, with the conclusion that peace efforts should be initiated.

LOST MOBILITY

The loss of the Caucasus oil fields, although they did not even go into

production, underscored the critical objective of German campaign. The "Stalingrad" offensive was also an offensive in the Caucasus. Hitler attempted both offensives concurrently because of the critical fuel shortages already experienced on the front. Stocks of diesel oil and motor gas had been falling since 1940. Meanwhile, both the size of the German armed forces and the intensity of war effort increased. Almost half of German crude oil came from Rumania, now intimidated by ground defeat and by ever approaching Soviet forces. Failure to seize this added oil capacity constrained future increases of German mobility and mechanization.

The greatest loss for Germany was freedom of action. There would be no more successful strategic offensives. In terms of men and resources Germany had lost the ability to act; they would *react*. The Kursk offensive would prove a desperate attempt to postpone the obvious. It failed partly because German units had to deploy to Italy.

For the next year Germany would rage a war of attrition. This would only succeed in delaying the final outcome until the next year. In the summer of 1944 Germany would be decisively beaten, to confirm that it was not strong enough to win such a war.

It is interesting to speculate about the extent to which unconditional surrender contributed to this hopeless warfare. The totalitarian leaders forced the German nation to wage a total war. For the intelligent Germans, as for the German allies, the biggest loss of the Stalingrad campaign was hope. They knew that Germany could not win a war of attrition but they also knew that a totalitarian government left them no other alternative then to wage a continued struggle against ever increasing numbers and resources.

In terms of future applications it is significant to note that the advantage of totalitarian control later passed to the principal enemy of the Germans. The modern Russian-communist leadership can control its vassal states by force. Obvious military or economic failure may not defeat totalitarian control. After June 1943 German-nazi force held the empire together, and partly succeeded despite the logical consequences.

156

German 20-mm. ANTIAIRCRAFT GUN used in ground fighting, 1942.

1 January 1943

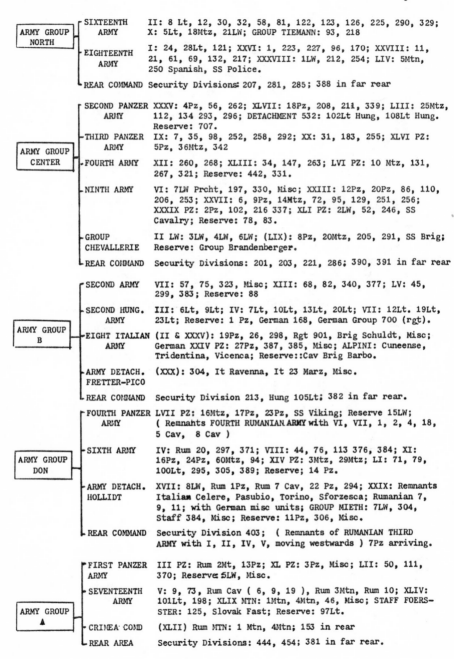

ARMY GROUP NORTH

SIXTEENTH ARMY	II: 8 Lt, 12, 30, 32, 58, 81, 122, 123, 126, 225, 290, 329; X: 5Lt, 18Mtz, 21LW; GROUP TIEMANN: 93, 218
EIGHTEENTH ARMY	I: 24, 28Lt, 121; XXVI: 1, 223, 227, 96, 170; XXVIII: 11, 21, 61, 69, 132, 217; XXXVIII: 1LW, 212, 254; LIV: 5Mtn, 250 Spanish, SS Police.
REAR COMMAND	Security Divisions: 207, 281, 285; 388 in far rear

ARMY GROUP CENTER

SECOND PANZER ARMY	XXXV: 4Pz, 56, 262; XLVII: 18Pz, 208, 211, 339; LIII: 25Mtz, 112, 134 293, 296; DETACHMENT 532: 102Lt Hung, 108Lt Hung. Reserve: 707.
THIRD PANZER ARMY	IX: 7, 35, 98, 252, 258, 292; XX: 31, 183, 255; XLVI PZ: 5Pz, 36Mtz, 342
FOURTH ARMY	XII: 260, 268; XLIII: 34, 147, 263; LVI PZ: 10 Mtz, 131, 267, 321; Reserve: 442, 331.
NINTH ARMY	VI: 7LW Prcht, 197, 330, Misc; XXIII: 12Pz, 20Pz, 86, 110, 206, 253; XXVII: 6, 9Pz, 14Mtz, 72, 95, 129, 251, 256; XXXIX PZ: 2Pz, 102, 216 337; XLI PZ: 2LW, 52, 246, SS Cavalry; Reserve: 78, 83.
GROUP CHEVALLERIE	II LW: 3LW, 4LW, 6LW; (LIX): 8Pz, 20Mtz, 205, 291, SS Brig; Reserve: Group Brandenberger.
REAR COMMAND	Security Divisions: 201, 203, 221, 286; 390, 391 in far rear

ARMY GROUP B

SECOND ARMY	VII: 57, 75, 323, Misc; XIII: 68, 82, 340, 377; LV: 45, 299, 383; Reserve: 88
SECOND HUNG. ARMY	III: 6Lt, 9Lt; IV: 7Lt, 10Lt, 13Lt, 20Lt; VII: 12Lt. 19Lt, 23Lt; Reserve: 1 Pz, German 168, German Group 700 (rgt).
EIGHT ITALIAN ARMY	(II & XXXV): 19Pz, 26, 298, Rgt 901, Brig Schuldt, Misc; German XXIV PZ: 27Pz, 387, 385, Misc; ALPINI: Cuneense, Tridentina, Vicenca; Reserve::Cav Brig Barbo.
ARMY DETACH. FRETTER-PICO	(XXX): 304, It Ravenna, It 23 Marz, Misc.
REAR COMMAND	Security Division 213, Hung 105Lt; 382 in far rear.

ARMY GROUP DON

FOURTH PANZER ARMY	LVII PZ: 16Mtz, 17Pz, 23Pz, SS Viking; Reserve 15LW; (Remnahts FOURTH RUMANIAN ARMY with VI, VII, 1, 2, 4, 18, 5 Cav, 8 Cav)
SIXTH ARMY	IV: Rum 20, 297, 371; VIII: 44, 76, 113 376, 384; XI: 16Pz, 24Pz, 60Mtz, 94; XIV PZ: 3Mtz, 29Mtz; LI: 71, 79, 100Lt, 295, 305, 389; Reserve: 14 Pz.
ARMY DETACH. HOLLIDT	XVII: 8LW, Rum 1Pz, Rum 7 Cav, 22 Pz, 294; XXIX: Remnants Italian Celere, Pasubio, Torino, Sforzesca; Rumanian 7, 9, 11; with German misc units; GROUP MIETH: 7LW, 304, Staff 384, Misc; Reserve: 11Pz, 306, Misc.
REAR COMMAND	Security Division 403; (Remnants of RUMANIAN THIRD ARMY with I, II, IV, V, moving westwards) 7Pz arriving.

ARMY GROUP A

FIRST PANZER ARMY	III PZ: Rum 2Mt, 13Pz; XL PZ: 3Pz, Misc; LII: 50, 111, 370; Reserve 5LW, Misc.
SEVENTEENTH ARMY	V: 9, 73, Rum Cav (6, 9, 19), Rum 3Mtn, Rum 10; XLIV: 101Lt, 198; XLIX MTN: 1Mtn, 4Mtn, 46, Misc; STAFF FOERSTER: 125, Slovak Fast; Reserve: 97Lt.
CRIMEA COMD	(XLII) Rum MTN: 1 Mtn, 4Mtn; 153 in rear
REAR AREA	Security Divisions: 444, 454; 381 in far rear.

24. GERMAN ARMY ORDER OF BATTLE, (April 1943)

15 April 1943

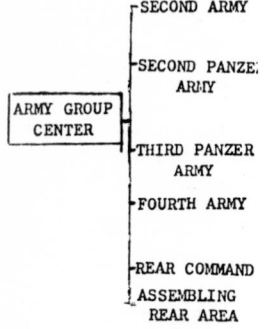

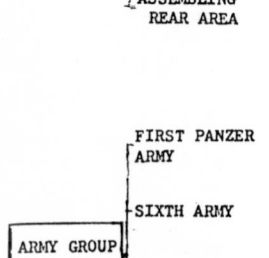

ARMY GROUP NORTH

SIXTEENTH ARMY

II: 16, 93, 123, 218; X: 8Lt, 18Mtz, 39, 126, 225; GROUP HOEHNE: 21LW, 32, 329; Reserve: 5Lt, 122.

EIGHTEENTH ARMY

I: 13LW, 227; III LW: 9LW, 10LW; XXVI: 1, 5Mtn, 11, 28Lt, 69, 212, 223; XXVIII: 12LW, 31, 61, 96, 121, 132; XXXVIII: 1LW, 23, 217; L: 170, 215, Span 250, SS Brig; LIV 21, 24, 58, 254, SS Police .

REAR COMMAND

Security Divisions: 207, 281, 285; 290, 388 in far rear.

ARMY GROUP CENTER

SECOND ARMY

VII: 26, 75, 68; XIII: 82, 88, 327, 340; Hung EAST: 1Sec, 105Lt, 205Sec; Reserve: Remnants 323 & 377.

SECOND PANZER ARMY

XX: 45, 72, 102, 707, 137, 251; XXXV: 34, 56, 262, 299; XLI: 20Pz: 86, 216, 383; XLVI PZ: 7, 78, 258; LIII: 25Mtz, 112, 211, 293; LV: 110, 134, 296, 339; DETACHMENT 532: Hung 102Lt, 108Lt; Reserve: 208, SS Cavalry.

THIRD PANZER ARMY

II LW: 2LW, 3LW, 4LW, 6LW; VI: 83, 206, 330; LIX: 263, 291, SS Brig; XLIII: 20Mtz, 205, 331; Reserve 201Sec.

FOURTH ARMY

IX: 35, 252, 342; XII: 98, 183, 260, 268; XXVII: 52, 197, 246, 256, 253; XXXIX PZ: 6, 95, 129, 337; LVI PZ: 14Mtz, 31, 131, 267, 321.

REAR COMMAND

Security Divisions 203, 221, 286; 390, 391 far rear.

ASSEMBLING REAR AREA

NINTH ARMY (XXIII): 2Pz, 4Pz, 5Pz. 8Pz, 9Pz, 12Pz, 18Pz, 36Mtz, 87, 292, 10Mtz.

ARMY GROUP SOUTH

FIRST PANZER ARMY

XXX: 38, 62, 333, 387 forming; XL: 7Pz, SS Viking; LVII PZ: 15, 17Pz; Reserve: III PZ: 3Pz, 19Pz 46, 257.

SIXTH ARMY

XVII: 294, 302, 306; XXIX: 15LW, 16Mtz, 336; XXIV PZ: 111, Staff 444Sec, 454 Sec; MIETH: 3Mtn, 304, 335; Reserve: 17, 23 Pz, 79.

ARMY DETACH. KEMPF

XLVIII PZ: 6Pz, 39, 106; LII: 57, 255, 332; RAUS: 167, 320, SS "DH"; Reserve: 11Pz, 168, GD, SS "R", SS "AH". SS CORPS, FOURTH PANZER ARMY Assembling

REAR COMMAND

Security Divisions 213, Staff 403; 153 ih far rear.

ARMY GROUP A

SEVENTEENTH ARMY

V: 4Mtn, 73, 125, Rum 10, Rum Cav Corps (6 & 9 Cav); XLIV: Rum 3Mtn, 9, Rum 19, 97, 101Lt; XLIX MTN: 50, 370; Reserve 13 Pz.

KERCH COMMAND

KERCH: Misc; TAMAN: Misc

CRIMEA COMD

(XLII): 153, Rum MTN CORPS: 1Mtn,,,2Mtn, 4Mtn; Reserve; Slovak Fast

GERMAN RECONNAISSANCE PATROL near the Don, 1942.

GERMAN PATROL returning with prisoners and wounded comrades.

PART FIVE
SMALL UNIT ACTIONS

XVI

INTRODUCTION

1. General

Proper combat training for officers and enlisted personnel is essential to military victory. The objective of peacetime training must be to improve their efficiency so that they can achieve optimum performance in time of war. This will be attained if every soldier knows how to handle his weapon and is fully integrated into his unit and if every leader is able to master any situation with which he might be faced. The better their preparation for war, the fewer improvisations commanders and soldiers will have to introduce in combat.

Every tactician and instructor recognizes the validity of these principles and tries to instill them in his trainees in the most realistic manner. Yet even the best-trained German troops had to learn many new tricks when war broke out and when they were shifted from one theater to another. In each instance they were faced with problems for which they were not sufficiently prepared. In unusual situations field commanders were sometimes compelled to violate certain regulations before they could be rescinded or modified by higher authority.

The preceding observations give an indication of the problems involved in preparing the German field forces for an encounter with an opponent whose pattern of behavior and thinking was so fundamentally different from their own that it was often beyond comprehension. Moreover, the peculiarities of the Russian theater were such that German unit commanders were faced with situations for which there seemed to be no solution. The unorthodox Russian tactics with which the Germans were not familiar were equally dis-

turbing, and Russian deception and trickery caused many German casualties. Several months of acclimatization were often necessary before a unit transferred to Russia was equal to the demands of the new theater. Occasionally a combat efficient unit without previous experience in Russia failed completely or suffered heavy losses in accomplishing a difficult mission that presented no problems to another unit familiar with the Russian theater, even though the latter had been depleted by previous engagements. This fact alone proved how necessary it was to disseminate the lessons learned in Russia, since this was the only method by which inexperienced troops could be spared the reverses and heavy casualties they would otherwise suffer during their commitment against Russian troops. To meet this need for training literature, a series of pamphlets and instructions based on German combat experiences in Russia was issued in 1943-44.

The actions contained herein describe the Russian soldier, his equipment, and his combat methods under a variety of circumstances and conditions as seen by his opponent—the German. The narratives are intended to supplement the theoretical knowledge of Russian combat doctrine during World War II that can be acquired from the study of manuals. Whereas the military doctrines of the nations vary little, the application of these doctrines differs greatly between countries. The chief characteristics of Russian combat methods during World War II were the savagery, fanaticism, and toughness of the individual soldier and the lavish prodigality with human life by the Soviet high command.

The actions here described are based solely on German source material, primarily in the form of narratives of personal experience. They were written under the direct supervision of General Franz Halder, Chief of the German Army General Staff from 1938 to 1942. General Halder, like many of our own high-ranking officers, has on numerous occasions expressed interest in small unit actions and has often stressed their importance in training junior leaders.

The German narratives, comprising over a hundred small unit actions, reached this Office in the form of 1,650 pages of draft translations done in the Historical Division, USAREUR. These were analyzed for content, presentation, and pertinence to the subject. The better ones were then rewritten, edited, and arranged in chronological sequence to give the best possible coverage to the different phases of the German campaign in Russia. Under the direction of Lt. Col. M. C. Helfers, Chief of the Foreign Studies Branch, Special Studies Division, Office of the Chief of Military History, this work, as well as the preparation of maps, was done by Mr. George E. Blau, Chief, and 1st Lt. Roger W. Reed, 1st Lt. Gerd Haber, Mr. Charles J. Smith, and Mr. George W. Garand of the Writing and Translation Section. Although the original German source material has undergone considerable revision, every effort has been made to retain the point of view, the expression, and even the prejudices of the original.

II. German Adjustments to the Russian Theater of War

Conversely, the German troops were ill prepared for a prolonged campaign in Russia. An immediate readjustment and a radical departure from the norms established in the western and central European theaters of war became necessary. As a first adjustment to local conditions the German Army revised the standards for selecting lower echelon commanders. Their average age was lowered and the physical fitness requirements were raised. Staff cars, riding horses, and every piece of excess baggage had to be left behind whenever a German unit had to go into action against Russian forces. For weeks at a time officers and men had no opportunity to change their underwear. This required another type of adjustment to the Russian way of life, if only to prevail in the struggle against filth and vermin. Many officers and men of the older age groups broke down or became sick and had to be replaced by younger men.

In comparison with the Russian soldier, his German counterpart was much too spoiled. Even before World War I there was a standing joke that the German Army horses would be unable to survive a single night in the open. The German soldier of World War II had become so accustomed to barracks with central heating and running water, to beds with mattresses, and to dormitories with parquet floors that the adjustment to the extremely primitive conditions in Russia was far from easy. To provide a certain amount of comfort during a term of service extending over several years was perfectly justifiable, but the German Army had gone much too far in this respect.

The breakdown of the supply system and the shortage of adequate clothing during the winter of 1941–42 were the direct outgrowth of German unpreparedness. The extraordinary physical fitness of the Russians, which permitted them to continue the struggle without let-up throughout the biting-cold winter, caused innumerable German casualties and thereby shook the confidence of the troops.

XVII

INFANTRY

I. General

The description of the course of the actual operations is not within the scope of this study. However, knowledge of the planning on which the invasion was based does afford a better understanding of the series of actions involving Company G of a German infantry battalion during the crucial winter of 1941-42. This unit helped to guard the life lines of the two German armies holding the Vyazma-Rzhev salient west of Moscow (secs. III, IV, and VI-VIII).

The infantry actions included in this chapter stress fighting under poor weather conditions, particularly in subzero temperatures, in the heart of European Russia. It was under such adverse conditions, which hampered armored operations, that German infantry battalions and companies demonstrated their capabilities and combat efficiency.

A series of five other actions describes the struggle of the 2d Battalion of a German infantry regiment that fought to the bitter end in the Stalingrad pocket during the winter of 1942-43 (secs. IX-XII and XIV). The remaining examples have been selected to complete the picture of German and Russian small infantry units fighting under unusual weather and terrain conditions.

II. German Limited-Objective Attacks South of Leningrad (September 1941)

After its lightning advance through the Baltic States during the early days of the Russian campaign Army Group North arrived at the gates of Leningrad, where the Russians fiercely contested every inch of ground. During the late summer of 1941 the Germans were slowly forging a ring of steel around the strongly fortified city. In

mid-September the 490th Infantry Regiment was given the mission of eliminating Russian centers of resistance approximately 15 miles south of Leningrad in the area north of the Izhora River between Romanovka and Slutsk. In the path of the regiment's advance stood an unknown number of Russian bunkers and defense positions established on the hills dominating the Izhora Valley. These positions had to be neutralized in order to secure the German lines of communication during the thrust on Slutsk. Late on 13 September the regiment crossed the river south of Gorki and spent the night in that village. The attack against the Russian-held hills north of the river was to start the next day, with the 1st and 2d Battalions advancing along the river valley and the 3d protecting the flank to the north (map 2).

Very little was known about either the terrain or the Russian fortifications in the area. The German maps, as well as previously captured enemy maps, were either inadequate or inaccurate. For this reason, the commander of the 3d Battalion decided to conduct careful terrain reconnaissance before attacking. The reconnaissance took the entire morning, and it was not until noon that the attack of the 3d Battalion against the Russian bunkers east of Gorki finally got under way. Attached to the forward elements were three demolition teams equipped with flame throwers and shaped charges. Only a few minutes were required to dispose of the first Russian bunker. While the engineers were preparing to attack the next bunker, two Russian howitzers in a cornfield west of Vilosi went into action. The regimental artillery was on the alert and destroyed the two howitzers and a nearby ammunition dump. By 1600 the demolition teams had captured the second bunker and were preparing to attack a third, which they presumed to be the last. Half an hour later this bunker was in German hands. The engineers were just about to withdraw and take a well-deserved rest when the 1st Battalion advancing farther to the south, discovered two additional bunkers, one of which was about 1,000 yards southwest of Vilosi. The demolition teams destroyed both bunkers in short order, thus paving the way for the 3d Battalion's advance toward Hill 312 northeast of Vilosi.

Continuing its attack, the 3d Battalion made some slight gains in the late afternoon of 14 September, but halted at 2015 after darkness set in and withdrew to Vilosi for the night. The other two battalions had made only little headway during the day, and spent the night of 14-15 September at the eastern edge of Vyarlevo. During the night Russian aircraft scattered bombs over widely separated areas, including some positions held by their own troops.

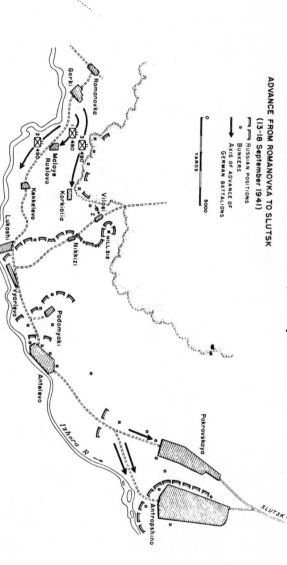

26. ADVANCE FROM ROMANOVKA TO SLUTSK, 13-18 September 1941

ADVANCE FROM ROMANOVKA TO SLUTSK (13-18 September 1941)

RUSSIAN POSITIONS
BUNKERS
AXIS OF ADVANCE OF GERMAN BATTALIONS

YARDS
0   5000

The seizure of strongly fortified Hill 312, scheduled for the next day, promised to be an arduous task. Although H-hour had originally been set for 0600, the attack had to be postponed until afternoon because the morning hours were needed for thorough terrain reconnaissance by two patrols sent out by the 3d Battalion.

One of the patrols, led by Lieutenant Thomsen, was to reconnoiter the hills between Korkiolia and Lukashi to determine whether and in what strength they were occupied by the Russians. The second patrol, under Sergeant Ewald, was to reconnoiter the area north of Hill 312 to determine the enemy's disposition and strength, and to probe for weak spots in his defense.

Patrol Thomsen was stealthily advancing southeastward from Korkiolia when it was suddenly intercepted and pinned down. In the ensuing exchange of fire the patrol was able to identify a number of Russian bunkers and field positions and to relay the necessary target data to the 3d Battalion CP. A short time later these Russian strong points were destroyed by the accurate fire of the regimental artillery. After having completed its mission, Patrol Thomsen returned to battalion headquarters.

By noon no word from Patrol Ewald had been received by the commander of the 3d Battalion. Since he could not postpone the attack on Hill 312 any longer, he ordered Lieutenant Hahn, the commander of Company I, to seize the hill.

At 1230 Hahn assembled the assault force, which consisted of Company I plus a machinegun and a mortar platoon, a demolition team consisting of two engineers equipped with flame throwers and shaped charges, and an artillery observer. Since Sergeant Ewald's patrol had not returned, only the two platoons led by Lieutenant Borgwardt and Sergeant Timm were available for the attack. In extended formation, the assault force advanced through the woods west and northwest of Vilosi and reached a point north of Hill 312 apparently without attracting the enemy's attention. From there, Lieutenant Hahn identified a bunker on top of Hill 312 and two positions on its northern slope. The fortifications were held in strength. Before he was able to conclude his observations, the enemy spotted the Germans, fired on them, and pinned them down.

The artillery observer attached to the assault force called for direct howitzer fire, whereupon the bunker received two hits which, however, appeared to do little damage. Hahn reported the situation to battalion headquarters and was ordered to continue the attack.

Platoons Borgwardt and Timm were to skirt Hill 312 and approach its base through the dense thicket that extended southward

from the forest edge to the hill. Platoon Borgwardt went to the right, Platoon Timm to the left. The latter was to support Borgwardt's advance up the hill and then dispose of the obstinate bunker on the crest of the hill as soon as Borgwardt entered the two slope positions. While the two platoons were moving out, the attached machinegun and mortar platoons went into position at the edge of the forest north of Hill 312. The howitzers gave the signal to attack by firing six rounds at the enemy bunker on top of Hill 312. Company headquarters personnel had to act as covering force since an enemy relief thrust was to be expected at any time.

Again the fire of the howitzers failed to put the bunker out of action. While the shells were exploding on and around the bunker, Borgwardt's men stealthily worked their way up the hill, creeping toward the two Russian positions whose occupants' attention was diverted by machinegun and mortar fire from the edge of the woods north of the hill. Platoon Borgwardt suddenly broke into the positions and caught the Russians completely by surprise.

While Borgwardt's men were engaged in seizing the two positions, Platoon Timm followed them up the hill and captured the bunker with the help of the engineers, whose flame throwers and shaped charges succeeded where the artillery had failed. Just as the operation seemed to have been brought to a successful conclusion, the personnel who had remained at the edge of the forest north of Hill 312 were attacked from behind by a force of about 50 Russians. Hahn ordered the newly arrived Patrol Ewald to hold off the Russians while the rest of the assault force followed the elements that had captured the hill. Upon arriving at the summit they immediately set up their weapons, took the Russians under effective fire, and repulsed their attack. From the top of the hill, Hahn saw the 1st Battalion, now no longer subject to flanking fire from Hill 312, penetrate the Russian positions west of Nikkizi. He immediately established contact with the battalion commander and made preparations to defend the hill against a potential Russian counterattack. This precaution had to be taken, for within the hour the artillery observer on top of the hill noticed Russian forces assembling for a counterattack in the woods north and northeast of Hill 312. However, the Russians lost all enthusiasm for an attack after the German artillery lobbed a few well-aimed shells into their midst.

After the capture of the hill on the afternoon of 15 September, the 3d Battalion continued its advance on the left of the 490th Infantry Regiment. Russian resistance was light, and the battalion had little difficulty in occupying Podonyaki since the Russians had evacuated the fortified position west of the village and had withdrawn to Antelevo.

On the morning of 17 September the 3d Battalion prepared to advance from the northwest toward Antelevo, which the Russians appeared to be defending in strength. The Russian positions west and north of the village were situated on high ground dominating the terrain over which the battalion had to advance; to the south and east Antelevo was protected by the Izliora River. At dawn a reconnaissance patrol of Company I identified two concrete bunkers as well as field emplacements in and around Antelevo. The northern and western sections of the village were held by one Russian battalion. German howitzers and antitank guns took the bunkers under fire, though only with little effect. Once again demolition teams were needed to destroy the enemy fortifications with shaped charges. The flame throwers, which previously had proved so effective, could no longer be used since the supply of flame-thrower fuel had been exhausted.

By an unexpected stroke of luck, the reconnaissance patrol managed to capture a Russian outpost whose telephone was still connected to the CP of the Russian regimental commander at Antelevo. The German battalion commander immediately interrogated the captured Russian telephone operator and obtained the latter's code name. His next step was to put his knowledge of Russian to the test. Using the code name of the Russian telephone operator, he called the Russian regimental commander. The latter was apparently misled, but did not divulge anything of value except that he was determined to hold Antelevo.

When the German officer became more insistent in his quest for additional information, the suspicions of the Russian commander were aroused, and he changed his tone. The German then tried a more direct approach and made an outright demand for the surrender of the Russian regiment at Antelevo. This was curtly rejected.

The commander of the 490th Infantry Regiment thereupon decided to mass his forces and seize Antelevo by direct assault. During the afternoon of 17 September he assembled the 1st and 3d Battalions west and north of the village, respectively, and launched an attack against the enemy stronghold after a strong artillery preparation. Again the demolition teams performed their task in an exemplary manner and quickly put one Russian bunker after another out of action. The Russians had apparently considered these particular bunkers impregnable, for once they were destroyed the enemy infantry fled in wild disorder, abandoning most of its equipment. By nightfall Antelevo was securely in German hands.

With the fall of Antelevo, Russian resistance seemed to disintegrate all along the regiment's route of advance, except for a brief encounter at the road fork south of Antropshino. There the Russians attempted to stop the regiment along prepared positions, but failed to do so. After this delay the German forces fanned out and reached Slutsk on 18 September, the 3d Battalion via Pokrovskaya and the 1st and 2d via Antropshino. Upon its arrival in Slutsk the regiment established contact with the 121st Infantry Division, which had previously captured the town.

A number of lessons may be learned from this operation. First, all regimental units had to conduct thorough terrain reconnaissance since their maps and those captured from the Russians were frequently either inadequate or inaccurate. Whenever one of the battalion commanders failed to reconnoiter the terrain thoroughly, his unit was in danger of being ambushed by the Russians.

The Germans were able to take the Russian bunkers with a minimum loss of time and men by employing skilled demolition teams. Each member of these teams had been thoroughly trained and was well versed in his task.

The capture of the Russian outpost on the morning of 17 September might have provided the Germans with information about Russian intentions and troop dispositions, had it been properly exploited. The battalion commander showed a lack of good judgment by using his average knowledge of Russian in an attempt to extract information from the Russian regimental commander. This was clearly a task for an expert interpreter who was skilled in methods of interrogation.

The Russians were fighting a delaying action during which they often failed to take advantage of the favorable terrain and of their prepared positions. The flight of the Antelevo garrison was indicative of how easily the Russians became demoralized when they were confronted by an unexpected situation. When the German demolition teams blew up the bunkers with shaped charges, the Russians panicked and instinctively took to flight, as happened so often during the early months of the campaign.

III. Company G Counterattacks During a Snowstorm (November 1941)

This action is typical of the fighting in the late autumn of 1941, when Russian resistance began to stiffen west of Moscow and the ill-equipped German troops had to rally all their energy to continue the advance toward the Russian capital.

In November 1941 the 464th Infantry Regiment of the German 253d Infantry Division was occupying field fortifications about 60 miles northeast of Rzhev. On the regiment's right flank was Hill 747 (map 3). Since the hill afforded an extensive view of the German rear area, the Russians had made repeated attempts to capture it in an effort to undermine the position of the 464th Infantry Regiment. The hill had changed hands several times, but was now occupied by the Germans. The presence of heavy weapons including assault guns, as well as reports of repeated reconnaissance thrusts, gave rise to the belief that the Russians were preparing for another attack against the hill. Accordingly, the regimental commander withdrew Company G from the sector it was holding and committed it on the regiment's right flank.

After reporting to battalion headquarters around noon on 15 November, Lieutenant Vielmann, the commander of Company G, accompanied by his platoon leaders, undertook a terrain reconnaissance. A heavy snowfall set in. As the group was returning from the reconnaissance mission, submachine gun and mortar fire was heard from the direction of Hill 747. The company commander attached little importance to this at the time. However, upon arriving at the battalion CP he learned that the Russians had taken advantage of the snowstorm and had seized the hill without artillery or mortar support in a surprise raid. An immediate counterattack by German troops failed to dislodge the Russians.

Vielmann thereupon received orders to recapture the hill in a surprise attack to be launched at 2200. Regimental headquarters attached a medium mortar platoon and a light howitzer platoon to the company and promised artillery support. Vielmann formed three assault parties and moved them into jumpoff positions close to the Russian line under cover of darkness. The infantry company to the right was to divert the attention of the defending force at the time of the actual attack, while the unit to the left was to support the attack with its fire. Artillery and heavy weapons were to open fire on specified areas at prearranged flare signals.

The German assault parties occupied their jumpoff positions without attracting the attention of the defending Russians. The party in the center, led by Vielmann, was only about 35 yards from the nearest Russian position. Close observation of the Russian defenses and the actions of individual soldiers indicated that a German attack was not anticipated. The Russian sentries were shivering from the cold and were by no means alert. Rations and supplies were being drawn. Not far from Vielmann's observation point a Russian detail was unloading furs and felt boots from a sled.

At 2200 the German assault parties, shouting loudly, broke into the Russian position. The attack confused the Russians, who dropped everything and attempted to make their way to the rear. Their escape, however, was prevented by the two assault parties that, at the

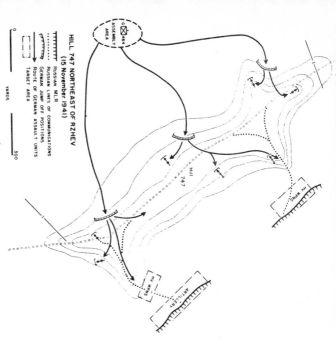

HILL 747
NORTHEAST OF RZHEV
(15 November 1941)

⎯⎯⎯ RUSSIAN MLR
········· RUSSIAN LINES OF COMMUNICATIONS
ⲧⲧⲧⲧⲧ GERMAN JUMP OFF POSITIONS
↝↝↝↝ ROUTE OF GERMAN ASSAULT UNITS
▭ TARGET AREA

0   300
⎣⎯⎯⎯⎯⎯⎯⎯⎯⎯⎯⎯⎦
        YARDS

After 45 minutes Hill 747 was completely in the hands of the Germans; their former MLR had been reoccupied and communications established with adjacent units. About 60 prisoners, 7 medium mortars, 5 heavy machineguns, 3 antitank guns, and large quantities of ammunition were taken. In the morning 70 Russian dead were found on the hill. Of the five German casualties, only one was severely wounded.

The manner in which the Russians exploited the snowstorm in carrying out a surprise attack without artillery or mortar support was typical of Russian infantry combat methods in wintertime.

The Russians launched their attack before winter clothing had been issued; some of the men wore only thin summer uniforms. As a stimulant, each Russian soldier was issued five tablets which had an effect similar to that of alcohol and a large ration of sugar cubes. In addition, the men were promised a special liquor ration upon completion of their mission. The sugar and tablets were presumably issued to counteract the discomfort caused by the temperature of 16° F. However, once the effects of these stimulants wore off, the men began to feel the cold acutely and their senses became numbed, as was observed in the case of the Russian sentries. During the German assault to retake Hill 747 the Russian defenders appeared to be as susceptible to the cold as were the Germans. This must be considered an isolated case, however, since the Russian soldiers were generally able to endure extremely low temperature. At the same time it indicates that some of the Russian units were insufficiently prepared for winter combat and had to improvise protective measures to overcome the rigors of the unexpectedly early winter weather.

IV. Company G Operates in Deep Snow (January 1942)

On 13 January Company G of the 464th Infantry Regiment was ordered to provide protection against Russian partisan raids on the division's supply line, which led from Toropets via Village M to Village O (map 4). To this end the company was reinforced by two heavy machineguns, two 80-mm. mortars, and one antitank platoon.

beginning of the attack, had skirted either side of the hill and severed the Russian lines of communications. Unaware of the fighting, the Russian heavy weapons and artillery remained silent throughout the attack. When the signal flare went up, the German artillery and heavy weapons opened fire, laying a barrage on the Russian-held side of the hill. Two Russian machineguns covering each flank put up fierce resistance before being silenced in the hand-to-hand fighting.

On the evening of 14 January the company, mounted in trucks, reached Village O, 5 miles east of Village M. Upon its arrival at Village O, a supply unit, which was fleeing eastward toward Rzhev before the powerful Russian offensive, indicated that strong contingents of Russian troops from the north had cut the German supply route in the forest west of Village N. Using civilian labor, the Russians had constructed a road at least 30 miles long that led south through the large forest bypassing Toropets to the east. The company commander, Lieutenant Viehmann, decided to establish local security in Village O, spend the night there, and continue westward on foot the next morning in order to see what was going on. During the night a few Russian civilians slipped out of the village, established contact with the Russian troops, and supplied them with intelligence regarding the German dispositions.

At dawn on 15 January, after posting security details, the company started out and arrived in Village M without having made contact with the Russians. As the company's advance element approached Village N, the Germans noticed a large group of soldiers in German uniform standing in the road, beckoning to them. That these soldiers were not Germans became evident when the antitank gun moving up behind the advance element was suddenly fired upon. The company's other antitank guns covered the advance element's withdrawal to Village M, where it rejoined the main body of the company. The prime mover of the lead gun was lost during this action. The Russians, however, did not follow up their attack.

In Village M the company set up hasty defenses against an attack from the north and west and tried to determine the strength and intentions of the opposing Russian force. From a vantage point in Village M it was possible to observe the eastern edge of Village N, where the Russians were building snow positions and moving four antitank guns into position. There was an exchange of fire but no indication of an impending Russian attack. During the hours of darkness Company G built snow positions along the western and northern edges of Village M, while the aforementioned supply unit

occupied Village R, about one mile east of Village M, and took measures to secure it, particularly from the north.

During the night of 15–16 January reconnaissance patrols reported that the Russians were continuing their defensive preparations in Village N and that their line of communications was the road leading north from there.

On 16 January between 0400 and 0500 a 50-man Russian reconnaissance patrol approached the northwest corner of Village M on skis. Although the Russian patrol had been detected, it was allowed to come very close before it was taken under fire. Approximately 10 men of the patrol escaped and three were taken prisoner; the rest were killed before they could reach the German position.

According to the statements of the three prisoners, two Russian divisions were moving south toward Village M. On 16 January Villages M and R were to be captured. What the prisoners either did not know or refused to tell, was that the Russians, attacking in force across frozen Lake Volga, had broken through the German positions west of the 253d Infantry Division 2 days before and had pushed on to the south. Thus, Viehmann was unaware of the true German situation.

Since the Russians in Village N remained passive, Viehmann decided to concentrate on defending his village against an attack from the north. The deep snow caused some difficulties; for instance, machineguns had to be mounted on antiaircraft tripods so that a satisfactory field of fire could be obtained.

About 0800 on 16 January the company's observation post identified three Russian columns moving south toward the forest north of Village M. Except for antitank guns these columns did not seem to be equipped with heavy weapons. Around 1000 the first Russians appeared at the southern edge of the forest, some 1,000 yards from the German defensive positions. At 1020 the Russian center and right-wing columns attacked with antitank guns and infantry. Just a short time before this attack Company G had dispatched two rifle squads to Village R to reinforce the supply unit there, since the Russian left-wing column was headed in that direction.

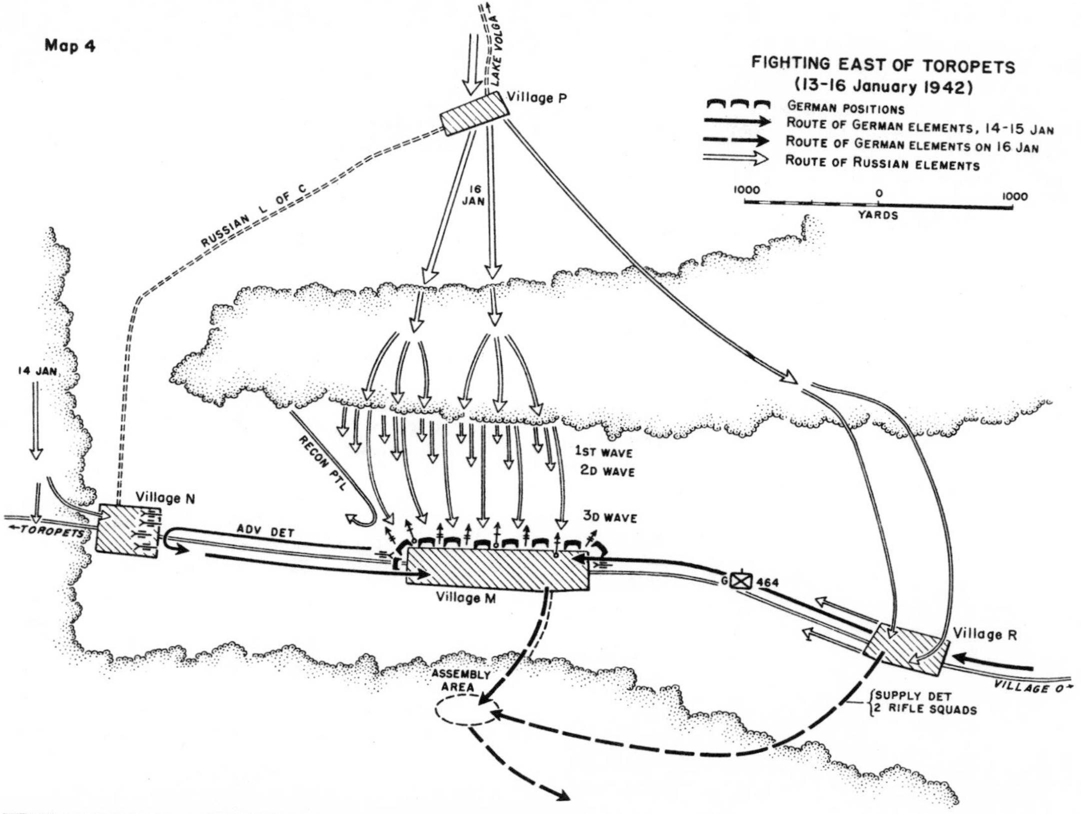

Map 4

28. FIGHTING EAST OF TOROPETS, 13-16 January 1942

FIGHTING EAST OF TOROPETS
(13-16 January 1942)

GERMAN POSITIONS
ROUTE OF GERMAN ELEMENTS, 14-15 JAN
ROUTE OF GERMAN ELEMENTS ON 16 JAN
ROUTE OF RUSSIAN ELEMENTS

1000   0   1000
YARDS

TO TOROPETS

14 JAN

Village N

ADV DET

RUSSIAN L OF C

RECON PTL

Village M

1ST WAVE
2D WAVE

3D WAVE

16 JAN

Village P

LAKE VOLGA

ASSEMBLY
AREA

GG 464

SUPPLY DET
2 RIFLE SQUADS

Village R

VILLAGE O

The first wave of Russian infantry, some 400 men strong, emerged from the forest on a broad front. It was evident that the 3-foot snow was causing them great difficulty. The concentrated fire of the German heavy weapons succeeded in halting the attack after it had advanced about 200 yards.

After a short while a second, equally large wave emerged from the forest. It advanced in the tracks of the first and carried the attack forward, over and beyond the line of dead. The Russian antitank fire became heavier, being directed against the German machinegun positions, which the Russians had spotted. As a result, several machineguns were destroyed; some changed their positions frequently in an effort to dodge the Russian fire. The Russians advanced an additional 200 yards, then bogged down under the effective German small arms fire. They sustained heavy losses which, however, were compensated for by the reinforcements pouring down south into the forest from Village P. Viehmann estimated that the Russians committed the equivalent of two regiments in this action.

By 1100 the Russian left-wing column had reached a point 150 yards from the German positions in Village R, where the terrain was more favorable for the attacker than that north of Village M. The supply unit and the two rifle squads defending Village R could no longer be reinforced because the road from Village M was under constant Russian fire.

Realizing that his position would become untenable within the next few hours, Viehmann ordered his men to prepare to evacuate Village M. A few men with minor wounds were detailed to trample a path through the deep snow from Village M toward the forest to the south in order to facilitate a quick withdrawal. The troops in Village R were also to withdraw to the same forest if pressed too heavily by the Russians.

The members of the third Russian assault wave emerged from the forest unarmed. However, they armed themselves quickly with the weapons of their fallen comrades and continued the attack. Meanwhile, Village R was taken and the Russians closed in on Village M from the east. The Germans were now very low on ammunition, having expended almost 20,000 rounds during the fighting.

About 1300 Company G, after destroying its mortars and antitank guns, evacuated Village M. Viehmann planned to make contact with the German troops in Village O by withdrawing through the forest south of Village M. He ordered the evacuation of the wounded, then withdrew with the main body of the company, and left behind a light machinegun and an antitank gun to provide covering fire and to simulate the presence of a larger force. After the gun crews had expended all the ammunition, they destroyed the breech operating mechanism of the antitank gun and withdrew toward the forest. About halfway there they were fired on by the Russians who had meanwhile entered Village M. The retreating Germans managed to escape without losses because the Russians did not pursue them into the forest.

During the next 3 days the company marched—with almost no halts for rest—through the deep snow that blanketed the dense forest, relying heavily on a compass in the absence of familiar landmarks. On 19 January, after bypassing Village O, which was found to be occupied by the Russians, it finally reestablished contact with the 253d Infantry Division. Only then did the company learn that all forces on the German front south of and parallel to Lake Volga had been withdrawn in the meantime.

In this action deep snow hampered the movements of both the attacking Russians and the defending Germans. Only by trampling a path in the snow before its withdrawal from Village M, did Company G avoid being trapped by the Russians.

The appearance of a Russian reconnaissance patrol in German uniform was a frequent occurrence; however, the number of disguised Russians encountered on 15 January in Village N was unusually large.

As so often happened during the winter of 1941-42, the Russians attacked in several waves on a given front, each successive wave passing over the dead of the preceding and carrying the attack forward to a point where it, too, was destroyed. Some waves started out unarmed and recovered the weapons from their fallen comrades.

VII. Company G Annihilates a Russian Elite Unit (March 1942)

During March 1942 Russian pressure from the north and west forced the Germans to make a limited withdrawal northwest of Rzhev. In late March the 2d Battalion of the German 464th Infantry Regiment, including Company G, established defensive positions in Village S, about 12 miles northwest of Olenino. The village was situated on level ground and was faced by forests to the north, east, and south (map **30**). The terrain to the west was open, permitting the defenders to detect at an early moment the approach of any Russian forces coming from that direction. Since the German forces in the area were not strong enough to establish a continuous defense line, the village was organized for perimeter defense. The battalion constructed snow positions above the ground, excavation of the frozen soil being impossible, and maintained contact with adjacent units by sending patrols through the forests around the village. On 25 March the low temperature was 11° F. and 3 feet of snow covered the ground. On that day the 2d Battalion repelled several attacks from the west, inflicting heavy losses on the Russians, who then intensified their patrol activity.

Before dawn on 26 March a reconnaissance patrol sent out by Company G returned from the forest bordering Village S to the north without having encountered enemy troops. The distance from the edge of the forest to the defense perimeter measured approximately 150 yards. Half an hour after the return of the patrol 100 Russians suddenly emerged from the forest and attacked Company G at the northwestern part of the defense ring. The Russians participating in the attack were armed with submachineguns and moved on skis, which made the small force exceedingly mobile in the snow-covered terrain. In addition, every third man carried a frangible grenade in his pocket, presumably for the purpose of setting fire to the village. Several Russians literally blew up when their frangible grenades were struck by bullets and exploded. Because of the severe cold some of the German machineguns failed to function, and the Russians succeeded in penetrating the German positions.

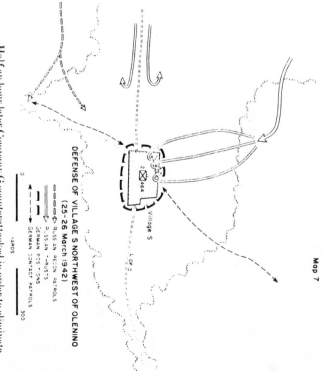

DEFENSE OF VILLAGE S NORTHWEST OF OLENINO
(25-26 March 1942)

RUSS IAN RECON PATROLS
RUSSIAN THRUSTS
GERMAN POS TIONS
GERMAN CONTACT PATROLS

Village S

2 ☒ 464

0   YARDS   300

Half an hour later Company G counterattacked in order to eliminate the penetration. The Russians fought tenaciously, and there was violent hand-to-hand combat. By 1200 Company G had recaptured the positions. Eighty-nine Russians were killed and nine, including two seriously wounded, taken prisoner. All of the attackers were NCO candidates who had been promised battlefield promotions if they captured Village S.

While Company G was mopping up the area, brief hand-to-hand fighting suddenly flared up at two points where prostrate Russians, suddenly coming to life, jumped to their feet and assaulted the German soldiers.

This example illustrates how effectively the Russian riflemen exploited the terrain when approaching the enemy, even in deep snow and extreme cold. The attack was conducted skillfully and silently, and fullest use was made of the element of surprise. The entire assault force rushed out of the forest and attacked in a single wave. However, when the surprise attack did not result in the immediate capture of the village but led to a struggle for the German positions, the operation lost its tactical value since the Russian unit had gone into battle without any support. Instead of breaking off the engagement and withdrawing, the Russians continued fighting until their entire force was wiped out.

This action, however, does not lend itself to generalization since a special Russian unit composed of noncommissioned officer candidates was involved. Except for the resistance offered to the German advance in the summer of 1941 by certain Russian elite formations, no other Russian units had fought so violently and tenaciously.

During World War II the training status of different Russian units showed such great variations that generalizations based on the performance of individual units are not permissible. As in any other army, there were both good and indifferent units among the innumerable divisions which opposed the Germans. Training courses at Russian service schools were conducted with great thoroughness, and even senior officers were subjected to the rigors of the ordinary training schedule. Training was not limited to the achievement of military proficiency; it was constantly overshadowed by political indoctrination designed to imbue every soldier with the ideological principles involved in the life-and-death struggle.

VIII. Company G Recaptures Hill 726 (October 1942)

During the spring and summer of 1942 the Germans strengthened the Rzhev salient and eliminated Russian forces that had gained a foothold west of the Vyazma-Rzhev rail line. The salient gradually became one of the strongest defense lines the Germans had built in Russia. In the early autumn Marshal Zhukov launched an offensive against the Rzhev salient to divert German forces from the Stalingrad front and to eliminate this potential threat to the Russian capital. In this action, which is the last one in the series concerning the fighting west of Moscow, Company G resisted the onslaught of fresh Russian troops who had recently arrived from training centers in Siberia.

In mid-September Russian infantry supported by tanks seized Hill 726, some 10 miles north of Olenino. Once the Russians had wrested it from the Germans, they withdrew their tanks and left an infantry company of about 75 men to defend the newly won position. This hill now constituted a dent in the German MLR and afforded a sweeping view of the German rear area, thus hampering movements. Its rapid recapture was of vital importance to the Germans (map ?).

The Russian defense system on the hill was not organized in a continuous line, but rather in the form of strong points. The positions were quite deep, afforded overhead cover, and were so well camouflaged that they could be detected only at very close range. The communication trenches leading to the rear were deep enough only for crawling. All machineguns were emplaced so as to deliver only frontal fire. Mortars were emplaced on the reverse slope of the hill, and large quantities of ammunition and hand grenades had been stored in the strong points. A belt of wooden mines—to which German mine detectors did not respond—extended almost completely around the hill. Gaps had been left in the mine belt to permit passage of friendly patrols. Before the attack German reconnaissance patrols were able to identify these lanes.

Company G made five or six attempts to retake Hill 726, but failed; in each case the attack was halted at the very beginning because of heavy casualties incurred from mines and massed mortar fire. The

Russians defended the hill with extreme tenacity. The company commander, Captain Viehmann, observed that the Russians confined their activity to the hours of darkness. During the day their positions appeared deserted. Russian reconnaissance patrols were very active, but only between midnight and dawn.

Viehmann decided to launch a surprise attack at dusk on 2 October. He selected 80 men who, together with two flame thrower teams, were to make up the assault detachments. Six machineguns were to follow directly behind. After seizure of the hill, an intrenching team was to move in with previously prepared barbed wire obstacles, set them up on the reverse side of the hill, and establish defensive positions. All men in the assault detachments were equipped with submachineguns and issued an ample supply of hand grenades. They were familiar with the terrain, including Hill 726 itself and the Russian MLR.

Under cover of darkness and unnoticed by the Russians, the assault troops moved from their assembly area into the jumpoff positions. At the scheduled time the two companies along the flanks of the German MLR facing the right and left sides of the hill as well as the machineguns located on the southern slope poured fire into the Russian positions. While the German troops in the MLR diverted the enemy's attention by sudden shouting, the assault elements attacked and penetrated the Russian mine belt through two previously identified gaps.

The defending Russians were taken completely by surprise. The fire and shouting coming from all sides confused them as to the true direction of the attack. They were further thrown off balance by the German flame throwers, despite the fact that the latter failed to function after only a few bursts.

Nevertheless, the Russians did not give way to panic or abandon their positions, but struggled to the bitter end. After about an hour of hand-to-hand fighting the entire hill was in German hands, as were 20 Russian prisoners. The initial German objective, to cut Russian communications to the rear, had been achieved early in the attack. The Russian MLR was thereby out of contact with the defenders on the hill, who apparently were not alert enough to summon assistance

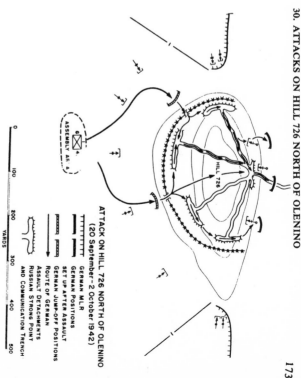

30. ATTACKS ON HILL 726 NORTH OF OLENINO

ATTACK ON HILL 726 NORTH OF OLENINO
(20 September–2 October 1942)

GERMAN MLR
GERMAN POSITIONS SET UP AFTER ASSAULT
GERMAN JUMP-OFF POSITIONS
ROUTE OF GERMAN ASSAULT DETACHMENTS
RUSSIAN STRONG POINT AND COMMUNICATION TRENCH

HILL 726

ASSEMBLY AREA

0   100   200   300   400   500
YARDS

from the rear before being cut off.

Once the hill was taken, the Germans immediately dispatched two listening sentries to points about 30 yards in the front of their lines, set up barbed wire obstacles, and otherwise prepared their defensive positions. Within 2 hours a continuous line of wire entanglements stretched across the crest of the hill.

About an hour after the completion of these defenses one of the sentries reported the approach of about 40 Russians. All intrenching work was immediately suspended and the defense positions were quickly manned. Soon thereafter the second sentry confirmed the report of the first. The gap in the wire obstacle line which had until then been left open for the men stationed at the listening post was closed.

At a given signal the Germans opened fire just as the screaming Russians began their counterattack. Rushing headlong into the wire entanglements, which they had failed to spot in advance, the Russians were cut down by German defensive fire concentrated on that zone. Only three of the attackers were able to regain the safety of their jumpoff position.

The next day the Russians directed heavy harassing fire against Hill 726, but made no further attempts to conduct a concerted infantry attack.

IX. The 2d Battalion Launches a Limited Counterthrust (November 1942)

The Battle of Stalingrad has often been referred to as the turning point in the German campaign in Russia. It was at Stalingrad that the Germans lost the initiative, never to regain it except for a few brief periods. The Russian strategy that led to the recapture of the city called for a double envelopment to trap the German Sixth Army in an area of 50 square miles. The initial blow was struck from the north, where three armored and two Russian cavalry corps annihilated three Italian and Hungarian divisions and crossed the Don at Sera-limovich. One of the Sixth Army units thrown into the battle to stem the Russian advance was a German infantry battalion, whose fate is described in the following series of actions.

In mid-November 1942 the 2d Battalion of the German 132d Infantry Regiment occupied defensive positions on the bluffs along the west bank of the Don River near Sirotinskaya (map 9). The battalion's 3 rifle companies averaged 50 to 60 men, while the strength of the heavy weapons company was approximately a hundred men. The combat efficiency and morale of the battalion, which had been fighting in Russia since the beginning of the campaign in June 1941, were high. On the evening of 18 November the 2d Battalion was relieved for movement on the 19th, and during the night it was relieved by a reserve unit. Before the regiment started its movement,

the 3d Battalion was dissolved because of insufficient manpower and its remnants were transferred to the other two battalions. No additional reinforcements were available.

The 1st and 2d Battalions covered the distance of 25 miles from Sirotinskaya to Verkhne-Buzinovka on foot and by truck. Although the movement was slowed down by a light snowfall, both battalions arrived at Verkhne-Buzinovka on the evening of 19 November. At the time of their arrival, weak German service elements were defending the northern and northwestern outskirts of the village in the face of heavy enemy pressure.

At dawn on 20 November the two battalions launched a counterattack, which was preceded by a heavy artillery preparation. The 2d Battalion, on the right, was to thrust to the north across a wide, overgrown ravine, while the 1st Battalion was to drive along the road leading northwest toward Platonov (map). The 1st Battalion's attack was to be supported by assault guns.

As always when they were on the defensive, the Russians proved to be tough opponents. Small detachments forming nests of resistance in the numerous depressions and recesses of the ravine were so well dispersed and concealed that the German artillery fire could have little effect. As a result, the 2d Battalion had to form small assault detachments to get the attack under way. The German machinegun and mortar teams worked together systematically. First, the high trajectory fire of the mortars drove the Russian soldiers from their concealment, then the machineguns pinned them down, and finally the men armed with submachineguns and hand grenades finished them off. As soon as a nest of resistance on one side of the ravine was neutralized, a Russian position on the other side was taken under flanking fire. Simultaneously, other German assault detachments worked their way forward across the bottom of the ravine, where the defenders were pinned down. By alternating punches, as does a boxer, the Germans slowly but surely pushed their opponents back approximately 2 miles. Toward noon the Russians abandoned the ravine altogether and withdrew northward. Their casualties had been heavy, and no less than 80 men had been taken prisoner. The

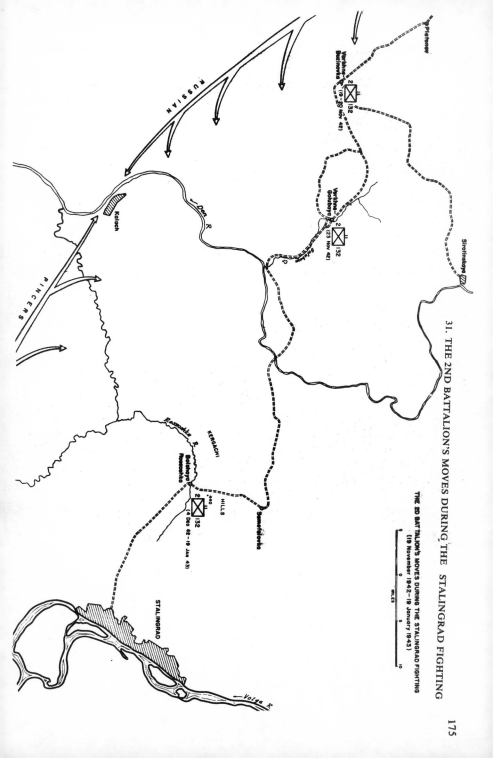

31. THE 2ND BATTALION'S MOVES DURING THE STALINGRAD FIGHTING

THE 2D BATTALION'S MOVES DURING THE STALINGRAD FIGHTING
(19 November 1942–19 January 1943)

175

32. BATTLES NEAR VERKHNE-BUZINOVKA

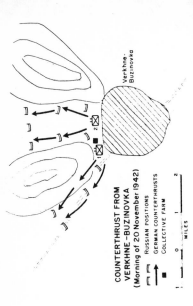

Map A

COUNTERTHRUST FROM
VERKHNE-BUZINOVKA
(Morning of 20 November 1942)

→ RUSSIAN POSITIONS
⇒ GERMAN COUNTERTHRUSTS
■ COLLECTIVE FARM

0   1   2
MILES

Verkhne-
Buzinovka

X. The 2d Battalion Switches to the Defensive (November 1942)

Toward 1300 on 20 November a long Russian march column consisting of infantry, cavalry, and artillery quietly approached the village along the road from Platonov. The column marched in close order without any advance guard. Surprised by the overwhelming strength of the approaching Russian forces, the two German battalions hastily took the most essential countermeasures. Using every possible means of concealment, the rifle companies split up into assault detachments and, abandoning the terrain they had captured during the morning, worked their way back to the edge of Verkhne-Buzinovka as rapidly as they could. As soon as a detachment arrived at the outskirts of the village, it was assigned the position it was to defend (map   ). Every available officer was given charge of a sector a few hundred yards in width. Being arbitrarily designated, some of these sectors comprised elements from several different units since there was no time to assemble the troops in their respective companies or work out a defense plan.

When the Russian column had approached to within 1,600 yards of the village, the German artillery, assault guns, and heavy infantry weapons opened fire with devastating effect. The stunned and confused Russians had great difficulty in getting off the road, which was soon blocked with burning vehicles and littered with debris. The German battalions thus gained an hour's respite during which they were able to close the gaps in their MLR at the outskirts of the village, place ammunition next to each weapon, set up a wire communication network, and extend their flank protection along the western edge of the village.

This incident was typical of the first phase of the Russian counteroffensive west of Stalingrad, during which higher headquarters, both German and Russian, often lost contact with their subordinate units. Caught in the tidal wave of Russian forces converging upon Kalach from the northwest, individual German units were still launching local counterattacks. They acted according to orders long superseded,

enemy forces opposing the 1st Battalion joined the withdrawal, giving way to German pressure.

ignorant of the fact that enemy forces had driven past them and that they were cut off. On the other hand, the Russians, equally ignorant of the general situation and of the exact front-line demarcations, advanced in the general direction of the northern arm of the pincers in massed columns without security or reconnaissance detachments, apparently under the impression that they were crossing territory that had already been mopped up by their predecessors.

After they had recovered from the surprise assault on their march column, the Russians assembled their forces for an attack on Verkhne-Buzinovka. At 1430, under cover of heavy artillery concentrations, wave after wave of massed Russian infantry began to descend upon the outskirts of the village. The collective farm occupied by a platoon of Company F was the first German outpost to change hands. The German regimental commander realized that Verkhne-Buzinovka could not be held for any length of time. He was aware, too, that a daytime withdrawal would undoubtedly result in heavy casualties for the Germans, whose escape route to the southeast passed through several miles of wide-open terrain, where the withdrawing rifle com panies would be exposed to merciless enemy fire for at least half an hour. There was no choice but to attempt to hold Verkhne-Buzinovka until nightfall. For the remainder of the afternoon, the defending force dispensed with aimed fire and turned its entire fire power to setting up a barrage. Heavy and light machineguns, mortars, even submachineguns and carbines laid down a curtain of fire which was heaviest around the collective farm, where the Russian infantry was assembling for the continuation of its attack. The 105-mm. guns were moved up to the northeast edge of the village. With all German artillerymen who could possibly be spared being used as riflemen, machine gunners, or ammunition carriers, the officers, aided by a few enlisted men, fired rapid salvos at a range of 250–350 yards. After 30 to 40 rounds had been fired from the same emplacement, a prime mover, waiting under nearby cover, moved the gun to another position, where it was quickly readied for action.

At the same time, the regimental commander initiated a ruse, which was to be highly successful. On the premise that the Russian sol-

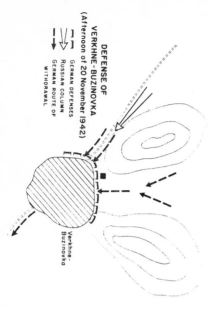

DEFENSE OF
VERKHNE-BUZINOVKA
(Afternoon of 20 November 1942)

GERMAN DEFENSES
RUSSIAN COLUMN
GERMAN ROUTE OF WITHDRAWAL

Verkhne-Buzinovka

Map 8

diers were usually underfed and therefore hungry and greedy, the German cooks were ordered to prepare lentil and pea soup from the stocks of legumes that had been left in one of the buildings. The legumes were emptied into large pots filled with water and placed over fires in front of the first houses the Russians would reach upon entering Verkhne-Buzinovka. Next, the Germans opened some mail bags containing packages from Germany addressed to a headquarters unit that had recently departed, and emptied their contents onto the streets of the village. By twilight the situation had become so critical that the Russians were expected to enter the village at any moment. The two German battalions now began their withdrawal. Platoon by platoon the companies disengaged and withdrew. The self-propelled assault guns and artillery pieces continued to fire at point-blank range and did not move out until just before the last rifleman. Then they drove straight to the southeast edge of the village, where the previously withdrawn companies had collected and established a provisional defense line. It was now that the ruse proved effective. The Russian soldiers, who at first had followed close behind the withdrawing German detachments, hesitated when they smelled the aroma of hot soup and saw all the packages on the ground. The temptation proved too much for them, and there was a general rush for the unexpected treat. The resulting delay enabled the German battalions to assemble their companies and carry out an orderly withdrawal from Verkhne-Buzinovka without being subjected to enemy pressure.

When a pocket comes into existence the situation of the encircled forces is usually confused. The individual units are temporarily on their own, facing almost unsurmountable difficulties. In such situations a determined and resourceful leader who does not hesitate to improvise and resort to ruses will be able to inflict heavy losses on the enemy, gain valuable time, and preserve the combat strength of his unit for further action.

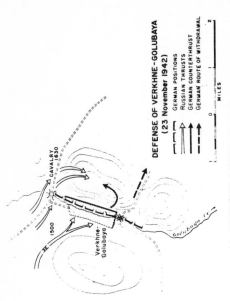

DEFENSE OF VERKHNE-GOLUBAYA
(23 November 1942)

GERMAN POSITIONS
RUSSIAN THRUSTS
GERMAN COUNTERTHRUST
GERMAN ROUTE OF WITHDRAWAL

0   MILES   2

XI. The 2d Battalion's Stand at Verkhne-Golubaya (November 1942)

The two battalions marched through the entire night. At 0200 on 21 November the company commanders were ordered to inform their men that the German Sixth Army had been encircled. While heavy snow was falling, the battle-weary troops halted along the road on which drifts were beginning to accumulate. The men realized the seriousness of the situation but were not dejected. The idea that the ring around the Sixth Army might not be broken did not occur to them at the time. They knew that difficult days and weeks lay ahead, but their confidence remained unshaken. On 22 November there was only isolated small-scale fighting, during which the two battalions withdrew to Verkhne-Golubaya where they arrived at 2300. Orders received from higher headquarters stipulated that the village was to be defended and that the enemy advance was to be delayed at Verkhne-Golubaya at least until the following evening.

At this time Sixth Army headquarters attempted to tighten its control over all German units in the Stalingrad pocket. In its effort to direct the employment of every unit, Sixth Army occasionally issued orders that went into too much detail and did not take the local situation sufficiently into account. The commander of the 2d Battalion, for instance, had selected the gently ascending hill west of Verkhne-Golubaya for establishing a defense position. Higher headquarters, however, ordered him to move his unit to the east bank of Golubaya Creek, as unfavorable a line for setting up a defense position as could be found in that area (map). The section of the village west of the creek obstructed the battalion's field of fire. The maneuvering space between the houses lining the east bank of the river and the steep slope adjacent was only about 200 yards in width. Also disadvantageous was the 800-yard gap between the 2d Battalion and the nearest German unit, which was committed northeast of the village. By noon of 23 November reconnaissance patrols had established contact with that unit, but the gap remained open.

33. DEFENSE OF VERKHNE-GOLUBAYA

A Russian force, consisting of 2 infantry battalions, 10 T34 tanks, and 2 cavalry troops approached Verkhne-Golubaya around noon. The 2d Battalion was exhausted from the recent fighting and hasty withdrawal and, despite the fire power delivered by its heavy weapons emplaced on the hills to the east, was unable to prevent the Russian infantry from gradually infiltrating the western section of the village.

Toward 1500 the 10 Russian tanks emerged from behind the hill situated west of Verkhne-Golubaya and drove straight toward the village. The Germans destroyed four, but the other six managed to penetrate the western section. In the bitter struggle that followed the 2d Battalion sustained extremely heavy losses. At dusk the German riflemen and machine gunners were handicapped by poor visibility, whereas the Russians were able to observe every German movement against the light background of the steep, snow-covered slope behind the village.

The struggle soon developed into a fire fight across Golubaya Creek. Two Russian tanks that had ventured too close to the creek were knocked out by German tank demolition teams which had to wade through the icy water to accomplish their mission. The situation reached a critical stage around 1630, when about 120 Russian cavalrymen outflanked the German positions from the north and rode toward the hill east of the village, thus threatening to cut the escape route of the German units still holding out in the village and of the heavy weapons section on the ridge of the hill. The commander of Company G, the right flank unit and a battalion staff officer, who happened to be at the company's CP at the time, were the first to realize the danger. They took immediate action without awaiting orders from battalion headquarters. Having gotten hold of every man they could find, they led their group to the top of the hill by the quickest route without taking cover or using concealment. On the hill the detachment of about 30 men was hastily organized for a counterthrust. The

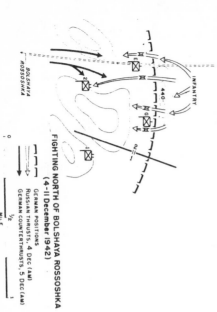

34. FIGHTING NORTH OF BOLSHAYA ROSSOSHKA

supply of ammunition was pitifully low. There were only 8 to 10 rounds of carbine ammunition per man, a machinegun with 80 rounds, 2 submachineguns with 20 rounds each, and a total of 6 hand grenades.

No time was to be lost, since the enemy was closing in fast. The German detachment advanced in extended formation. The Russians, dismounting at the foot of the hill, started to move up. Darkness was falling when the clash occurred, the opposing elements having approached to within 20 yards of each other. Shouting "Hurrah!" at a given signal, the German detachment fired a few rounds and threw the six hand grenades in the direction of the enemy. The Germans then sought cover and took their time in directing well-aimed small arms fire at the enemy. The Russians, surprised by the suddenness with which the Germans struck, suffered considerable losses since they had advanced in close formation. The initial random fire led them to believe that they were facing a strong German force, while the deliberate fire that had followed pinned them down and helped the Germans to save their ammunition.

This resolute German counterthrust, carried out by a few men without an adequate supply of ammunition, had succeeded in intercepting the Russian enveloping movement. Both officers and six of the men were wounded, but reinforcements and ammunition reached the detachment on the hill within the hour. Under the protection afforded by the detachment, the battalion was able to break off the engagement in Verkhne-Golubaya that same night and withdraw to the southeast without further incident.

The fighting at Verkhne-Golubaya demonstrated once again that the selection of a defense line solely on the basis of map study by a higher headquarters rarely takes all terrain features into account. In the above instance, the German position lacked depth and space for maneuver. The heavy machineguns, for example, which had been emplaced halfway up the slope of the hill east of the village, could not be shifted to alternate positions because movement by any crew member was conspicuous against the white background. In view of the narrowness of the battle position, the battalion and company commanders were unable to organize an effective defense of the village because their only choice was to establish their CP's either in the village or in the MLR, where they could not see what was happening on the wings of their units, or on top of the hill, from where they were unable to exercise proper control. As a result, German losses were heavy, with each company losing one-quarter to one-third of its strength and much of its equipment. This was all the more regrettable because the losses had been sustained in a relatively insignificant defensive action. Had it not been for the hill detachment's well-timed counterthrust, the consequences might have been disastrous for the battalion.

The mistakes made by Sixth Army headquarters in this instance were typical of those made during the second phase of an encirclement. The Sixth Army had decided to shorten the defense perimeter in accordance with an integrated plan. During this phase isolated units which had been fighting at outposts within the pocket gradually established contact with their neighbors. The defense lines solidified, even though the front was not continuous. In many instances, however, the planning was too hasty and superficial; units were ordered to occupy sectors as if the front were a continuous line. At Verkhne-Golubaya, for example, higher headquarters made the mistake of designating a sector from a map without on-the-spot reconnaissance, thus denying the lower echelon commanders any exercise of initiative. Moreover, since every man would be needed for the defense of the pocket to whose outer boundary his unit was gradually converging and which had to be held as long as possible, the 2d Battalion commander should have been allowed to use his own judgment in order to hold casualties to a minimum.

The last week of November was marked by several minor engagements similar to the one at Verkhne-Golubaya. During their gradual eastward withdrawal across the Don toward Stalingrad, the German man units repeatedly became involved in bitter fighting that flared up suddenly. In the process they slowly drew closer to one another and began to form a continuous front. The troops were subjected to extreme hardships, spending cold nights without sleep, making difficult marches without adequate rations, and fighting without sufficient ammunition against a far superior enemy. Often the soil was

frozen so solid that the men were unable to dig in. This difficult period was the acid test of whether or not a unit had *esprit de corps* and discipline. Some newly organized divisions, which had recently arrived from Germany, showed early signs of disintegration. Men who lost their leaders discarded their weapons, plundered ration dumps, stole alcoholic beverages, and staggered aimlessly over the snow-covered paths. Stragglers and isolated service troops roamed around as fugitives from discipline. On the other hand, the older, seasoned regiments—and they represented the majority—continued to give a good account of themselves, even after their officers had become casualties. Those noncommissioned officers who had participated in innumerable engagements since the crossing of the Bug River in June 1941 formed the backbone of resistance. In units that still had their officers the comradeship between officers and enlisted men became closer than ever. The company commanders did their best to provide the men with food and shelter and set an example of endurance and courage. Once Sixth Army assumed control over all personnel in the pocket, it disbanded those units whose combat value was doubtful and distributed their personnel, as well as any excess service troops and stragglers, to reliable regiments, where high morale and strict discipline prevailed and which could exercise a beneficial influence on the troops assigned to them.

XIII. Infantry Succeeds Where Armor Failed (December 1942)

Toward the end of November 1942 the German Fourth Panzer Army with headquarters at Zimovniki, due east of Rostov, was responsible for organizing and directing the relief thrust on Stalingrad. By 27 November, under the command of the LVII Panzer Corps, the reinforced 6th Panzer Division was moving toward Stalingrad via Kotelnikovo, while advance elements of the 23d Panzer Division were preparing to join the advance.

In the steppe north of Kotelnikovo the Russians had deployed a cavalry corps on the right and an infantry corps on the left in order to protect the approaches to Stalingrad. Behind these two corps and

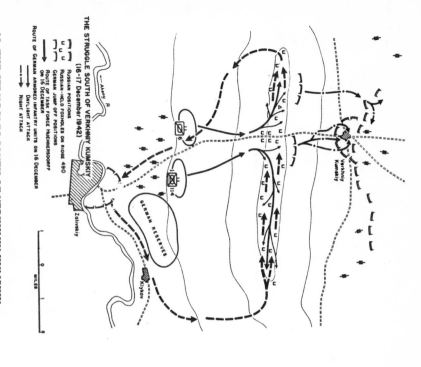

35. THE STRUGGLES SOUTH OF VERKHNIY KUMSKIY

THE STRUGGLE SOUTH OF VERKHNIY KUMSKIY
(16-17 December 1942)

RUSSIAN POSITIONS
RUSSIAN-HELD FOXHOLES ON RIDGE 490
GERMAN JUMP OFF POSITIONS
ROUTE OF TASK FORCE HUEHNERSDORFF ON 16 DECEMBER
ROUTE OF GERMAN ARMORED INFANTRY UNITS ON 16 DECEMBER
DAYLIGHT ATTACK
NIGHT ATTACK

MILES

north of the Aksay River loomed the powerful Russian Third Tank Army, often called Tank Army Popov after its able commander.

During the first half of December the German relief force steadily battled its way northeastward. With 200 tanks and self-propelled assault guns, the 6th Panzer Division, overran the Russian cavalry and infantry corps, and by 12 December forward elements crossed the shallow river bed of the Aksay against only weak opposition and established a bridgehead opposite Zalivskiy (map   ).

About 8 miles north of the river the Russian tank army was concentrating its forces in the town of Verkhniy Kumskiy. When the 6th Panzer Division continued northward and drove into the village during the afternoon of 12 December, the Russian armored forces reacted violently. A furious tank battle ensued during which the village repeatedly changed hands in the following 24 hours. When it became apparent that the Russians were gradually concentrating numerically superior forces, including motorized infantry and scores of antitank guns, the Germans quickly withdrew to the Aksay. The Russians, however, had suffered such heavy tank losses that they did not pursue, but rather contented themselves with establishing defensive positions along Ridge 490, which stretched across the steppe about 2 miles south of Verkhniy Kumskiy.

By 16 December the two panzer divisions had repaired most of their disabled tanks. On orders from army, an armored task force composed of elements from both panzer divisions was to launch a flanking attack against the Russian-held ridge. The intrenched Russian motorized infantry forces were to be rolled up from east to west.

Composed of one tank regiment and one armored infantry battalion of the 6th and one tank company of the 23d Panzer Division, Task Force Huehnersdorff, so named after its commander, moved out from Zalivskiy and ascended the gentle slopes of the Aksay Valley via Klykov. After reaching the eastern end of the enemy-held ridge the tanks began to move westward along the crest of the ridge without encountering opposition. The Russian infantrymen, hiding in their deep foxholes and narrow trenches in groups of two to four men, permitted the tanks to pass over them. However, as soon as the German armored infantry at the tail end of the column had passed them, the Russians fired antitank grenades at the lightly armored vehicles at point-blank range, inflicting heavy losses. Repeatedly, the tanks had to stop and come to the assistance of the armored infantrymen who tried to flush out the Russian nests of resistance. But even the tanks were ineffective against the Russian infantrymen, who were so well concealed by the tall, brown steppe grass that they could not be dislodged by the tankers or infantrymen from their armored vehicles. In most instances the German soldier was hit by a sniper's bullet before he ever got close to his hidden opponent. German planes were as powerless as the tanks, whose ineffectiveness in this situation was only too obvious. Although the lead tanks were able to reach the opposite end of the ridge by midafternoon, the majority of the Russians were still in their positions. Having failed in its mission and suffered considerable losses, the task force had no other choice but to return to the bridgehead.

This experience induced the commander of the 6th Panzer Division to revise his plans for the next day. Not tanks but infantrymen on foot would have to dislodge the enemy from the ridge. He formed an assault force that same night (16/17 December) and assembled it north of the bridgehead directly in front of the armored artillery regiment.

The left wing was formed by the seasoned 6th Armored Reconnaissance Battalion, the right by the 1st Armored Infantry Battalion of the 114th Infantry Regiment (Mechanized). The two battalions were reinforced by engineer assault detachments, flame-thrower teams, and mine-clearing details. The tanks and remaining armored infantry elements were assembled in the rear between Zalivsky and Klykov, where they stayed in reserve, ready to follow up the assault force.

At 0800 on 17 December the massed guns of the artillery regiment opened fire. As the hail of shells came down on the ridge it obliterated the Russian observation post. The dried-out steppe grass burned fiercely and reddish clouds of dust enveloped the whole ridge, de-

priving the Russians of all visibility. After a short time, however, the fires died out because a light snowfall prevented them from spreading.

Meanwhile, the first German assault wave moved up to the ridge. When a signal flare was set off to indicate it was entering the Russian defensive positions, the artillery fire was shifted. The assault detachments had opened a gap at the center of the ridge. The difficult task of ferreting out the enemy force dug in on the ridge had thus begun.

Several squadrons of German dive bombers, flying in relays, came over and headed in the direction of Verkhniy Kumskiy, where they blasted Russian artillery positions, silencing one battery after another. Directly overhead, Messerschmitts and Ratas tangled in dogfights, during which three of the Russian fighters were shot down near the ridge.

Paying little heed to the air action, the assault forces fanned out from the initial point of penetration and moved forward. Machine gunners and sharpshooting riflemen stalked the hidden Russians like game and fired well-aimed bullets at anything that moved. Whenever Russians from a nearby foxhole returned the fire, they were silenced by a well-placed hand grenade. The fortified positions were neutralized by the flame-thrower teams. Whenever a particularly fanatic Russian force could not be flushed out by the assault troops, they fired a signal flare to pinpoint the target for the German artillery pieces and mortars.

By noon the reconnaissance battalion had cleared all enemy forces from its zone of action, and an hour later the armored infantry battalion had done likewise on the eastern part of the ridge. An attack on Verkhniy Kumskiy could be envisaged. Reconnaissance patrols reported that the village and the slopes facing it to the north were occupied by strong Russian forces. As the patrols approached Verkhniy Kumskiy, they encountered hostile fire from all directions. German reconnaissance planes identified numerous antitank guns and dug-in tanks along the outskirts and in well-concealed positions in the hills. Russian tanks were observed to be moving toward the village from the west.

During the rest of the afternoon the Russian positions and gun emplacements in and around the village were shelled by German artillery. Until nightfall dive bombers, flying in waves, made low-level attacks against tank concentrations, dug-in tanks, and batteries of antitank guns. After darkness the armored infantry units resumed their northward drive. With special assault detachments leading the way, infantrymen felt their way along routes that had been reconnoitered during the daylight hours. The smoldering ruins of bombed and shelled houses in the village illuminated the area and facilitated orientation. Like phantoms, the assault detachments crept up to the first houses and observed Russian field kitchens preparing rations. This was the ideal time for a surprise raid!

Upon a given signal the German assault detachments stormed the village from three sides. Seized by panic, some surprised Russians ran for their lives. Many were too stunned to move and were taken prisoner as the German infantrymen pursued the disorganized remnants into the hills to the north. The Russian tanks tried to make a dash to the north in order to escape the approaching German tank-demolition teams, but many failed to get started in time and were destroyed. Scores of Russian antitank guns and disabled tanks, as well as a great store of heavy equipment, fell into German hands.

The Russian stronghold of Verkhniy Kumskiy was thus taken by the Germans at the cost of negligible losses. Where a task force of almost two tank regiments had failed the day before, an armored reconnaissance and an armored infantry battalion achieved a decisive success. Without this success, the relief thrust on Stalingrad would have bogged down much earlier than it eventually did, and the men in the pocket would have lost all hope.

XIV. The 2d Battalion's Final Struggle in the Stalingrad Pocket (January 1943)

The third and final phase of the operations along the periphery of the Stalingrad pocket began immediately after Christmas 1942. At that time the pocket had a diameter of approximately 22 miles. The life expectancy of the encircled Sixth Army depended on its ability to defend this perimeter. If the Russians succeeded in breaking through the German ring at any point, they would split the encircled army into smaller pockets, capture the remaining airfields, and thus cut off the supply by airlift. Ration and ammunition dumps would fall into their hands, and the German resistance would crumble. Although sporadic fighting might continue, such isolated German resistance would merely have nuisance value and could be eliminated in the course of mopping-up operations.

This explains the ferocity with which both sides fought to gain a decision. The stakes were high, and the Germans needed cool-headed leaders. Whereas German unit commanders could envisage the possibility of a voluntary withdrawal during the first and second phases of the encirclement, defense in place was mandatory during the third. At this stage Russian front-line propaganda took over. On New Year's Day Russian psychological warfare teams went to work. Night after night loudspeakers blared forth speeches by German refugees speaking from a studio in Moscow, who read appeals, ostensibly from German mothers and wives, imploring their loved ones to give up the fight. German prisoners, who had been confined in model Russian camps, were sent back across the lines to their former units to report the excellent treatment they had received.

The prospect of relief from the outside had meanwhile grown dimmer. Nevertheless, the men in the pocket refused to give up hope, even though there was every indication that the Sixth Army was doomed. Living conditions in the pocket went from bad to worse. The German infantrymen had to stay in their foxholes, exposed to snow and rain, extreme cold, and sudden thaw. Again and again the rations had to be cut. At first every man was issued one-third of a loaf of bread per day, then a quarter, and later a fifth. This monotonous diet was occasionally supplemented by a few slices of sausage and a meat broth obtained by boiling horse meat. Only the wounded were given half a bar of chocolate and some brandy immediately after the evacuation to revive their spirits.

Constant Russian pressure resulted in a steadily growing number of casualties. The 2d Battalion's combat strength diminished gradually. When the Russians resumed their large-scale attacks early in

184

January 1943, the battalion had only 3 officers and about 160 men left. In mid-January the executive officer was killed in close combat during a German counterattack. On the following day the battalion commander committed suicide as the result of a nervous breakdown. On 19 January the battalion's last remaining officer, a platoon commander of Company G, launched a final desperate counterthrust and led the last 13 men of the battalion to their death. A few days later, at the beginning of February 1943, the battle of Stalingrad came to an end.

XV. Sudden Initiation Into Russian Winter Combat (February 1943)

After they had liquidated the Stalingrad pocket, the Russians launched a powerful counteroffensive which quickly carried them westward. At the beginning of February Soviet tanks took Slavyansk against virtually no German, opposition since the entire sector had been stripped of German troops except for a few service units. In an effort to stem the tide the XL Panzer Corps, including two panzer and one infantry divisions, was moved up from the south and ordered to drive the Russians back across the Donets River.

Typical Russian winter weather prevailed in the Konstantinovka area south of Slavyansk. Blankets of deep snow covered road and countryside alike, and the temperature reached a low point of −49° F. at night. Such conditions alone were enough to tax to the utmost the fortitude and hardiness of even the fittest German soldier.

The 679th Regiment of the 333d Infantry Division, forming part of the XL Panzer Corps, had not seen previous combat in Russia. Upon detraining at the railhead in Konstantinovka at 0400 on 12 February, the 3d Battalion received orders to launch an immediate thrust toward Kramatorskaya (map). The battalion assembled, and the forward elements started to move out without delay. At 0800, after having advanced barely a mile east of the Torets River, the battalion point ran straight into an oncoming Russian tank force. After a brief clash the German detachment was annihilated and the advance party put to rout. Deeply impressed by this sudden turn of

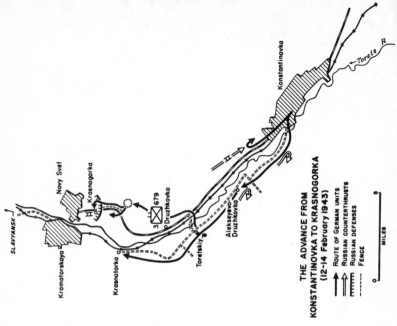

THE ADVANCE FROM
KONSTANTINOVKA TO KRASNOGORKA
(12-14 February 1943)

⟹ Route of German units
⟹ Russian counterthrusts
━━━ Russian defenses
⌐⌐⌐ Fence

0 _____ 5
MILES

36. THE ADVANCE FROM KONSTANTINOVKA TO KRASNOGORKA

events, the main body of the German battalion, which was just then moving out of Konstantinovka, began to waver and was seized by an acute case of tank jitters.

The regimental commander realized that he had to act immediately. Fear of tanks had gripped the battalion, suddenly converting gallant troopers into quivering cowards. What could he do? The overall situation was none too favorable since the 2d Battalion was not due to arrive for 12 hours and the 1st Battalion would take at least another 24 hours.

When the regimental commander discovered that a self-propelled gun was undergoing repairs in Konstantinovka, he immediately commandeered it. Realizing that the danger of encountering enemy tanks was greatest east of the Torets, he chose the road running along the west bank as the new axis of advance.

The regimental and battalion commanders mounted the assault gun and proceeded to lead the advance northward. The men were heartened by the sight of their two commanders speeding northward along the new route without encountering enemy opposition. They quickly regained confidence and, falling in behind their leaders, moved forward with new courage. Against light enemy resistance the battalion fought its way to Alekseyevo-Druzhkovka, and during the night the newly arrived 2d Battalion closed up and moved into the same town.

On 13 February, as a result of the previous day's experience, the regimental commander decided to employ the 2d Battalion as lead element in order to condition the unit to combat in Russia. In an effort to simulate greater strength, all motorized vehicles were ordered to follow the lead battalion in plain view of the enemy. This deception could be used only because enemy interference from the air was not expected.

Toward evening the 2d Battalion arrived at Krasnotorka without major incident. During the night, however, the battalion suffered heavy casualties from frostbite when the battalion commander, who was unfamiliar with the severe Russian winter weather, ordered sentries to be posted in the open outside the village. The deception,

however, had been successful, judging by an intercepted Russian radio message in which the enemy command was warned that strong German motorized formations were advancing toward Kramatorskaya.

The regimental commander moved the 1st Battalion, the last one to arrive, to Toretskiy with orders to capture Krasnogorka the next day. At dawn the 1st Battalion crossed the river, passed through Druzhkovka, and moved into a hollow about 2 miles south of Krasnogorka. The cross-country march in deep snow was exhausting because the motorized equipment constantly bogged down and had to be pulled out by wreckers. Nevertheless, the battalion arrived in its jumpoff position by 1000.

The situation facing the battalion commander was exasperating. Ahead of him lay strongly defended Krasnogorka, from where a few enemy tanks were firing in his direction. Between him and his objective loomed a vast expanse of snow that was more than 3 feet deep. Despite promised support from a medium artillery battery, a direct frontal assault on the town was bound to fail and involve heavy casualties. From afar off the Russians could observe the individual German soldiers cautiously inching their way forward, their silhouettes clearly outlined against the white background, and could pick them off at will. Although the regimental commander shared his apprehensions, the attack had to be launched and Krasnogorka had to be taken.

The only landmark that broke the monotony of the flat landscape was a high, snow-covered fence extending for about 2 miles along the right side of the road from the turn to the village. This fence, which actually looked more like a wall of snow, might conceal the troops while they worked their way toward the objective in single file, hugging the fence until they reached Krasnogorka. Although far from an ideal solution to the problem of carrying out a frontal assault on the village, this plan was the only apparent way out. To deceive the Russian garrison and divert its attention, one company was to be echeloned in depth and advance on Krasnogorka en a wide front on the left side of the road. While this company was launching its diversionary attack, the rest of the battalion crept to within 500 yards of the objective. The Russians fell for this ruse and concentrated the fire of their multibarrelled rocket launchers, self-propelled guns, and mortars on the single company, which was promptly pinned down. Meanwhile, the main assault force continued its advance along the snow fence, infiltrated into Krasnogorka, and seized it in short order. Because of the deep snow, the battalion took 2 hours to cover the 2-mile stretch along the fence. The Russians were taken completely by surprise and beat a hasty retreat to Kramatorskaya. A few days later the regiment, committed as a unit for the first time, followed up this initial success by seizing Slavyansk after overcoming stiff Russian resistance.

One of the lessons to be learned from the above action is that infantry units lacking combat experience against tanks should not be committed without adequate support from antitank weapons. Unless this precaution is taken, the strength of the unit will be uselessly dissipated and its morale will suffer unnecessarily.

The regimental commander had to make several decisions which were in contradiction to standing operating procedures and had to introduce improvisations that fulfilled the needs in unexpected situations. When he and the battalion commander mounted the assault gun and drove ahead of the column, they contravened all standing regulations. This daring exploit, assisted by a good measure of luck, helped to turn a dispirited unit into an aggressive one.

In this instance the Russians let themselves be deceived too easily. They had obviously failed to obtain essential reconnaissance information and grew panicky when the Germans suddenly launched the coup de main on Krasnogorka.

I. General

In 1941 the Russian armored command was in the process of re-organizing and converting to new equipment. Only selected personnel were assigned to this arm of the service, and the outdated heavy and light tanks were being replaced with medium models, primarily T34's, which mounted a 76-mm. gun and were exceptionally fast and powerful.

Before 1941 the principal function of the Russian tank unit was to support the infantry. The successes achieved by German armor during the blitzkrieg in Poland, France, and the Balkans led the Russians to a reevaluation of their doctrine affecting armor, and the Russian planners turned to the idea of using armor in a strategic role along the German lines.

During this transitional period the Russian armored command was suddenly confronted with the German invasion. The first year of the war saw the Russians suffering heavy losses in desperate attempts to stem the tide which threatened to engulf them while at the same time they were trying to carry through fundamental changes in their armored tactics and equipment.

In hastily passing from one stage to the next, Russian armored tactics and techniques developed along lines that seemed, at least to the German foe, entirely unorthodox. It was this very unorthodoxy that baffled the Germans and enabled the Russians to achieve successes, which began to sap the German strength long before Russian armor reached its full effectiveness. At the beginning of the campaign the Russians were forced to commit their armor piecemeal, usually in units no larger than a regiment. By early 1942 the independent tank brigade appeared on the field of battle, and eventually the Russians organized armored armies.

The T34 was constantly improved during the war years, particularly with regard to its radio and sighting equipment, its armor, and, above all, its armament, which was eventually changed to an 85-mm. gun.

The technological improvements in Russian tanks were the result of many factors. The developments in German armor were without doubt known to the Russians, sometimes even in the blueprint stage. Captured German tanks became available early in the war, as did the latest United States and British thought on tank design. Of all the factors involved, it was perhaps the delivery of materiel under lend-lease agreements that had the most important impact on Russian tank construction.

The imbalance which resulted from the simultaneous effort to attain both technical perfection and tactical skill was most obvious in the conduct of battle by the small unit. In one action the Russians might demonstrate a conspicuous lack of flexibility, while in another they might prove masters in maneuvering mobile units. The records show instances where tank strength was woefully wasted, and, on the other hand, an example of how a single Russian tank tied down an entire German combat team for 48 hours.

In the actions selected for the purpose of this study there is no pattern that lends itself to generalization. If they do convey a unified impression, it is that the Russian is aware of the need for constant changes in armored tactics to keep in step with technological improvements, and that he is extremely flexible in the application of these tactics. He is a master of camouflage. He will dig in his tank as readily as he digs in an antitank gun, and will usually succeed in removing it after it has been bypassed. He seeks ever to preserve mobility. He will hit and run; he will hit and stay; he will use his tanks as decoys, for traps, in ambush. He will always do the unexpected. The Russian tanker, who knew his native soil better than he knew his field manuals, eventually drove the German invaders all the way back to Berlin.

The following small unit actions show clearly the way in which the Russians overcame their early mistakes and developed an effective

188

fighting force. In these examples of armored combat, descriptive details are fewer than in infantry engagements at a similar level. This comparative lack of detailed information reflects the very nature of tank warfare, which takes place at a rapid pace and therefore offers fewer clues to permit a reconstruction of events. The absence of details, however, in no way diminishes the intrinsic value of the material presented.

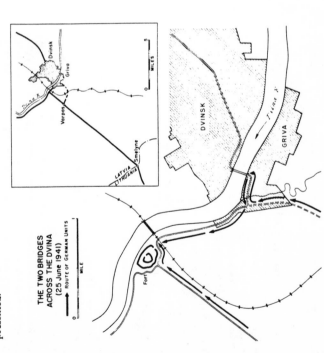

THE TWO BRIDGES
ACROSS THE DVINA
(25 June 1941)

→ ROUTE OF GERMAN UNITS

0 _____ 1
MILE

III. German Armored Engineers Capture Two Bridges (June 1941)

While elements of the 6th Panzer Division were thus momentarily delayed, the 8th Panzer Division, which was also part of Army Group North, spearheaded the German attack farther south, taking the Russians completely by surprise. The 8th Panzer Division sped northeastward in the face of sporadic and constantly diminishing enemy resistance, leaving Russian units at its flanks and rear to be mopped up later by the German infantry. On the evening of 24 June the division reached Smelyne, a village on the Lithuanian-Latvian border, 12 miles southwest of Dvinsk. It had advanced over an excellent highway through open and gently rolling terrain.

Late on 24 June the division commander made an estimate of this situation. The division's immediate objective was the city of Dvinsk, situated on the north bank of the Dvina (map 18). However, in order to capture the city the division first had to seize the 2 bridges spanning the river, which was approximately 250 yards wide in this area. While the highway bridge was needed for the division's advance, the other, a railroad bridge situated about a mile downstream, was to be used as an alternate should the Russians succeed in demolishing the highway bridge. German air reconnaissance had indicated that the Russians intended to defend Dvinsk and that the two bridges across the Dvina had been prepared for demolition. The destruction of these bridges, however, would delay the division's advance and thus upset the Army Group's timetable. Consequently, the two bridges had to be seized in a surprise raid before the Russians could destroy them.

The division commander decided to act without delay and ordered the commander of the division's advance guard and Lieutenant Schneider, CO of Company C, 59th Armored Engineer Battalion, to report to his CP immediately. After the two officers arrived there, he briefly outlined the general situation and then issued the following verbal orders :

One platoon of Company C, divided into four assault detachments, will launch a surprise, attack against the two bridges at Dvinsk. The detachments will jump off at 0130 on 25 June and head for the bridges in the four Russian trucks that the division captured earlier today. The Russians must be led to believe that the trucks are friendly, so that the assault detachments can get within striking distance of the bridges without being challenged.

Once the detachments have reached the bridges, they will immediately cut all cables leading to the bridges from both banks to prevent the enemy from setting off the demolition charges electrically, cut all detonating cords leading to the charges, and defend the bridges against Russian counterattacks.

The main body of Company C will also jump off at 0130, but will proceed somewhat more slowly so as to arrive at the bridges about 15 minutes after the assault detachments, which it will relieve. Company C will be followed by the division's advance guard, which will arrive at the highway bridge at 0305. Since the highway bridge should be firmly in German hands by this time, the advance guard, consisting of one armored infantry battalion and one tank battalion, will cross over into Dvinsk and spearhead the division's northeastward advance.

Gentlemen, I have confidence in your ability to execute this difficult mission successfully and wish you luck. If there are no questions, that is all.

Preparations for the impending mission were quickly made. Schneider organized the 4th Platoon of his company into four assault detachments, each consisting of 10 men equipped with machineguns, submachine guns, hand grenades, and wire cutters.

The main body of Company C was to march in the following order: 1st and 2d Platoons, each equipped with five special engineer tanks. These vehicles were Mark II tanks, each armed with a 20-mm gun and a machinegun. At the back of each tank a special boom had been mounted for the purpose of depositing demolition charges and removing obstacles.

The seven half-tracks of the 4th Platoon, equipped with frame-type rocket projectors, were to follow the first two platoons. On the march the half-tracks were to be occupied only by the drivers, since the other men of the 4th Platoon were to form the assault detachments.

The 5th Platoon, composed of combat engineers equipped with demolition charges, was to follow in trucks.

Company C's 3d Platoon was engaged in bridge construction elsewhere and was not available for the operation.

Company C moved out of its bivouac near Smelyne at 0130. With their headlights on, the trucks carrying the assault detachments sped northeastward at 40 m. p. h. over the hard-surfaced road in the direction of Dvinsk. The company's tanks and half-tracks followed the trucks at a lower rate of speed. Initially, everything proceeded according to plan. The assault detachments did not encounter any Russians and continued toward the bridges at unabated speed.

At Varpas, 2 miles from the river, the first three trucks turned east and continued toward the highway bridge, while the fourth truck headed straight for the railroad bridge. The detachments passed several Russian infantrymen, but the latter apparently assumed that the trucks were friendly and did not challenge them.

a. *The Struggle for the Highway Bridge.* After turning east at Varpas, the three trucks continued on at full speed, reaching Griva on the south bank of the Dvina at 0215. The southwestern outskirts of Griva were occupied by a Russian rear guard of about 50 men, who let the trucks pass through. Only a short distance separated the assault detachments from the bridge, and the men became tense. At the approach to the bridge Russian sentries blocked the road and challenged the first truck, which then slowed down. It seemed to the detachment commander that his luck had finally run out. Since deception was no longer possible, only quick action could save the day. The driver of the first truck pulled up close to the Russian sentries as if to stop. Then, at the last moment, he stepped on the gas, and the truck lurched forward with a roar and headed across the bridge, followed by a second truck. A few of the Russians standing in the path of the trucks managed to jump out of the way. Others, less fortunate, were run over. Those that were able to do so, leaped to the aid of their injured comrades. In the confusion, little attention was paid to the third truck, which had halted at the approach to the bridge. At a given signal, its occupants suddenly jumped the dazed Russians with knives and bayonets, killing them all. Four of the men then rushed to the bridge and cut all the wires they could locate. The first truck meanwhile succeeded in crossing the bridge without being attacked; the second, however, which had stopped briefly at the middle of the bridge to drop off a wire-cutting detail, received small-arms fire from the north bank and quickly moved on to the far end of the bridge where it joined the first. The wire-cutting detail had barely completed its work when enemy machineguns and antitank guns on the north bank of the Dvina opened fire, pinning the men down. The two detachments at the north end of the bridge also drew fire and suffered their first casualties. At 0230 the Russians launched a strong counterattack in an attempt to drive the two detachments from the north end of the bridge. In the ensuing close combat both sides suffered heavy losses. Ten minutes after the trucks had first rolled onto the bridge the Russian rear guard arrived from Griva and attacked the detachment at the south end. However, despite their numerical superiority, the Russians were unable to dislodge the three assault detachments from the bridge, although they did prevent the German engineers from conducting a systematic search for the demolition charges. Even though the Germans had cut all cables on the bridge, making it impossible for the Russians to set off the charges electrically, there was still the danger that they would set them off by means of detonating cords if they succeeded in getting onto the bridge.

At 0240, just as the assault detachments began to run short of ammunition and hand grenades, they were relieved by the main body of the company. During the 20 minutes of fighting the three assault detachments, which altogether numbered 30 men at the outset, had suffered heavy casualties. One officer, one NCO, and three privates were killed, and four men were wounded.

With the arrival of the main body of the company, tanks of the 1st and 2d Platoons went into position on the south bank and began to fire at Russian troops in Dvinsk. Ten minutes later the half-tracks of the 4th Platoon joined the special engineer tanks and fired rockets into Dvinsk. Large fires soon broke out in the city.

After a brief struggle the remnants of the Russian rear guard on the south bank surrendered. A strong Russian force, which had assembled north of the bridge for a counterattack, was caught in the German barrage and dispersed before the attack could get under way.

By 0255, when the division's advance guard arrived, Company C had accomplished its mission of seizing the highway bridge intact. At 0305 the division's advance guard began to cross the bridge and push on into Dvinsk against fierce Russian resistance.

There remained only one more task to be carried out by Company C: the removal of the demolition charges on the bridge. A hasty check indicated that the Russians had prepared each of the three spans for demolition. However, the check did not reveal any charges at the piers.

While a detail was preparing to remove the charges, one of the men suddenly noticed a puff of smoke nearby and discovered that a Russian had crawled onto the bridge, apparently unnoticed, and had lighted a detonating cord. Jumping forward, the engineer wrenched the cord from the charge only 10 seconds before the explosion would have taken place. At almost the same time a similar incident occurred near the north end of the bridge. Here the detonation was also prevented just in time.

With the company's mission at the highway bridge accomplished, Lieutenant Schneider was able to turn his attention to the railroad bridge, where the noise of battle was audible, indicating that the 4th Assault Detachment had run into trouble. Schneider dispatched Company C's 2d and 5th Platoons to that bridge by way of the road which ran parallel to the river.

b. The Struggle for the Railroad Bridge. When the first three assault detachments, en route to the highway bridge, turned east at Varpas shortly after 0200, the other truck continued north on the main highway, which led directly to the railroad bridge. Several hundred yards short of the bridge, at the intersection with the road that parallels the river, there was an old fort whose outer wall the truck had to pass. As the vehicle turned right onto the river road it received small-arms fire from the fort. In a matter of seconds the truck caught fire and was hastily abandoned. The detachment then attempted to fight its way toward the bridge on foot, a distance of some 500 yards. However, the men were soon pinned down by the Russian fire, despite which they slowly and laboriously crawled toward the bridge. Just as the detachment had inched close enough to rush the bridge, there was a terrific explosion. Apparently aware of German intentions, the Russians had detonated charges attached to the steel piers. As the smoke cleared, it became evident that the demolition had not been very effective. The bridge was still intact. The wood planking and the rail ties had, however, caught fire, and there was danger that the fire might set off additional charges, which would normally be placed beneath certain girders of the truss sections. Quick action on the part of the assault detachment was therefore necessary if the fire was to be extinguished and the bridge saved.

At 0330 the 2d and 5th Platoons of Company C arrived at the east entrance to the fort, which was blocked by a heavy steel gate. Since the fire at the railroad bridge was still unchecked and fire-fighting equipment could not be brought up as long as the Russians kept the bridge under fire, the two platoons were ordered to take the fort by direct assault.

The men of the 5th Platoon, who had dismounted and tried to place a demolition charge next to the gate, drew heavy Russian small arms fire. An estimate of the situation indicated that it would be inadvisable to approach the gate without the protection of armor. Accordingly, one of the 2d Platoon's special engineer tanks was ordered to back up to the gate and lower a 110-pound HE charge from its boom. As soon as the charge had been deposited and the tank had moved to a safe distance, the charge was set off. The terrific explosion destroyed the gate and stunned the Russians in the immediate vicinity. However, as the German tanks advanced through the breach, they again drew fire. Their progress was further impeded by a second wall, whose gate, also of steel, was on the side facing the river. Again a special engineer tank had to be brought up with a 110-pound HE charge, which was set off with the same results as the first. At this point a few Russians surrendered. The remainder of the garrison, about 20 in number, continued to resist from the CP, which was lo-

cated in a structure at the very center of the fort. While the Russians in the fort were trying desperately to repulse the German attack, Company C's fire-fighting equipment proceeded to the railroad bridge and quickly extinguished the blaze. Using shaped charges and hand grenades the 5th Platoon finally succeeded in driving the Russians from their last foothold within the fort. At 0400 the fight for the fort came to an end. Of the company of Russians that had held the fort, 70 had been killed or wounded and 30 taken prisoner.

The entire action had been carried out with great speed, only half an hour having elapsed between the initial assault on the fort and its capture. When interrogated, Russians captured at the fort stated that they had been ordered to hold out as long as possible, even if the bridge were demolished. They were to keep the Germans from moving up bridge equipment over the highway and to delay the German advance as long as possible.

With both bridges firmly in German hands, Company C's mission was accomplished. In the fierce fighting which continued until evening the 8th Panzer Division captured Dvinsk and continued its northeastward advance toward Leningrad.

The preceding example illustrates to what extent the commitment of armor in situations where speed is imperative can result in major successes. The seizure of the two bridges at Dvinsk was possible mainly because the four captured Russian trucks were sent ahead of the main body of Company C, thus taking the Russians by surprise and preventing them from demolishing the bridges before the Germans could reach them.

The selection of Company C for this mission was justified because its special engineer tanks and half-tracks had sufficient fire power to pin the Russians down north of the highway bridge and pave the way for the division's advance into Dvinsk. During the fighting for the fort, the special engineer tanks once more proved invaluable in destroying the two gates. Only armor could get close enough to the gates to place the demolition charges in the face of the heavy Russian small-arms fire.

IV. Russian Tank Trap (July 1941)

By the beginning of July 1941 the 3d Panzer Division, which was part of Army Group Center, had reached the Dnepr River north of Zhlobin and was preparing to attack across the river. On 6 July the division's tank regiment, then in reserve, was ordered to relieve an infantry division which had encountered strong Russian resistance while attacking Zhlobin from the southwest. The infantry attack had bogged down about 2½ miles southwest of the town (map 19).

The terrain around Zhlobin was gently rolling grassland alternating with swampy ground. The weather was warm and sunny.

The tank regiment commander decided to employ 2 battalions, each with about 40 tanks. According to his plan the 1st Battalion was to advance straight toward Zhlobin. The 2d Battalion was to follow the 1st up to a point approximately 1 mile from the Russian MLR

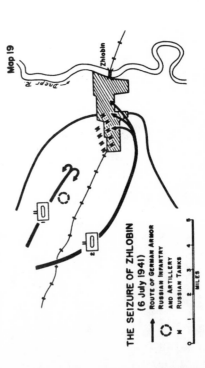

Map 19

THE SEIZURE OF ZHLOBIN
(6 July 1941)

→ ROUTE OF GERMAN ARMOR
⋀ RUSSIAN INFANTRY
⊙ AND ARTILLERY
N RUSSIAN TANKS

MILES
0   1   2   3

38. THE SEIZURE OF ZHLOBIN

northwest of Zhlobin, turn southward, cross the railroad tracks, and drive southeastward to smash the Russian forces which—so he presumed—were holding positions immediately south of the town. This two-pronged thrust would put him in possession of Zhlobin and simultaneously relieve the German infantry.

The march column advanced according to plan. About 2½ miles northwest of Zhlobin the 1st Battalion penetrated the Russian MLR against weak resistance, overran some Russian infantry elements, and then bypassed an artillery battery. Suddenly, when the lead tanks were only a mile from the outskirts of the town, they received devastating fire from Russian tanks which had been cleverly concealed among houses, farmyards, and barns at the edge of the town. The Russian tanks, lying in ambush, had held their fire until the last moment. When the 1st Battalion tanks veered to escape the onslaught, they received point-blank fire from the artillery battery they had bypassed. The Russian artillerymen had turned their pieces on the German battalion. In all the Germans lost 22 tanks as a result of this ambush.

The 2d Battalion had meanwhile received desperate calls for assistance over the radio, but could not come to the rescue because the high railroad embankment obstructed its path. The battalion commander therefore decided to bring relief by a direct thrust on Zhlobin. Upon finding the Russian left flank open, the battalion entered the town from the south and destroyed 25 of the 30 Russian tanks without suffering any losses. The Russians had not expected a thrust from this direction and had devoted all their attention to fighting the 1st Battalion.

The failure of the 1st Battalion's frontal attack must be ascribed to its laxity in reconnaissance before attempting to relieve the infantry division. Moreover, tanks on an independent mission should be accompanied by armored infantry. In this instance armored infantry might have been able to capture the Russian artillery battery.

Had the 2d Battalion followed the 1st, the artillery battery could have been neutralized and immediate assistance given to the 1st Battalion. In obscure situations it is better to advance in depth in order to meet possible surprise with unfettered forces than to advance on a relatively wide front where contact may be lost and separate elements of one's forces may be pinned down. In the ambush of the 1st Battalion the discipline of the Russians, combined with their characteristic craftiness, more than compensated for their inferiority in training and equipment. An ambush is indeed an economical operation against a careless foe.

VI. The Struggle for Shelter (December 1941)

The winter of 1941–42 was particularly severe and the fighting on many sectors of the front centered around inhabited localities that could offer shelter from the cold. In mid-December a German patrol captured an operations order that revealed that the Russians planned to attack southwestward along a road leading from the direction of Lisichansk, on the Donets, with the intention of disrupting the German lines of communication. On 18 December the 203d Infantry Regiment moved into a new battle position in and around Berestovaya, a village situated along the expected Russian axis of advance. The regiment organized its center of resistance around the stone buildings in the center of the village (map 21).

The 203d had been engaged in heavy defensive fighting for several weeks, and its combat efficiency had dropped sharply. The average strength of the infantry companies had been reduced to approximately 50 riflemen, and the regiment had lost about one-third of its heavy weapons.

Sprawling villages and a few trees were predominant features of the rolling landscape around Berestovaya, whose stone houses—rare in this part of Russia—provided ample shelter against December temperatures, which averaged about 15° F. The snow cover varied from 4 inches to several feet in depth.

From 18 through 22 December the Russians deployed their forces and pushed back one German outpost after another, an indication that a major attack was imminent. On the evening of 22 December the 2d Battalion was hit by a Russian infantry force of regimental

strength. German defensive fire succeeded in stopping the Russian advance on both sides of the Lisichansk-Belogorovka road; however, a German strong point on F Company's left flank was overrun and Russian elements penetrated Berestovaya as far as the 2d Battalion command post. The battalion commander then committed his reserves and restored the situation.

On 23 December the Russians made unsuccessful piecemeal attacks in company to battalion strength against the 2d Battalion sector astride the Lisichansk-Belogorovka road. After darkness had fallen, the Russians fired a brief artillery concentration against the forward positions of G company in the area east of the road; then they attacked the company with 2 battalions of infantry supported by 10 tanks and broke through near Hill 676. German artillery was then brought to bear on the Russian armor, forcing it to withdraw, and the infantry, deprived of tank support, was unable to advance. The Germans thereupon committed Companies I and K of the reserve battalion and sealed off the Russian penetration.

On the 24th the Russians, using only infantry, attacked along the road and, for the first time, against the left flank of the adjacent 1st Battalion.

On Christmas morning the Russians attacked along the road and eastward with two battalions of infantry, but were stopped by artillery fire. Shortly afterward, two Russian assault groups, each consisting of one to two companies supported by mortar fire, debouched from draws northwest of Berestovaya and attacked A and C Companies. Despite their numerical inferiority, the Germans managed to repulse these attacks.

About 1400, in the face of a sharp east wind, 12 Russian tanks suddenly emerged from the same draws and made a surprise attack toward Berestovaya from the west. Accompanied by infantry, the tanks advanced slowly and brought the German strong points under fire. Within an hour the tanks had broken through Company A's position, where 40 men were trying to hold a 1,000-yard-wide sector. A few of the tanks broke off from their accompanying infantry and moved southward toward the railroad embankment, but withdrew after two tanks had been lost to antitank fire.

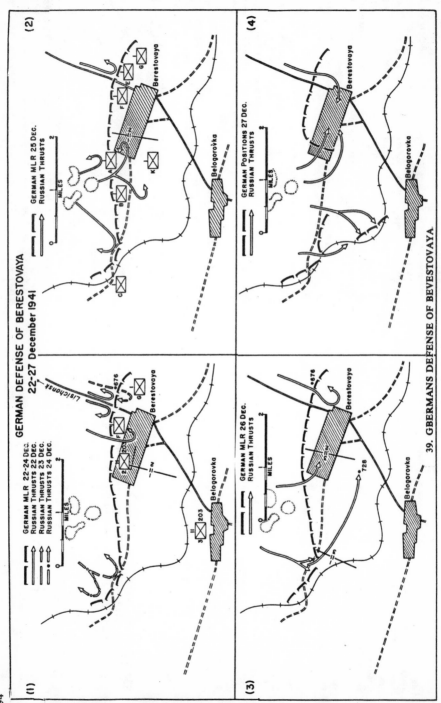

GERMAN DEFENSE OF BERESTOVAYA
22–27 December 1941

39. GERMANS DEFENSE OF BEVESTOVAYA.

194

Company K counterattacked from the south and cleared the village of those elements that had broken through its defenses. Headquarters Company of the 3d Battalion and I Company were moved up from Belogorovka and committed; by 2100 the German MLR was restored.

The heavy casualties that had been suffered in the action up to that point forced the 203d Infantry Regiment to reorganize the three battalions being assigned adjoining sectors, with the 3d Battalion in the center, flanked by the 1st and 2d on the left and right, respectively. Each battalion held one company in reserve.

At dawn on the 26th the Russians began heavy attacks in the area between Berestovaya and that portion of the rail line due west of the village. Seventeen Russian tanks, accompanied by infantry, moved against the right wing of the 1st Battalion, smashing B Company's position. As the Russians reached the railroad embankment they were halted by German artillery fire. Some of the Russian tanks moved on southeastward toward Hill 728, a conspicuous plateau in the otherwise rolling terrain. The hill offered no cover to the Germans who could not hold it against the Russian tank fire and therefore withdrew southward to the railroad. In order to strengthen the regiment's defenses, division moved one infantry battalion and a squadron of dismounted bicycle infantry to Belogorovka.

German ground-support aircraft were committed during the early morning hours with but little success—the situation on the ground was so confused that accurate bombing and strafing was impossible. At 0930 the Russians penetrated Berestovaya from the west and at noon the regimental commander gave the 2d Battalion permission to withdraw from the village. However, with the arrival shortly thereafter of reinforcements and five assault guns, the battalion was able to withstand Russian pressure until 1600, when Russian infantry, together with a few tanks, made a fresh attack along the road. The Germans lost two strong points near Hill 676 as the Russians broke through. With the aid of the reserve battalion and the assault guns, the 2d Battalion was able to throw the Russians back. By midnight the 2d Battalion's MLR was restored, but contact had been lost between the 3d and 1st Battalions, the latter having taken up a new defensive position close to the railroad embankment.

At dawn on the 27th the Russians launched an attack fully as powerful as that of the preceding day. Striking from the gap between the 1st and 3d Battalions, a strong infantry force supported by at least 20 tanks attacked the 1st Battalion's positions along the railroad embankment. The battalion's eight 37-mm. antitank guns on the embankment were ineffectual against the Russian T34 tanks and were soon knocked out, whereupon the Germans were forced to give up the embankment.

Toward 1100, after a strong artillery preparation, Russian infantry with tank support attacked from the area just west and northwest of Berestovaya and succeeded in reaching the center of the village. The Germans then counterattacked and recaptured it, following which another Russian force enveloped it by sweeping around the south side.

At 1400, a Russian infantry force, accompanied by several tanks, broke into Berestovaya from the west. Shortly afterward a tank-infantry force attacked along the Lisichansk-Belogorovka road and entered the village from the east. The commander of the 2d Battalion then ordered the evacuation of Berestovaya during the night. The night withdrawal was carried out without interference. The Russians, who had suffered heavy losses, continued to attack the next day, but were so weak that the Germans had no difficulty in stopping any attempt to advance.

This action exemplifies the tenacity with which both parties fought for villages or other permanent-type shelter during the bitter winter of 1941–42. The German defense of Berestovaya was facilitated by the existence of stone houses, which were not as easily destroyed as the usual Russian structures of wood, clay, or straw.

Throughout the course of their repeated attacks the Russians dissipated their offensive strength without forming points of main effort. Tanks were employed exclusively in support of infantry, a characteristic often evident during the first few months of the war. The Russians could have seized Berestovaya with much less effort if they had tried to envelop it from the beginning. An early Russian thrust to the dominating terrain of Hill 728 would have isolated the German forces in and around Berestovaya and made a prolonged defense impossible.

VII. Seesaw Battle in Subzero Temperatures (January 1942)

The beginning ascendancy of Russian armor over its German counterpart is exemplified in the following action, during which the Russian tank units showed themselves more aggressive than usual. In January 1942 the German front near Kursk ran north and south about 20 miles east of the city (map   ). Because of heavy snowfall cross-

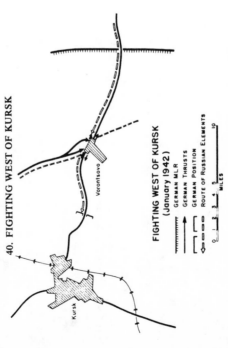

40. FIGHTING WEST OF KURSK

FIGHTING WEST OF KURSK
(January 1942)

········· GERMAN MLR
⟶ GERMAN THRUSTS
▭▭ GERMAN POSITION
⊏⊐⊏⊐ ROUTE OF RUSSIAN ELEMENTS

0 1 2 3 4 5 10
MILES

country movements was hampered by deep drifts, and temperatures dropped to −30° F. as sharp winds swept across the rolling countryside.

Since there were no woods in the area, visibility was good, except in low places. The monotony of the landscape was relieved only by a number of villages and towns.

Exposed for the first time to the rigors of a Russian winter, the Germans struggled desperately against the elements, as their tanks,

trucks, and automatic weapons broke down in the bitter cold. Timber for the improvement of the positions was scarce; accordingly the exhausted German infantry units, then employed along broad sectors, concentrated their defense in village strong points.

The Russians, taking advantage of their numerical superiority and greater experience under winter conditions, sought to undermine the German defense by a series of local, limited-objective attacks.

In the sector of the German 16th Motorized Infantry Division, Russian reconnaissance patrols had skillfully identified a weak spot at the boundary between two regiments. A combined arms team of Russian armor and infantry succeeded in breaking through the German MLR where it crossed the east-west road leading to Kursk, through which a railway and highway vital to German supply movements ran parallel to the front.

Exploiting the breakthrough, a force of about 25 T34 tanks with infantry mounted on them drove on toward Kursk and easily captured the communities in its path which were held solely by German service units. The Russian thrust continued into the next day, when it was stopped about 5 miles from Kursk by a hastily assembled German force. Several attempts to close the gap in the MLR with weak local reserves failed, and the Russians were able to follow up their tank force with two or three battalions of infantry, including some mounted in trucks.

The town of Vorontsovo, situated on the road leading to Kursk, was occupied by a weak Russian force. A German tank battalion, whose tank strength had fallen to 22, was released from another sector and sent in from the north against the right flank of the breakthrough force. The battalion took Vorontsovo by a *coup de main*, whereupon the Russians had to discontinue their westward advance.

After receiving meager reinforcements in the form of one 88-mm. antiaircraft gun and a battalion of infantry replacements that had just arrived from the zone of interior, the Germans conducted harassing raids in the areas east and west of Vorontsovo, effectively interfering with the supply of those Russian troops that had been cut off west of the town. On the third day of the action these isolated Russian forces attacked with infantry and tanks but were repulsed.

On the following day, during a driving snowstorm, the Russians attacked Vorontsovo from both the east and west, the thrust from the west being supported by tanks. Taking advantage of their greater ground clearance and lower ground pressure, the Russian tanks swept across terrain that the Germans had considered impassable for armor.

The young German infantry replacements, untested in battle, lacked experience in hand-to-hand fighting in villages and towns. They had not yet learned to fight in conjunction with tanks and were quickly overcome. Inferior in fire power and mobility to their Russian opposites, the German tanks were almost completely wiped out, and Vorontsovo was once again in Russian hands.

The Russian attack on this key town from two opposite directions was perfectly coordinated. The Germans never found out whether the two Russian forces had established radio contact or whether, perhaps, they were assisted by civilians who had remained in the town. Executed in a driving snowstorm, the Russian attack achieved surprise because the German precautions were inadequate. Extensive reconnaissance and security measures are elementary precautions that must be taken, regardless of the weather. To be derelict in these essentials is to risk lives.

The German counterattack was inadequately supported and led, and the inexperienced infantry were more a hindrance than a help in the operation. An armored unit on an independent mission must be accompanied by seasoned troops equipped with the necessary supporting weapons.

IX. Feint, Ambush, and Strike (July 1942)

The following actions took place in July 1942 on the central front during an attack by two panzer divisions supported by two infantry divisions. The Russians held well-fortified positions protected by extensive mine fields. At some points the Russian defensive system reached a depth of 3 miles. The German objective was to thrust toward the Resseta River, in the vicinity of which additional Russian

fortifications were under construction. Aerial photographs taken before the attack was launched did not reveal the presence of any Russian tanks.

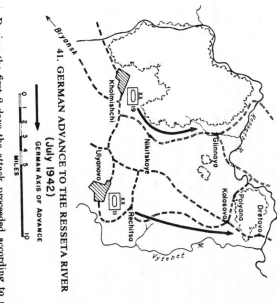

41. GERMAN ADVANCE TO THE RESSETA RIVER (July 1942)

During the first 2 days the attack proceeded according to plan. The two infantry divisions crossed the mine belt and fought their way through the Russian positions. On the third day the two panzer divisions were moved up and committed in the direction of the Resseta. The 11th Panzer Division was at full strength, whereas the 19th had only 60 percent of its prescribed T/O & E. Only about half the armored infantry units were motorized, the others had to march on foot. The Russians, meanwhile, had moved up reinforcements, including tanks. Their air forces, particularly the fighter-bomber squadrons, were quite active.

The fighting took place in or near very dense forests, where visibility was poor. The watercourses could be forded at several points. The weather was warm and sunny.

When the 19th Panzer Division attacked northeastward from Kholmishchi, the forward armored elements ran into strong Russian antitank defenses south of Nikitskoye (map). In devising their defense system, the Russians had taken full advantage of the concealment offered by the terrain and vegetation. One German armored column drove straight into an antitank gun front disposed on a semicircle facing south. The Russian guns, emplaced in pairs for mutual support, were dug in so that the muzzles were just above the surface of the ground. Between each pair of guns was an additional antitank gun mounted on a two-wheeled farm cart. The cart-mounted guns were camouflaged, but no effort had been made to conceal them.

As the German tanks advanced, the dug-in guns fired a volley, then ceased. Seeking the source of the fire, the Germans noticed the guns mounted on carts, and moved toward the newly discovered targets. As soon as a German tank turned to bring the cart-mounted guns under fire, it was hit from the side by Russian antitank fire from the concealed positions. The cart-mounted guns were dummies. Several of the tanks were lost in the action before the Germans succeeded in knocking out all the real antitank guns. In emplacing the dummy guns, the Russians were careful to leave just enough of the gun visible to make it an attractive target. Taken in by this ruse, the Germans turned their tanks to face the decoys, thereby exposing tracks and lateral armor, the most vulnerable parts.

After elements of the 19th Panzer Division had pushed through Nikitskoye, they ran into trouble north of the town, where they were repeatedly attacked by groups of five to seven Russian tanks emerging from the large forest adjacent to the division's left flank. After allowing the German armored point to pass, the Russian tanks pounced upon the wheeled vehicles which followed. Whenever the Germans counterattacked, the Russian tanks immediately withdrew into the forest, only to emerge at another point. The tanks used in this operation were of an older type, no match for their German counterparts

in open terrain. Hence the Russians used them—and with telling effect—only for hit-and-run operations. These Russian tactics cost the Germans a large number of casualties and caused considerable delay.

The German division commander thereupon ordered one tank battalion to cover the left flank of the advancing column. Echeloned in depth and supported by armored engineers, the tanks proceeded to comb the edge of the forest. In this manner the column was protected against any further surprise attacks.

When committing tanks in densely wooded areas, the Germans found it expedient to have them accompanied by infantry or engineers because the tank crews were unable to see or hear enough to proceed safely on their own.

Meanwhile, the 11th Panzer Division, driving toward the Resseta on the right of the 19th, attacked northeastward from Ulyanovo according to plan. As the leading tanks approached the village of Rechitsa, several T34's suddenly debouched from deep gullies and attacked the German armor from the left flank. After a stiff fight the T34's disappeared into the gullies only to renew their attacks at another point farther north.

The Russian medium tanks sent in pursuit were suddenly hit by flanking fire delivered from nearby gullies. In seeking the source of this fire the Germans observed that the Russians had dug in heavy tanks in such a way that only the turrets and guns were visible. The Russian heavies held their fire until the German tanks were within range or, when bypassed by the Germans, rolled backward out of the gullies and raced northward.

Although the Russian tanks were outnumbered, their tactics, well suited to the terrain, took a heavy toll of German armor. The Russians skillfully exploited the superior fire power of their heavy tanks and the maneuverability of their T34's in a way that compensated for the slowness of the former and the shortage of the latter.

At first the 11th Panzer Division commander tried to cope with these unusual tactics by committing artillery and antitank guns. When these proved ineffective, he asked for air support. Reconnaissance planes, protected by fighters, hovered over the area, maintaining constant radio contact with division headquarters. At least one reconnaissance plane circled at all times above the division's axis of advance and reported the hideouts of the Russian tanks by radio or flares. This information was relayed to the German tank commanders. As a result of good air-ground teamwork, the Russian armor was driven back after suffering heavy losses.

Despite the initial setback, this armored action was brought to a rapid and successful conclusion. Once the reconnaissance planes had established the presence of Russian armor, they kept the hostile tanks under observation until the latter were annihilated by their German counterparts or were withdrawn toward the north.

But the 11th Panzer Division had not seen the last of the elusive T34's. As the division attacked Kolosovo, its last objective before reaching the Resseta, the Russians dispatched twenty T34's from the direction of Dretovo, less than a mile from the river.

As soon as they established contact with the advancing elements of the German armor just north of Kolosovo, the T34's began to withdraw, fighting a delaying action. After the German tank formations had all passed through Kolosovo, they were brought under heavy antitank fire from the woods north of the town. Most of the German armor then swung to the left, toward the forest, while the remainder held to the main axis of advance. As the German tanks that had veered off were approaching the immediate vicinity of the forest, an entire brigade of T34's broke out of Polyana, west of Kolosovo, and hit the German tanks from the flank and rear, forcing them to withdraw to Kolosovo, which changed hands several times during the bitter tank battle that ensued. Only after the German division commander had thrown in all his artillery and antitank guns were the Germans able to obtain a firm hold on the town.

The advance and subsequent withdrawal of the twenty T34's slowed the German northward advance, setting up a perfect target for the antitank guns north of Kolosovo. This antitank-gun ambush, insufficient in itself to hurt the German division seriously, diverted the attention of the Germans while the Russian tank brigade struck a punishing blow against the German flank and rear. The three phases of the Russian tactical plan—the feint, the ambush, and the strike of the tank brigade—were perfectly coordinated. On the other hand, if the German air and ground reconnaissance had operated effectively, the panzer division commander would have been warned of the Russian intentions in time.

During the actions which took place south of the Resseta River, the Russians revealed their skill in adapting armored tactics to different types of terrain. Despite numerical inferiority they were able to inflict severe losses and delay the German advance.

In contrast to the engagements that were fought during the winter of 1941-42, Russian tanks appeared in brigade formation in the early months of 1942. The majority of these newly formed units were composed of T34's, occasionally interspersed with a few light tanks and some 52-ton KV's. The armored brigades had no organic infantry, artillery, or antitank units. In most instances they were employed to penetrate the German MLR, to widen the gap, and to achieve a breakthrough in depth. Rifle brigades or divisions were usually coupled with the armored brigades, either during the first phase of the attack—when the infantrymen rode into battle mounted on tanks—or after a penetration had been achieved to widen the gap and secure the flanks. For the latter purpose the Russians employed both foot and motorized infantry. Even on foot Russian infantrymen often kept pace with the advancing armor and proved capable of consolidating and holding the territory gained by the tanks.

X. Ambush Without Followup (December 1942)

In December 1942, when the Germans were putting up a desperate struggle in the Stalingrad pocket, their drive into the Caucasus had been stopped about 300 miles from the Baku oil fields. The German 3d Panzer Division was in the area northeast of Mozdok covering the left flank of the First Panzer Army, which had gone over to the defensive. In front of the division's right wing a continuous line of defense had been formed which dwindled to a mere security line as it ran northward toward the division boundary (map 24). The Russian forces north of the Terek River were steadily receiving reinforcements and their reconnaissance patrols constantly probed the weaker

The division commander divided his forces into two groups: Task Force M was to mount the attack and Task Force F was to hold. The attack force, under one of the regimental commanders, comprised two tank companies, one infantry company mounted in armored personnel carriers, two armored reconnaissance platoons, and one battery of self-propelled 105-mm. howitzers.

On 5 December Task Force M moved out. After a slow march of about 7 miles over difficult terrain, it encountered stiff resistance from dug-in Russian infantry. About 3 hours later the Russian defenses were finally overcome, but further movement that day was rendered impractical by the approach of darkness. Just before nightfall German air reconnaissance reported Russians in unknown strength about 3 miles southeast of the site selected for the bivouac. To the east and northeast, however, no enemy forces were reported.

Early on the morning of the 6th the task force fanned out in two columns toward the reported enemy concentration. The tank companies formed the left column; the armored infantry company, somewhat weakened by the previous day's engagement, the right. Some infantrymen were assigned to protect the artillery battery that covered the advance.

After an advance of about 1 mile the German columns ran into Russian infantry, which was well supported by mortars and antitank guns. As the Russian infantry engaged the task force frontally, 15 Russian tanks suddenly emerged from a hollow and fired point blank on the flank of the German left column. One of the two German tank company commanders was killed and two tanks were knocked out. It was only by virtue of the fact that the Russians did not attempt to pursue their advantage that the task force was able to disengage.

Here was an instance where the Russians skillfully withheld their tanks until the German armor was pinned down by frontal fire. The task force was not strong enough to be deployed in depth. Had it been, an attack could have been mounted against the Russian flank.

The Germans failed to perform ground reconnaissance and to secure their flanks during the advance.

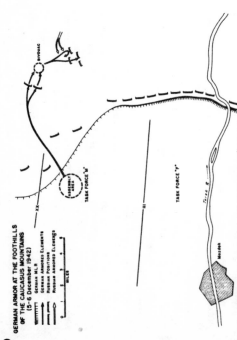

GERMAN ARMOR AT THE FOOTHILLS OF THE CAUCASUS MOUNTAINS
(5-6 December 1942)

German MLR
German Armored Elements
Russian Positions
Russian Armored Elements

MILES

BIVOUAC
TASK FORCE "M"
TASK FORCE "F"

sectors of the division front. Between the division and Stalingrad, 250 miles to the north, there was only a German armored infantry division and "Group Velmy," a motley unit composed of non-German volunteers.

The steppe in this area was devoid of vegetation and habitation, the monotony of the desertlike terrain being relieved only by small hills.

42. GERMAN ARMOR AT THE FOOTHILLS OF THE CAUCASUS MOUNTAINS

At noon on 4 December the division was ordered to attack the Russian forces to its left while continuing to provide flank protection for the army's left. The attack was set for the next day.

Carrying out simultaneous holding and attack operations presented a serious problem, in that the division was understrength and had sufficient gasoline for an operational radius of only 100 miles.

Appendix

List of German Military Leaders (July 1940— Nov 1942)

BOCK, Fedor von
Grade: Field Marshal—19 Jul 40.
Assignments: CG, Army Group B—Oct 39-31 Mar 41.
CG, Army Group Center—1 Apr-18 Dec 41.
CG, Army Group South—17 Jan-13 Jul 42.

BRAUCHITSCH, Walther von
Grade: Field Marshal—19 Jul 40.
Assignment: CinC of the Army—4 Feb 38-19 Dec 41.

FROMM, Friedrich
Grade: Generaloberst (General)—19 Jul 40.
Assignment: CG, Replacement Trining Army—End of 39-21 Jul 44.

GOERING, Hermann
Grade: Reich Marshal—19 Jul 40.
Assignment: CinC of the Luftwaffe—1 Mar 35-23 Apr 45.

GREIFFENBERG, Hans von
Grades: Colonel—3 Oct 38.
Generalmajor (Brigadier General)—1 Aug 40.
Generalleutnant (Major General)—1 Apr 42.
Assignments: Chief, Operations Division, Army High Command—26 Aug 39-24 Oct 40.
Officers Reserve Pool—25 Oct 40-15 Jan 41.
CofS, Twelfth Army—15 Jan-10 May 41.
CofS, Army Group Center—10 May 41-5 May 42.
C of S, Army Group A—5 May 42-1 Aug 43.

GUDERIAN, Heinz
Grade: Generaloberst (General)—19 Jul 40.
Assignments: CG, Second Panzer Group—May-5 Oct 41.
CG, Second Panzer Army—5 Oct-22 Dec 41.

HALDER, Franz
Grade: Generaloberst (General)—19 Jul 40.
Assignment: Chief, Army General Staff—1 Nov 38-24 Sep 42.

HITLER, Adolf
Assignments: CinC of the Armed Forces—2 Aug 34-30 Apr 45.
CinC of the Army—19 Dec 41-30 Apr 45.
CG, Army Group A—9 Sep-22 Nov 42.

HOTH, Hermann
Grade: Generaloberst (General)—19 Jul 40.
Assignments: CG, Third Panzer Group—16 Nov 41-5 Oct 41.
CG, Seventeenth Army—5 Oct 41-25 Apr 42.
CG, Fourth Panzer Army—1 Jun 42-15 Nov 43.

JODL, Alfred
Grades: Generalleutnant (Major General)
General der Artillerie (Lieutenant General)} 19 Jul 40.

Assignment: Chief, Armed Forces Operations, Staff (Office)—26 Aug 39-8 May 45.

KEITEL, Wilhelm
Grade: Field Marshal—19 Jul 40.
Assignment: CofS, Armed Forces High Command—4 Feb 38-8 May 45.

KINZEL, Eberhard
Grades: Lieutenant Colonel—1 Mar 39.
Colonel—1 Feb 41.
Assignments: Chief, Eastern Intelligence Division—26 Aug 39-1 May 42.
Officers Reserve Pool—1-23 May 42.
CofS, XXIX Corps—23 May-12 Nov. 42.

KLEIST, Ewald von
Grade: Generaloberst (General)—19 Jul 40.
Assignments: CG, First Panzer Group—Jun-5 Oct 41.
CG, First Panzer Army—5 Oct 41-21 Nov 42.

KLUGE, Guenther von
Grade: Field Marshal—19 Jul 40.
Assignments: CG, Fourth Army—1 Sep 39-26 Dec 41.
CG, Army Group Center—18 Dec. 41-12 Oct 43.

KUECHLER, Georg von
Grades: Generaloberst (General)—19 Jul 40.
Field Marshal—30 Jun 42.
Assignments: CG, Eighteenth Army—5 Nov 39-15 Jan 42.
CG, Army Group North—16 Jan 42-31 Jan 44.

LEEB, Wilhelm von
Grade: Field Marshal—19 Jul 40.
Assignments: CG, Army Group C—Jul 40-Mar 41.
CG, Army Group North—1 Apr 41-16 Jan 42.

LIST, Wilhelm
Grade: Field Marshal—19 Jul 40.
Assignments: CG, Twelfth Army—1 Sep 39-Oct 41.
CG, Army Group A—26 Jun-10 Sep 42.

MANSTEIN, Fritz Erich von
Grades: Generalmajor (Brigadier General)—1 Apr 39.
Generalleutnant (Major General)—1 Mar 41.
Field Marshal—1 Jul 42.
Assignment: CG, Eleventh Army—18 Sep 41-21 Nov 42.

MARCKS, Erich
Grades: Generalmajor (Brigadier General)—1 Jun 40.
Generalleutnant (Major General)—1 Mar 41.
General der Artillerie (Lieutenant General)—1 Oct 42.
Assignments: CofS, Eighteenth Army—5 Nov 39-10 Dec 40.
CG, 101st Light Infantry Division—10 Dec 40-28 Jun 41.
Officers Reserve Pool—28 Jun 41-15 Mar 42.
CG, 337th Infantry Division—15 Mar-28 Sep 42.
CG, LXVI Corps—28 Sep-Nov 42.

MODEL, Walter
Grades: Generalleutnant (Major General)—1 Apr 40.
General der Panzertruppen (Lieutenant General)—28 Oct 41.
Generaloberst (General)—1 Feb 42.
Assignments: CofS, Sixteenth Army—23 Oct 39-13 Nov 40.
CG, 3d Panzer Division—13 Nov-28 Oct 41.
CG, XLI Corps—28 Oct 41-15 Jan 42.
CG, Ninth Army—16 Jan 42-5 Nov 43.

PAULUS, Friedrich
Grades: Generalleutnant (Major General)—1 Aug 40.
General der Panzertruppen (Lieutenant General)—1 Jan 42.
Generaloberst (General)—30 Nov 42.
Assignments: CofS, Sixth Army—3 Sep 40.
ACofS, Operations, Army High Command—3 Sep 40-16 Jan 42.
CG, Sixth Army—16 Jan 42-1 Feb 43.

RAEDER, Erich
Grade: Grossadmiral (Fleet Admiral)—1939.
Assignment: CinC of the Navy—1935-43.

REICHENAU, Walter von
Grade: Field Marshal—19 Jul 40.
Assignments: CG, Sixth Army—Oct 28-3 Dec 41.
CG, Army Group South—3 Dec 41-17 Jan. 42.

RICHTHOFEN, Wolfgang von
Grade: Generaloberst (General)—Mar 42.
Assignments: CG, VIII Air Corps—End of 39-23 Jun 42.
CG, Fourth Air Force—24 Jun 42-10 Jun 43.

ROMMEL, Erich
Grades: Generalmajor (Brigadier General)—1 Aug 39.
Generalleutnant (Major General)—7 Feb 41.
General der Panzertruppen (Lieutenant General)—1 Jul 41.
Generaloberst (General)—1 Feb 42.
Field Marshal—22 Jun 42.
Assignments: CG, 7th Panzer Division—15 Feb 40-14 Feb 41.
CG, Afrika Corps—14 Feb-1 Sep 41.
CG, Panzer Group Afrika—1 Sep 41-30 Jan 42.
CG, Panzer Army Afrika—30 Jan 42-22 Feb 43.

RUNDSTEDT, Gerd von
Grade: Field Marshal—19 Jul 40.
Assignments: CG, Army Group A—20 Oct 39-15 Mar 41.
CG, Army Group South—1 Apr-3 Dec 41.
CG, Army Group D (West)—8 Mar 42-2 Jul 44.

SODENSTERN, Georg von
Grade: Generalleutnant (Major General)—1 Feb 40.
General der Infanterie (Lieutenant General)—1 Aug 40.
Assignments: CofS, Army Group A—15 Feb 40-15 Mar 41.
CofS, Army Group South—1 Apr 41-15 Jul 42.
CofS, Army Group B—15 Jul 42-14 Feb 43.

STRAUSS, Adolf
Grade: Generaloberst (General)—19 Jul 40.
Assignment: CG, Ninth Army—30 May 40-15 Jan 42.

THOMAS, Georg
Grade: General der Infanterie (Lieutenant General)—1 Aug 40.
Assignment: Chief, Armed Forces Economics Office—1 Sep 39-17 Nov 42.

WAGNER, Eduard
Grades: Colonel—1 Oct 37.
Generalmajor (Brigadier General)—1 Aug 40.
Generalleutnant (Major General)—1 Apr 42.
Assignment: CofS, Supply and Administration Division, Army High Command—23 Aug 39-1 Oct 40.
Chief, Supply and Administration Division—1 Oct-22 Jul 44.

WARLIMONT, Walter
Grades: Colonel—1 Feb 38.
Generalmajor (Brigadier General)—1 Aug 40.
Generalleutnant (Major General)—1 Apr 42.
Assignments: Chief, National Defense Division, Armed Forces High Command—26 Aug 39-31 Dec 41.
Deputy Chief, Armed Forces Operations Staff—1 Jan 42-6 Sep 44.

WEICHS, Maximilian von
Grade: Generaloberst (General)—19 Jul 40.
Assignments: CG, Second Army—23 Oct 39-13 Jul 42.
CG, Army Group B—13 Jul 42-10 Jul 43.

ZEITZLER, Kurt
Grades: Colonel—1 Jan 39.
Generalmajor (Brigadier General)—1 Feb 42.
General der Infanterie (Lieutenant General)—24 Sep 42.
Assignments: CG, XXII Corps—26 Aug 39-5 Dec 40.
CofS, First Panzer Army—5 Dec 40-24 Apr 42.
CofS, C-in-C West—24 Apr-24 Sep 42.
Chief of the Army General Staff—25 Sep 42-20 Jul 44.